BICYCLING THE BACKROADS
OF NORTHWEST OREGON

Second Edition

BICYCLING THE BACKROADS
OF NORTHWEST OREGON

Second Edition

Philip N. Jones and Jean Henderson

THE
MOUNTAINEERS

5 4
5 4 3 2

Published by The Mountaineers
1011 SW Klickitat Way, Seattle, Washington 98134

Published simultaneously in Canada by Douglas & McIntyre, Ltd., 1615 Venables Street, Vancouver, B.C. V5L 2H1

Published simultaneously in Great Britain by Cordee, 3a DeMontfort Street, Leicester, England, LE1 7HD

Manufactured in the United States of America

Edited by Kris Fulsaas
Maps by Philip N. Jones and Kenneth Winkenweder
Cover photograph: Oregon covered bridge by Kirkendall/Spring
Cover design by Elizabeth Watson
Cartoons and drawings by Dale Martin
Typography by Graphics West

Library of Congress Cataloging in Publication Data
Jones, Philip N.
    Bicycling the backroads of northwest Oregon / Philip N. Jones, Jean Henderson.
    — 2nd ed.
        p.   cm.
    Includes index.
    ISBN 0-89886-340-6
    1. Bicycle touring—Oregon—Guidebooks. 2. Oregon—Description and travel—1981- I. Henderson, Jean. II. Title.
    GV1045.5.07J66   1992
    796.6'4'09795—dc20   92-18259
                                                                                            CIP

CONTENTS

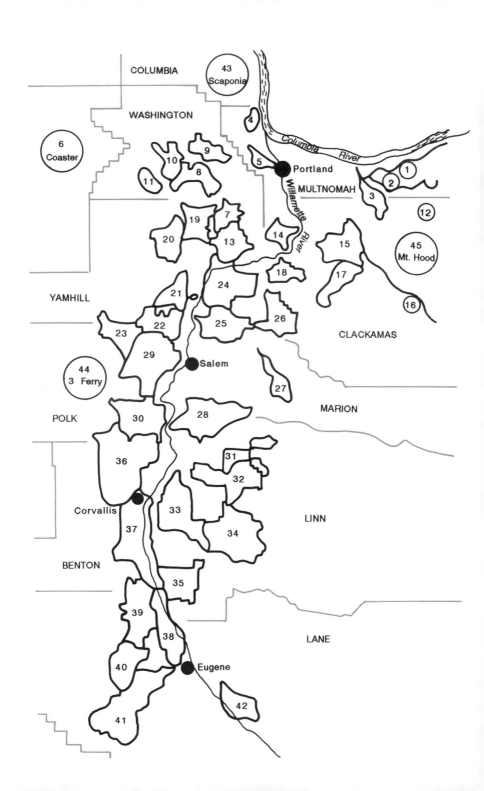

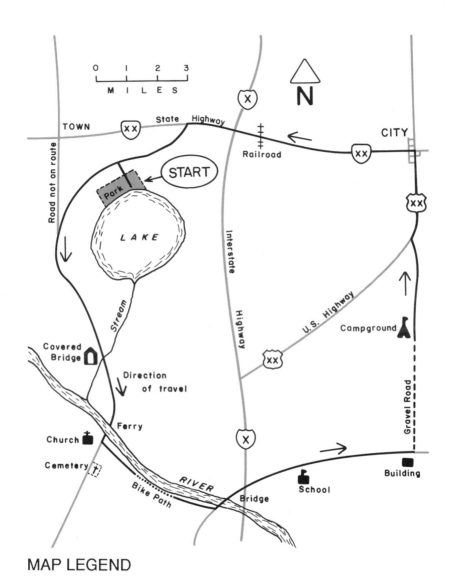

MAP LEGEND

PREFACE

Pioneers who came west to Oregon in the 1840s found adventure, discovery, and a new life. They also faced hardships so severe they are difficult for us to imagine. In putting together the original version of this book, Philip Jones offered a similar experience on a much smaller scale. Thanks to him, cyclists seeking backroads, adventure, discovery, and new fitness found the Willamette Valley. And they did it without the hardships.

Patterned after the successful series of Washington state bicycling guides for scenic backroads, by Erin and Bill Woods of Redmond, Washington (published by The Mountaineers Books), this volume extended this tradition into the Willamette Valley.

In accepting co-authorship of this second edition, I first cycled the trips Phil Jones had described. Then I added two I had led for Seattle Mountaineers. In researching this book's more than 2300 miles, my partner, Ken Winkenweder, and I used as our guide the first edition of the publication. We pedaled about 3000 miles, much of it on backroads. Each mile seemed to bring a new discovery and a yearning to learn more about Oregon, its people, and its geography. Every element of our touring was an unforgettable experience. We especially enjoyed Brownsville, covered bridges, and fantastic mountain and valley vistas. Each season had its own special flavor. But as much as we'd like to share it all, our exact experiences can't be duplicated. Happily, using this guide, your unique experiences can be only a few pedal strokes away. We encourage you to get going.

Seeking to retain the original flavor of Phil Jones's book, I have added information and route changes to enhance enjoyment and discovery for every cyclist. Every effort has been directed toward maintaining the format, standards, and quality set by both Phil Jones, and Bill and Erin Woods.

I am indebted especially to Ken Winkenweder for accompanying me every mile by bicycle, making excellent suggestions, and creating new and revised maps; to Ella Mae (Mom) Winkenweder for providing a base of operations (as needed) in McMinnville; to Phil Jones for the opportunity to co-author this book; to Roger Aasen and other friends in the Mountaineers Bicycling Group for their support and help; and to Bill and Erin Woods for the foundation they have laid. Any errors are mine and I would appreciate having them called to my attention so they may be corrected.

Jean Henderson

A NOTE ABOUT SAFETY

Safety is important in all outdoor activities. No guidebook can alert you to every hazard or anticipate the limitations of every reader. Therefore, the descriptions of roads, trails, routes, and natural features in this book are not representations that a particular place or excursion will be safe for your party. When you follow any of the routes described, you assume responsibility for your own safety. Under normal conditions, such excursions require attention to traffic, road and trail conditions, weather, terrain, the capabilities of your party, and other factors. Also, many of the lands in this book may be subject to development and/or change of ownership. Conditions may have changed since the book was written that make your use of some of these routes unwise. Always respect posted private property signs and avoid confrontations with property owners or managers. Keeping informed on current conditions and exercising common sense are the keys to a safe, enjoyable outing.

The Mountaineers

INTRODUCTION

A collection of forty-five bicycle trips in Northwestern Oregon, principally in the Willamette Valley from the Portland area south to Eugene, this book includes routes from 12 to 178 miles in length. Mostly loops, the routes are designed to bicycle in a few hours. Also included are a few tours in the Columbia Gorge area, one along the Oregon Coast, and some linear trips. Four rides in the book are for multiday journeys. These are the Oregon Coaster, Mount Hood Loop, Three-Ferry Figure Eight, and Scaponia.

Strike out along the county and rural roads, bicycle lanes, or secondary highways of Oregon. Pedal into rolling hills, flatlands, or deep gorges. The people and life-styles are as varied as the terrain and weather patterns. The history stems from hardy pioneers who sought a better life in the West. Visit parks, old soda fountains, festivals, country stores, historic buildings, lakes, and covered bridges decorating foothills, farmland, forests, side valleys, small towns, and ethnic settlements. Your miles of pedaling will enhance physical fitness and your appreciation of Oregon. We wish you all the enjoyment we have found pedaling the beautiful, bountiful backroads of Northwest Oregon.

The Trip Descriptions

Each ride in the book includes a capsule summary. Use the summary to match rides to your abilities and interests, paying particular attention to both visual and narrative information provided.

Elevation and distance graphs illustrate the route's altitude profile, but don't be put off by a route that first appears too long or hilly. Almost every route has shortcuts or shorter options. Tailor the ride's length and difficulty to your needs by reviewing the accompanying text, mileage logs, and map sketches. Some options are described in the text and logs, and others may be readily apparent in the sketch maps.

Starting and en route times are estimated and should not be considered rigid. Based on averages for the novice cyclist, these assume a fairly slow pace with frequent stops at points of interest. Strong riders or seasoned racers may complete the routes in half the estimated times.

Starting times are recommended to permit riders to complete the routes by mid- to late afternoon. Consider, however, the advantages of starting very early in the morning. Traffic is almost nonexistent, permitting the cool morning air to be enjoyed in solitude, and leaving the hot afternoon riding to the late risers. Cyclists who can stand the initial agony of crawling out of bed at dawn will find their efforts rewarded. In winter, the opposite advice may be better: Wait for the day to warm up a bit, then choose a short ride that will end well before the chilly late afternoon.

Each route also includes a map and a mileage log. In theory, either one should be sufficient for a selected route. In practice, both the map and the mileage log should be followed, particularly in unfamiliar territory or on routes with frequent turns or numerous intersections.

Mileage logs in this book describe the routes in tenths of a mile. Used in tandem, maps and logs provide adequate information for following the exact route. These can be followed with a cyclometer (bicycle computer), but don't expect an exact match to distances printed in the book. Bicycle computers vary, partly because of differences in wheel and tire sizes.

A watch and a compass are two other pieces of optional equipment that can assist in following a mileage log. With experience, most riders develop a feel for how fast they are riding and, using a watch, can estimate distances traveled with a surprising degree of accuracy. In this book, maps have a scale of miles and a north arrow, while mileage logs frequently mention compass directions. When in doubt about intersections where road signs are missing, twisted, or otherwise confusing, check both the log and the map. Then consult a compass, if necessary.

The mileage logs describe each of the loop trips in a particular direction, i.e., clockwise or counterclockwise. Any route may be ridden in the opposite direction, but some that pass through cities and towns may require slight modification when one-way streets are encountered.

The mileage logs usually mention bike lanes or paths, when available along the routes. These are recommended in the interest of safety. Throughout the book, a bike route on the shoulder of a road, whether designated by a painted line or protected by small cement dividers, is referred to as a bike lane. A paved path separate from the roadway is referred to as a bike path.

Accurate road and street names often are difficult to determine. Especially in rural areas, many roads are unmarked, or are signed with names different from those on local maps. Although Oregon Department of Transportation maps purport to show the correct official name for every road in the state, those may not appear on street signs. In this book, the road and street names usually are the ones on local signs. Be cautious, however. Signs can be missing, altered, or, through the efforts of local pranksters, twisted ninety degrees. Where signs conflict with available maps, or where more than one name appears on different signs, the mileage log shows alternate names in parentheses. Maps show the most commonly used names. To avoid losing the route, consult both the map and the mileage log.

A turn onto a gravel road is a signal that you are probably off-route. Few of these rides involve gravel roads, and the ones that do are marked clearly on both the map and the mileage log.

To take shortcuts or side trips away from the itineraries described here, consult the map. It shows whether nearby roads are paved or gravel. On recommended variations, the roads have been inspected. In other cases, the pavement status is based in part on information derived from Oregon Department of Transportation maps, which are generally accurate.

Also keep in mind that roads and intersections are changing constantly as highway departments fiddle with the landscape. Don't be surprised to find roads realigned, intersections rearranged, or new highways built. A close eye on the map and the mileage log should make most changes readily apparent and wrong turns avoidable. The others will make for interesting stories.

Facilities available along the routes are described for rider enjoyment. Stores, and sometimes restaurants, are mentioned when they appear in rural locations, but no attempt is made to list their hours. Carrying food is always a good idea when cycling.

Public parks are mentioned whenever they appear along the routes or within striking distance. Nearly all have rest rooms, if only outhouses, but many of those facilities are open solely during summer months. Drinking water and camping facilities are mentioned in the mileage logs, but again, water often is disconnected and campgrounds closed in the off-season. Carry a water bottle and refill it at every opportunity.

Choosing a Bicycle

Almost any bike can be used to ride the routes described here. It doesn't have to be fancy or expensive. A forty-pound balloon-tired bike will get you to your destination just as surely as a twenty-pound racing bicycle, but it may take a bit longer. If you've got an old bike gathering dust in the garage, get it out, dust it off, make sure it is safe to ride, and start pedaling. You eventually may want to graduate to a better bike, but don't stay home for want of it now.

When it's time for a new or upgraded bicycle, here is a tip: Concentrate on lightness and the frame. A good, light bike really isn't as fragile as it may appear. Extra weight is mostly located in nonfunctional places. Once you have a good frame, you can vary components to suit your riding style and needs.

When considering bike lightness, the frame is a good example. Most stress is at the joints where frame tubes come together. On expensive "double-butted" frames, the tube wall's thickness is greatest at each end, where strength is needed, and narrower in the midsection, where the stress is much less. Significant weight is thus saved without loss of strength.

Bicycle choices are abundant in today's marketplace. Before selecting a bike, consider your riding style, the length and type of trips, and the need to carry gear. Road frames are designed for touring, racing, or a combination of the two. Hybrid bicycles primarily meet the demands of commuters and mountain cycles are designed for off-pavement use.

Touring frames are more stretched out and flexible than their racing counterparts, and thus produce a smoother ride. Extremely responsive, a stiff racing frame would be less comfortable on long rides and unable to carry much gear. Sport-touring frames absorb some of the road shock of a racing frame without sacrificing the benefits of responsiveness, and can be equipped with panniers (saddlebags). Mountain bikes can be ridden on pavement, but their weight and bigger tires require more effort than touring and racing frames.

Bicycle frames are graduated to fit different-size bodies. Measured in inches or centimeters from the spindle (the axle on which the pedals rotate) to the point where the seat post enters the frame, most frames are sized between 18 and 25 inches.

To determine if a particular frame fits, straddle the bike, standing between the handlebars and the seat. If the bike fits, you should be able to lift the front wheel an inch or two off the floor. Frames may also be measured by standing in a wide, equidistant stance over the top tube. Clearance between you and the top tube should be 1 to 2 inches on a road bike, but as much as 4 inches on a mountain bike. (Some say 3 inches is ideal.) This extra mountain-bike clearance allows for more responsiveness and for sitting behind the saddle to hold down the back wheel on steep descents.

Frame and wheel sizes should not be confused. While frame sizes vary, nearly all road or hybrid bicycles with gearing use 27-inch-diameter wheels, or their slightly smaller metric equivalent, 700-millimeter wheels. Mountain bikes and some youth or inexpensive adult bikes use 26-inch wheels.

Bicycle fitting is not complete with selection of the correct frame size. Competent advice from someone who can examine the bike and the rider at the same time is advised.

Saddle height on all bikes is generally adjusted by balancing on the bike. With the ball of the foot on a pedal, the leg should bend slightly when the pedal is at its lowest position.

Handlebars can also be adjusted, and should generally be slightly lower than the saddle. Long- or short-armed riders might also consider changing the length of horizontal extension of the handlebar stem. This change requires a new stem, but helps avoid undue strain on the neck or hands.

After properly fitting the frame to the rider, examine the bike. Rims, handlebars, pedals, cranks, and front sprockets on a heavy, inexpensive bike will all be steel. A light bike uses aluminum (actually aluminum alloy) for these parts. Frames also can be constructed from either steel or aluminum alloy. On a light bike, parts commonly made of steel, with the exception of the frame, are the axles, spokes, parts of the saddle, and a few others. If you can't tell the difference between aluminum and steel, carry a small magnet when shopping for a bike.

Remember, the finest, lightest components can't make up for a heavy frame and vice versa. Nevertheless, don't focus so much on weight that you lose track of components and how they work together. Components on most bikes can be exchanged for lighter or higher-quality parts. If your budget limits your choice of bikes, buy the best frame—the bicycle's heart and soul. Components can be added or switched as your finances and technology advancements in the industry allow, watching for compatibility with existing equipment.

A key component is the crankset. This consists of front chainrings (sprockets), cranks (the arms on which the pedals are mounted), and bearings that attach to the bottom bracket of the frame. On an inexpensive bike, crank arms are attached to the spindle (bearing axle) with steel cotter pins. Higher-quality bikes have aluminum cranks attached to the spindle with bolts that screw directly into the ends of the spindle. In addition to being significantly lighter and more durable, cotterless cranks are much easier to maintain.

Now that bicycling is the top recreational activity nationwide, many advancements developed for racing have been adapted for touring. Once tires and rims were a compromise of durability, weight, and air pressure. Riders chose between two extremely different types of rims and tires: "clinchers" and "sew-ups" (or tubulars). "Clincher" bicycle tires were durable, but heavy, and would accept only moderate air pressures. "Sew-ups" were light, high-pressure, and extremely susceptible to punctures.

Today there are many types of narrow clincher rims and tires that combine the best attributes of both clinchers and sew-ups. While traditional clincher rims and tires were 1¼ inches wide, the new designs are 1 inch or 1⅛ inch wide, weigh almost as little as some sew-ups, and accept air pressures up to 150 pounds per square inch. The high pressure and narrow width provide a fairly stiff ride with a small loss in traction, but the corresponding reductions in weight and rolling resistance are very appealing. Some models also incorporate lightweight linings or impregnated chemicals as extra barriers to small punctures.

To choose tires and rims, look for what works best for the situation and what is compatible with the bicycle. Then consider personal preferences. Narrow rims require slender tires and inner tubes. Also, it generally is true that 1-inch tires will not fit on 1¼-inch rims and vice versa, but 1⅛-inch tires will generally fit on any rim. If you prefer the liveliest, lightest bike possible, choose 1-inch rims and tires. If luggage is to be carried, or gravel roads ridden, 1⅛-inch tires could be used with the 1-inch rims. Heavy loads and truly rough roads require wider rims. Most riders find the lighter equipment an excellent choice for average tours on good roads. The 1¹/₈-inch tires are particularly useful in upgrading older bikes with 1¹/₄-inch rims.

Another issue to resolve before your tour is the bicycle's saddle. Many bikes languish in garages and basements because of the pain inflicted by their saddles. Shop around, compare different models, and solicit recommendations from other cyclists—then choose. Traditional saddles are made solely from a piece of stiff leather, but present several drawbacks. They are susceptible to damage from water (especially in the Northwest), and the less-expensive models wear out quickly. A well-broken-in leather saddle often is extremely comfortable, if only to the person who broke it in.

Plastic saddles with a padded leather cover require no break-in period. Neither do they improve in comfort over time. "Anatomical" leather/plastic saddles, with extra padding in contact areas, have become popular.

Selecting Bicycle Gearing

Gears for the bike should also be chosen carefully. A multispeed gearing system consists of a crankset with two or three chainrings in the front and a freewheel (or cluster) with five, six, or seven sprockets in the rear. By selecting various sizes of chainrings and rear sprockets, gearing systems can easily be designed for particular types of riding or terrain. Yet many bicycles are delivered with poorly chosen gear ratios. Riders also often fail to examine gearing in light of their particular needs.

Most bikes now have at least 12, 15, or 18 speeds. For illustrative purposes this discussion uses the traditional 10-speed arrangement. Actually, a 10-speed bike has eight usable gears. The two others are basically not usable due to excessive wear caused by chain angles from the outside chainring to the inside freewheel sprocket (or vice versa).

To maximize usefulness of the remaining gear combinations, choose well. Racers want gears tightly grouped so cadence isn't lost in shifting. Most tourists prefer a wider range of gears, particularly in the low-end range. Low (or granny) gears are for climbing hills or mountain passes, carrying a heavy load, or pedaling into a head wind. Higher gears are for the flats, downhill, or when riding with a tail wind.

A gear ratio is a specific front chainring compared with a given rear sprocket. The combination is stated as if the pedals were connected directly to a certain diameter wheel measured in inches. Thus, riding a bicycle with a 50-inch gear would require the same effort as riding a tricycle with a 50-inch-diameter front wheel. The smaller the wheel or gear, the easier the pedaling, but the more revolutions required to cover a given distance. For example, a 30-inch gear, which is quite small, might be a good choice for climbing steep hills, while a 100-inch gear is most suitable for high-speed descents.

Figure these gear inches by dividing the number of front chainring teeth by the number of rear sprocket teeth, then multiplying by the diameter of the wheel (usually 27 inches). You can also do what most riders do: Consult gear charts in bicycle catalogs and manuals.

To examine gearing, first count the teeth on each of the bike's chainrings and rear sprockets. Next list the ten ratios resulting from combining each of the two chainrings with each of the five rear sprockets. After eliminating the two gears considered unusable, look closely at the remaining eight. What is the range between the highest and lowest? A low of 40 inches and a high of 100 might be considered a good compromise. Personal preferences, including what has felt comfortable over varied terrain, are more important than someone else's rule. A wider range may mean unacceptably large jumps between gears, but may be necessary in mountainous terrain. A smaller range will not provide gears most riders prefer to use in hilly country, but will afford incremental adjustments useful in flat farm country. Riders who can rely on strength, rather than low gears, to get up hills, may prefer close-range gearing. Novices (or those planning to climb long, steep hills) will sacrifice the midrange gears for a very low one.

Next, how do those eight gears spread over the range? If two are nearly identical (only 2 or 3 inches apart), one is being wasted. If two are more than 15 inches apart, with no other gear in between, your ability to make small adjustments is limited. On a touring 10-speed, ideally no gear is more than 15 inches, or less than 5 inches, from the next higher or lower one. This is particularly true for the middle gears, but ideals are difficult to realize without sacrificing other factors.

Another consideration is whether both the front and rear derailleurs must be used each time the gears are shifted. Such "double-shifting" would be fatal to a racer, but is merely inconvenient to the tourist.

The size of the lowest gear is of more importance to the tourist. If extremely steep hills are anticipated, the rider is not in condition, or heavy baggage will be carried, a very low gear should be sought. In such situations, a 30-inch, or lower, gear might be considered. Some cyclists believe a 40-inch gear is adequate under most conditions, but the subject will be debated as long as cyclists ride.

If the gears on your bike are not what you want, your fitness or riding habits change, or you are planning to ride over unusual terrain, gearing can be changed fairly easily. Front chainrings and/or rear sprockets can be replaced, but the latter are much less expensive. Keep in mind that a gear change may also require adjustments in the derailleur and chain length.

Bicycle Accessories

Adding accessories to your bicycle should be done sparingly, since many contribute little more than weight and clutter. However, serious consideration should be given to toe clips, cleats, and step-in bindings. Simply to keep the rider's feet in place, all give more control, security, and pedaling efficiency. Today's marketplace offers many options of shoe and cleat combinations for racing, commuting, touring, or mountain biking.

Novices are often reluctant to try toe clips, but those who do usually keep them. With touring-type shoes, toe clips are simple to use and do not require tight strapping of the feet. Cleats and step-in bindings attach more positively. Some newer models allow stepping in on both sides of the pedal and are also comfortable for walking.

An essential accessory, whether you are embarking on a tour or taking neighborhood rides, is a good tire pump mounted on the bike. Choose your pump carefully, since some models are not capable of high pressures and others reach them only when powered by a professional weightlifter. Also make sure that the pump fits the valves of your bike: Schrader valves are the same type used on automobile tires, while Presta valves are narrower. Combining the pump with a patch kit and an extra tube for your bicycle helps guarantee a ride instead of a walk, in case of a puncture.

Another accessory especially useful in the Northwest is fenders. These greatly extend the bicycling season and most models are featherweight. Besides adding comfort in the rain, fenders help avoid "skunk" stripes created when mud from the rear wheel becomes airborne.

Other accessories include rear-view mirrors, goggles, carry bags, and water bottles. Now available for all types of helmets or handlebars, rear-view mirrors enhance riding safety, especially in traffic. Some models also are available for eyeglasses.

Goggles not only protect eyes from flying debris, but also avoid sudden blinding caused by cold air. The best models protect 100 percent from the sun's ultraviolet rays, are nonshattering, and come in dark or clear shades.

Bags are very useful for carrying food, extra clothes, maps, bicycle essentials, and tools. Training racers usually carry the bare necessities in their pockets or tied under their saddles, but most day tourists enjoy a pack. Select from many designs and colors, but pay particular attention to function. A rear rackpack or bag is favored. It won't create drag because it sits or hangs in the slipstream behind the cyclist. Handlebar bags, which are great for holding maps and logs, catch the wind and sometimes sag onto the front wheel.

Carry water in a bottle mounted on the bike frame. The bottle and its frame cage are inexpensive and can be color coordinated with the bike and accessories. Frequent drinks en route help avoid dehydration.

Clothing

Bicycling requires proper clothing. Aside from helmets, "proper" doesn't necessarily translate into the latest high-tech gear. Specialized fibers in jazzy colors work for cycling because they can be easily seen by motorists and offer protection in changing weather. In western Oregon the usual challenge is keeping warm and dry, but occasionally the problem is keeping cool. Clothing for these situations may be items you already use for hiking, skiing, or walking around the neighborhood.

Many riders have adopted knitted wool or synthetic (Lycra) shorts with a padded seat. Because they fit snugly, have no seams at the crotch, and wick moisture away from the body, these shorts reduce chafing. This can be important, even if the outside temperature is mild. In cold weather, tights of polypropylene, wool, Lycra, or a combination of fibers can be added or worn instead of shorts. Leg warmers, which attach to the shorts, are also available.

Other riders "make do." In cool weather they carry either pants or long underwear, which are fine if cotton is avoided. Once wet, cotton can chafe, add weight, and actually steal body heat. Instead, try knickers made from old wool dress slacks, available from military surplus or second-hand stores. In the event of a fall, knickers, long pants, or leg warmers also help prevent abrasions.

Shirts, or jerseys as cyclists prefer to call them, can also be specially designed wool or synthetic knit. Pockets on the back for food and other items and bright colors add to their utility. Arm warmers are available to instantly turn short-sleeved versions into longer-armed ones. Other types of shirts, blouses, and T-shirts work, but pay particular attention to fiber content. Some fibers hold moisture next to the body, keeping the rider wet and cold.

A tip for assuring added warmth in weather changes year-round is to carry ear warmers or a headband. Small and light, a wool or polypropylene hat or ear cover easily fits under the helmet or into a bike bag. Use the headband on hot days to absorb brow perspiration.

On a long ride, bicycling gloves add comfort and protect hands in the event of a crash. Most cycling gloves have padded palms to absorb vibrations, but are fingerless. For colder days, new fiber combinations provide warmth and function. Some models even have rubberized palms to minimize slippage. Avoid gloves with tight cuffs; in damp weather they are difficult to get on and off.

Light leather or synthetic cycling shoes with very stiff soles and metal or plastic cleats are the choice of racers and many tourists. On the other end of the spectrum, many recreational riders wear conventional running shoes. These work best if they have a thick sole and a narrow heel. Flared heels or rough soles are problematic on the bicycle pedal, especially with toe clips.

Other shoes are specially designed for bike touring. The appearance

Howard, I don't think you were meant to wear Lycra.

and walking comfort of running shoes is combined with soles sufficiently stiff to provide comfortable long-distance pedaling. These touring shoes do not have cleats, but some have grooves to grip the pedal.

Since most bike shoes are not suitable alone for winter use, a wide range of booties or shoe covers are available. Many do not keep the feet dry, but do offer warmth. Soles can be cut to allow for cleats or step-in bindings.

Actually, rainy weather presents a new set of challenges for all clothing. Remaining dry is easier if a breathable, waterproof fabric, such as Gore-Tex, is chosen for outerwear. If the rain is not particularly cold or heavy, wool usually keeps the rider fairly comfortable. Items that are waterproof, but not breathable, have limited use since they hold in body moisture. In any kind of weather, an extra windbreaker, rain jacket, or sweater should be carried on the bike, just in case.

Maintenance and Tools

One of the joys of bicycling is the relative simplicity of maintenance and repairs. Even persons with minimal mechanical inclination or ability can learn to do repairs. Leaving them to others means missing out on a satisfying aspect of bicycling, not to mention being at the mercy of circumstances if the bike breaks down far from a repair shop.

Even if you don't enjoy working on your bike, and would rather pay someone else to do it, certain basics are necessary. Learn to spot dangerous conditions like frayed brake cables, worn brake blocks and tires, and loose fenders. Be aware of subtle symptoms, such as a funny clicking noise, a soft brake lever, or an unresponsive derailleur, and know what to do about it.

Understanding basics won't take long. Begin with a good bike repair book. *Anybody's Bike Book*, by Tom Cuthbertson, published by Ten Speed Press, is just one of many excellent examples. It doesn't cover everything, but it is close enough. Then cultivate a relationship with a bike addict or a repair person at your local shop. That helps those tricky one-of-a-kind problems. A good bike shop will cheerfully answer your questions and help find those little parts that never seem to be available. Bike repair classes also are offered at bike shops, park departments, or evening college programs.

Specialized tools are generally not needed, but the few essential ones are not expensive. Buy a few light tools to carry for touring. An ultralight tool kit might include the following:

1. Two or three tire irons, preferably of aluminum or plastic rather than steel, or a "Quick Stik" for prying clincher tires off rims.
2. A patch kit for repairing punctured tubes. Carry both a patch kit and a new tube. Many riders don't bother to fix punctures on the road, but simply install a new tube.

3. An allen wrench or two to fit the bike.
4. A small screwdriver.
5. Twenty-five cents. The 10-cent phone call is long gone.

A lengthy ride would justify carrying a heavier tool kit, which might also include some of the following:

6. A small (6-inch) adjustable wrench, such as a crescent type, or a few socket wrenches.
7. An extra brake cable and small, sharp cable cutter.
8. A spoke wrench.
9. Extra spokes. These can be taped to the frame or even bent and stuffed inside the handlebars.
10. A freewheel remover.
11. A chain tool.

This list could go on endlessly, limited only by the countless mechanical failures one can imagine, but the temptation to carry an extensive tool kit should be resisted. Instead, keep your bicycle on a regular maintenance schedule. Many on-the-road mechanical difficulties can be traced to neglect.

Safe Riding

Bicycling is a safe sport, but awareness of potential dangers is still required. The single most significant danger is the careless motorist. Many motorists watch for vehicles only as large as theirs. Anything on the road smaller than another car is either invisible or, even worse, seen but disregarded.

To battle this, arm yourself on three fronts: Wear bright clothing and ride defensively and responsibly. Bright clothing should include a helmet. Taking to the roads, or even bike paths, without one puts the rider unnecessarily at risk. Choose a helmet with either an ANSI or a Snell rating, or, better yet, one with both. Styles, colors, and weights vary, but be sure the helmet fits properly on your head and buckles snugly under your chin.

Ride defensively by seeking to avoid situations in which safety can be compromised. Be aware of traffic on the road—on foot, in motorized vehicles, or on bicycles. On a broad, busy highway, stay on the shoulder, out of the flow of traffic. Be prepared to relinquish the right of way, if necessary to avoid a moving vehicle.

Ride responsibly by maintaining a straight line, rather than constantly pulling in and out of traffic. Check oncoming traffic before moving around objects in your path and signal assertively and often to motorists and other cyclists. Cyclists demand roadway rights, but should also show respect for motorists. Maintain the image of an adult pursuing a serious form of transportation and act lawfully, predictably, and courteously.

Signal turns, obey traffic signs and lights, and ride single file when being overtaken by cars.

Oregon laws grant cyclists substantial roadway rights. The statutes specifically state bicycles are vehicles and, as such, have all rights and responsibilities accorded motorists. Laws allow cyclists to use any portion of the lane, if they can keep up with the flow of traffic. In faster traffic, when the lane is too narrow to allow cars to pass safely, cyclists may ride in the road, legally forcing motorists to pass them in the oncoming lane. While this kind of "offensive" riding is legal, it should be practiced only when necessary, with caution, and in the interest of safety. Obstructing a line of traffic is illegal. Otherwise, cyclists must keep up with traffic or stay to the right. On one-way streets, cyclists may keep to either the right or the left.

Courteous and responsible riding is also required. This includes obeying all traffic signals, signaling all turns, and riding two abreast only when the normal flow of traffic is not impeded. Since bicycles do not have brake lights to indicate slowing or stopping, cyclists should communicate through arm signals. One innovation provides that cyclists may signal a right turn by simply extending the right arm horizontally, rather than the left one upward.

Statutes also address the use of bike paths. The law allows cyclists to choose between the roadway and the bike path, even when both are present. Use of a bike path can be mandated only if local government has held a public hearing to determine if reasonable rates of speed are suitable on that specific bike path.

Safe riding also requires safe equipment. Wear a helmet and inspect your bike frequently for mechanical problems. Bombing down steep hills is great fun, but a mechanical failure or blowout at 40 miles per hour turns delight to disaster.

Cyclists should also consider advocating safe riding. Urge that roads and other public facilities be designed for safe use by bicyclists. Maintain awareness of what is occurring in the bicycling community and let your voice be heard through an organization that lobbies for your views.

Maps for Touring

The ideal bicycling map is small enough to be conveniently carried and used on the road, but sufficiently detailed to show every road and inter-section. Maps should also name every road accurately, and indicate which are paved. Topographic contour lines, along with cultural facilities such as small towns and public parks, should be included. Ideal bicycling maps do exist, but most have compromised one or more of these qualities. The maps in this guide approach the ideal, but also have compromises. They are intended to guide riders with a minimum risk of wrong turns.

U.S. Geological Survey (USGS) topographic maps are available from certain government offices and bookstores. Most are printed in scales either too large—the area covered is so small that several sheets must be carried—or too small—roads are not shown in sufficient detail. For ex-ample, the scale on the USGS 1:250,000 series maps is too small, and the scale on the 1:24,000 series (7.5-minute) maps is too large. The 1:62,500 series (15-minute) is a good compromise in terms of both size and detail, but few, if any, maps in that series have been updated recently. (Even-tually, the 15-minute series will be phased out entirely.) Moreover, none of the topographic maps indicate paving on backroads.

A series of 1:100,000, 60-minute metric topographic maps are being produced by USGS in a 31-inch-by-22-inch size. The scale is excellent for bike touring, cultural features are up-to-date, and the maps are easy to carry. Drawbacks are a relatively high price and the lack of pavement information on backroads.

The most reliable, although not always perfectly accurate, information about pavement is available from maps published by state highway de-partments in cooperation with the Federal Highway Administration. These inexpensive maps are published on a county-by-county basis, although some of the larger counties require more than one sheet for coverage. Of the several scales, three should be of interest to bike tourists.

The General Highway Series, although quite large (36-inch-by-42-inch), shows every public road with a generally accurate indication of paving, but doesn't give road names. For those who prefer to have road names shown, a separate Road Index Series is published in the same scale, but pavement status is not indicated. Given a choice between the two, riders who wish to avoid gravel roads will prefer the General Highway Series. As the highway department revises its maps, the need to make that choice will slowly disappear, since General Highway Series maps revised recently bear most road names, and the Road Index Series now show pavement status. In a few years, when maps for all thirty-six counties have been revised, either of the two series will suffice.

A third series, probably the most useful to bicyclists, consists of the

General Highway Series in a smaller size (17.5-inch-by-20-inch). This "half-size" series is less expensive and easier to carry. Printed in color, it is quite easy to read. An atlas of black-and-white, 8.5-inch-by-11-inch "quarter-size" maps is also available for a few dollars. These are particularly useful for photocopying and carrying on the road.

All Oregon Department of Transportation maps lack detail in cities and towns, and do not include the road names and pavement status on the same maps. Not to fear, however, for a new series of maps of cities and towns is available, along with aerial photos of most urban areas. Or, for the ultimate in map trivia, straight-line maps of state highways are available. These show every intersection, railroad crossing, bridge, and culvert, all measured to within 1/100th of a mile.

At this point, consider an addition onto your house to store maps. If you still are interested, write for a free map index and ordering information from the Oregon Department of Transportation, Map Distribution Unit, Room 17, Transportation Building, Salem, Oregon 97310. For maps in Washington, write the Washington Department of Transportation, Public Transportation and Planning, Highway Administration Building, Olympia, Washington 98504.

County maps are also available commercially under several brand names. While not as inexpensive as highway department versions described above, they do show most roads with corresponding names on the same map. Some detail in cities and towns is also included. Most commercial maps are quite large, however, and difficult to use on the road. On some, pavement status either is not indicated or does not appear to be as accurate as on state maps. Others appear to be reprinted substantially from state maps. Shop around among available brands to find one combining features you need.

For bicycling within cities, city street maps are generally adequate. City maps published by the state are excellent, but many communities also provide free guides. These are available from local visitors bureaus or chambers of commerce offices.

In addition, larger cities in the Willamette Valley publish street maps for cyclists. The *Salem Bicycle Map* is available from the City of Salem, 555 Liberty Street SE, Room 325, Salem, Oregon 97301, (503) 588-6211. The *Eugene Bicycle Map* is available from the Eugene Bicycle Coordinator, 858 Pearl Street, Suite 300, Eugene, Oregon 97401, (503) 687-5298. Order *Corvallis Area Bikeways* from the Corvallis Department of Community Development, P.O. Box 1083, Corvallis, Oregon 97339, (503) 757-6941. Only the Corvallis map is free. Maps generally are available at local bike shops and bookstores.

The Portland metropolitan area is covered by an excellent bike map, *Getting There By Bike*. Available for a fee from the Metropolitan Service District, 2000 SW First Avenue, Portland, Oregon 97201, (503) 221-1646, it is also sold in local bike shops and bookstores.

For biking outside of cities, the State of Oregon publishes two specific brochures and offers state highway maps. *Oregon Bicycling Guide* highlights cross-county and state routes for cyclists, and the Oregon Coast route and facilities are detailed in *Oregon Coast Bike Route*. Obtain these free from bike shops or the State Department of Transportation, Bicycle Program Manager, Room 200, Transportation Building, Salem, Oregon 97310, (503) 378-3432.

The Astoria-to-Idaho route was established in 1976 by Bikecentennial. Detailed maps and guides for this and several other cross-country routes are listed in a catalog of maps and books available from Bikecentennial, P.O. Box 8308, Missoula, Montana 59807.

For riders heading north into Washington, Cascade Bicycle Club of Seattle publishes the Seattle-to-Portland (STP) route map. Developed for the annual and popular STP, it is available from Cascade Bicycle Club, P.O. Box 31299, Seattle, Washington 98103, (206) 522-3222, or from Bikecentennial.

MULTNOMAH COUNTY
1 Columbia River Highway

Starting point: Lewis and Clark State Park near Troutdale, just south of I-84, exit no. 18
Distance: Up to 49.8 miles
Terrain: Hilly
Total cumulative elevation gain: 1900 feet
Recommended time of year: Any season, except when freezing conditions exist in the Columbia River Gorge
Recommended starting time: 9:00 A.M.
Allow: 6 hours

Points of interest:
Columbia River Gorge
Eight state parks
Vista House at Crown Point
Columbia River Highway bridges
Numerous waterfalls

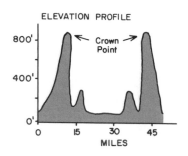

Started in the late 1800s by bicyclists who were tired of cycling on muddy roads, the "Good Roads" movement gained strength in the early 1900s when automobiles became available to the masses. In the Northwest the movement was championed by railroad attorney Sam Hill, who had a vision of a beautiful highway built through the Columbia River Gorge, a road to be constructed in complete harmony with its surroundings.

Construction began in 1913 with the political and financial assistance of lumberman Simon Benson and a newly formed state highway commission. Lumberman John Yeon helped by serving for two years without pay as Multnomah County Roadmaster, and Samuel Lancaster, back from a tour of roads in the Alps with Sam Hill, was hired as supervising engineer.

Opened in 1915, the highway was acclaimed both an engineering marvel and an aesthetic masterpiece. Sensitive design by Lancaster, together with painstaking skills of immigrant stonemasons, created a highway to be respected. It was not only a key transportation route, but also a special roadway to be savored at a slow pace, mindful of the inspired craftsmanship that created it. Despite the awesome terrain of the gorge, nowhere did the slope of the road exceed 5 percent, nor were any of the curves on a radius of less than 100 feet. Careful placement of the roadbed, miles and miles of hand-built stone railings, dozens of beautiful bridges (of which no two were identical), and several basalt tunnels (one with arched windows) were features that brought widespread acclaim to the highway.

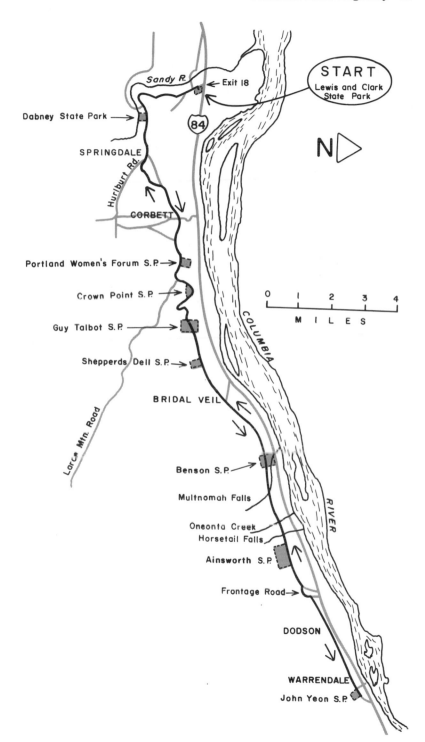

Following World War II, however, the public wanted more than "good roads." They wanted interstate freeways, making the picturesque Columbia River Highway obsolete. Construction of what now is Interstate 84 began in 1948, and eventually destroyed much of Lancaster's work.

Today, the western half of the highway from Troutdale to Warrendale remains intact, as does the easternmost section from Mosier to The Dalles. In between, from Warrendale to Mosier, the original highway has been badly segmented by the addition of the freeway. Many segments have been destroyed, and others have been abandoned, neglected, or, at best, poorly preserved.

The ride described here covers the intact western half of the highway, starting near Troutdale, slowly climbing up over Crown Point, and then descending to near-water level, to pass at the feet of many of the gorge's spectacular waterfalls. Although the entire western section of 24.9 miles is described as an out-and-back trip of 49.8 miles, it can be shortened by a U-turn at any point, or the ride could begin at any of the parks or waterfalls along the highway. For example, the climb over Crown Point can be avoided by starting at Latourell Falls, just east of there. The ride also can be lengthened to 3 or 4 days. For specifics on that option, please see Trip No. 45, the Mount Hood Loop.

One caution: Designed for Model T's, the Columbia River Highway is narrow and twisting, with segments of aging pavement. On sunny days the road may be populated by tourists who pay more attention to scenery than to the road. Ride carefully.

MILEAGE LOG

0.0   Lewis and Clark State Park (day use only; water available). Leave the parking lot and turn left. Follow this road past the Troutdale bridge at 0.3 mile and the Stark Street bridge at 2.9 miles. The entrance to Dabney State Park (day use only; water available) is on the right at 3.3 miles.

4.6   Springdale. Bear right, following the signs to Crown Point.

4.8   Bear left at the intersection with Hurlburt Road.

6.3   Corbett.

8.8   Portland Women's Forum State Park (day use only; water available). Probably the most famous view of the gorge is from this park at Chanticleer Point. Enjoy seeing Beacon Rock in the distance and look at what is coming as you proceed into the gorge.

9.2   Intersection with Larch Mountain Road. Bear left.

10.0   Crown Point State Park, consisting of the Vista House, was conceived by Lancaster as an observatory from which the gorge "could be viewed in silent communion with the infinite." On weekends and during the summer months visitors can enjoy interesting displays of gorge fauna and flora, and old photos of the area. The displays and volunteers make this a worthwhile stop. (Rest rooms; water available). The highway curves around the front of Vista House and then drops (at a 5 percent grade) under a picturesque archway through a series of Lancaster's graceful 100-foot curves.

12.4 Latourell Falls day use area, part of Guy Talbot State Park (day use only; water available). Walk your bike up a short path for a full view of the falls. Also note the craftsmanship of the highway bridge over Latourell Creek. It is probably the only braced-spandrel, concrete-arched bridge in the state, and one of the first built in the United States.

13.7 Shepperds Dell State Park (day use only; water not available). A short path at the east end of the bridge gives excellent views of the bridge and Shepperds Dell Falls. In spring there are lots of plants to be viewed close up.

14.7 Bridal Veil Bridge. This small bridge is supported by its solid railings, rather than from below, to allow clearance for the three log flumes and the small dam that once lay beneath it.

15.3 Bridal Veil. Continue east on the **Columbia River Highway**, rather than turning left to the freeway.

17.9 Wahkeena Falls, part of Benson State Park.

18.5 Multnomah Falls, the highest in Oregon at a combined height of 620 feet (store, concession; water available). On both sides of the falls, the highway traverses steep ground on concrete viaducts. The lodge was constructed in 1925.

20.8 Oneonta Creek. The present highway bridge was built in 1948 to replace the original 1914 structure, now used as a wayside. Note evidence of the tunnel to the east, which was closed when the new bridge was built.

21.1 Horsetail Falls.

21.6 Ainsworth State Park picnic area. An overnight camping area is located at mile 23.8 (water available).

22.4 Intersection with I-84. Turn right, following the signs toward I-84 eastbound. A short section of the old highway was destroyed by this interchange's construction.

22.7 Turn right on **Frontage Road**. At mile 22.8, Frontage Road rejoins the old alignment of the Columbia River Highway.

23.1 Dodson. The large barn on the south side of the road was built circa 1870. Above it sits a basalt formation known as St. Peters Dome.

24.0 Warrendale.

24.9 John Yeon State Park (day use only; water not available). East of this point, the old highway was destroyed by construction of I-84. This is the eastern end of the ride described here. Make a U-turn and proceed west, retracing the route back to Lewis and Clark State Park.

49.8 Lewis and Clark State Park. End of ride.

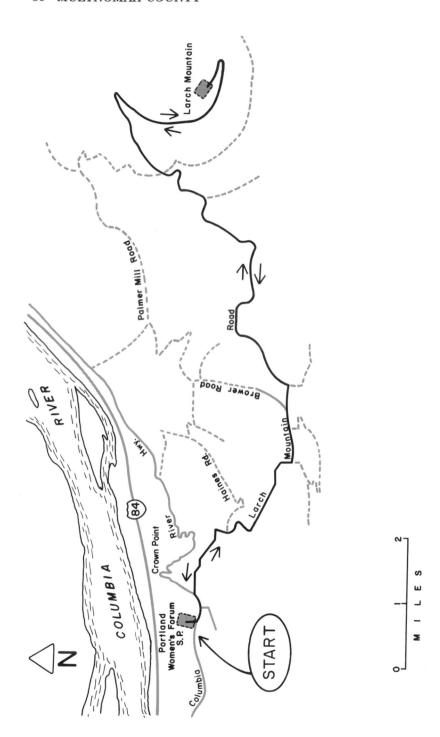

2 Larch Mountain

Starting point: Portland
Women's Forum State Park
(Chanticleer Point), 1 mile west
of Crown Point on the Columbia
River Highway
Distance: 30.2 miles
Terrain: Very hilly
**Total cumulative elevation
gain:** 3220 feet
Recommended time of year:
Any season except winter
Recommended starting time:
11:00 A.M.
Allow: 4 hours

Points of interest:
Chanticleer Point
Summit of Larch Mountain
Views of major peaks in
Washington and Oregon

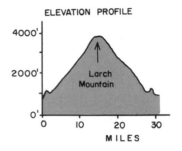

The Columbia Gorge has a complex geologic history. Its steep walls are believed to have been created by the uplifting of the Cascade Range. Heavy rains enabled the Columbia to cut slowly through the range as it rose. Massive floods further enhanced the river's ability to cut a channel lined with steep basalt cliffs. Due to the steep terrain, fairly high peaks now stand short distances from the sea-level Columbia. Larch Mountain is an excellent example: More than 4000 feet high, it lies only 3.5 miles from the Columbia.

This ride follows a well-paved road to within a few feet of the summit of Larch Mountain, a former volcano. The route does not begin at sea level, but starts 840 feet above the river at Portland Women's Forum State Park, a prominent viewpoint. Even so, the ride presents a 3000-foot climb, averaging more than 100 feet of elevation gain in each mile. While the road is never truly steep, it climbs at a steady rate, with very few level stretches.

For those who might prefer to begin at sea level, start the ride at Lewis and Clark State Park near Troutdale, for a round trip of 47.8 miles and a cumulative elevation gain of 4050 feet. (The ride from Lewis and Clark State Park to Portland Women's Forum State Park is described as the first 8.8 miles of Trip No. 2.)

The road ends at a Forest Service picnic ground near the mountain's summit. For the best views, walk your bike up a short trail, then carry it up a few steps or stow it in the woods to visit Sherrard Point, just north of the true summit. On clear days mounts Rainier, Adams, and St. Helens in Washington and mounts Hood and Jefferson in Oregon can be seen from this point.

Descending Larch Mountain is speedy, perhaps taking less than one-half hour. Check your brakes before you start, and be careful of the frequent curves and occasional traffic.

Larch Mountain was apparently named for the larch, a tree unusual because, unlike most evergreens, it is deciduous, losing its needles in the fall. In late September, as their needles begin to drop, larches turn a beautiful yellow hue. That's no reason to ride up Larch Mountain in September, however, since not a single larch tree has been found there. In Oregon, larches grow only on the east side of the Cascades.

Due to the location and elevation of Larch Mountain, weather should play a key role in planning this ride. The Columbia Gorge is noted for terrible and rapidly changing weather conditions. Consult a current forecast and if conditions turn for the worse during your ride, consider a quick descent. This advice is particularly important during periods of cold weather, when snow and freezing rain are always strong possibilities in the gorge.

When snow comes to the gorge, Larch Mountain generally cannot be ridden for some time thereafter, since the road is usually not plowed beyond mile 7.0. If in doubt about weather or snow conditions, call the Forest Service's Columbia Gorge Ranger Station in Troutdale, (503) 695-2276, or the Columbia Gorge National Scenic Area office in Hood River, (503) 386-2333.

MILEAGE LOG

0.0 Portland Women's Forum State Park. Park at Chanticleer Point, the lower (northern) end of the park, and then ride south, out of the park, toward the Columbia River Highway.

0.1 Turn left on the **Columbia River Highway**.

0.5 Bear right on **Larch Mountain Road**. Follow Larch Mountain Road all the way to the picnic ground near the Larch Mountain summit.

15.1 Larch Mountain parking lot and picnic ground (water not available). A 0.25-mile trail leads to a viewpoint. After lunch or a rest, retrace the route back down to your car.

29.7 **Columbia River Highway**. Turn left.

30.1 Turn right into Portland Women's Forum State Park.

30.2 Chanticleer Point. End of ride.

3 Sandy River Gorge

Starting point: Lewis and Clark State Park near Troutdale, just south of I-84, exit no. 18
Distance: 39.4 miles
Terrain: Very hilly
Total cumulative elevation gain: 2700 feet
Recommended time of year: Any season, except during possible snowy conditions
Recommended starting time: 10:00 A.M.
Allow: 5 hours

Points of interest:
Lewis and Clark State Park
Dabney State Park
Sandy River Gorge
Bull Run Gorge
Roslyn Lake

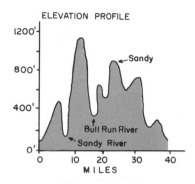

ELEVATION PROFILE

The Sandy River and its tributary, the Bull Run, have cut deep gorges into the foothills west of Mount Hood. This ride descends into the Sandy Gorge three times and the Bull Run once, in each case making a steep climb back out again. Since the three climbs each involve elevation gains of several hundred feet, and one rises more than 1000 feet, this is not a flatlander trip, despite traverses of several flat plateaus between each gorge. The plateaus, by the way, offer rewarding views of Mount Hood and surrounding foothills.

The several descents are not only long and steep, but some are also on narrow, fairly rough roads. Make certain your bike is in good condition, paying particular attention to its brakes and tires.

The ride visits or passes within striking distance of at least five parks. Lewis and Clark and Dabney state parks are along the lower Sandy River, while Oxbow and Dodge county parks are farther up the Sandy River Gorge. Roslyn Lake Park, operated by the public utility company that created the man-made lake, lies on a plateau between the Sandy and Bull Run gorges.

The trip begins at Lewis and Clark State Park near the mouth of the Sandy and then climbs slowly past Dabney State Park to Springdale, where it turns south to make a sudden and very steep drop, returning to the Sandy River. At its lowest point, the road skirts the river near Oxbow Park and then climbs steeply out of the gorge to the flat farmland surrounding the nearly nonexistent community of Aims.

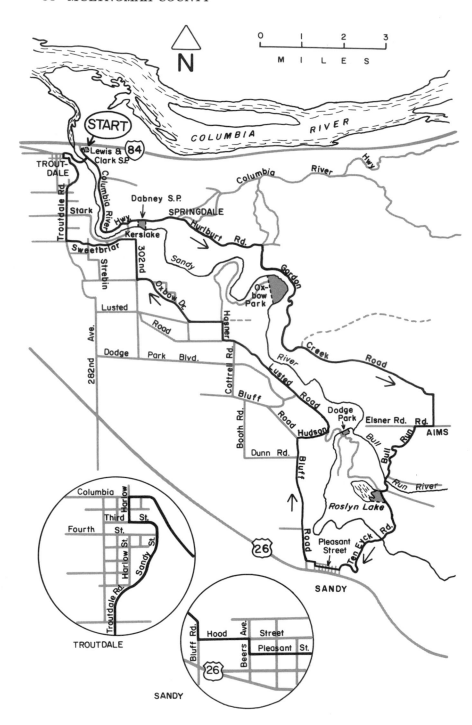

Flat pedaling is short-lived. The road makes another sudden and steep drop, this time to the Bull Run River, and then immediately climbs 350 feet to Roslyn Lake. After another short, flat section, the route drops back into Sandy Gorge, leaving the cyclist to grind up to the town of Sandy and onto the farmland north of there. This climb can be the most rewarding because a choice of parks and eating facilities, plus a view of where you've been, are on top. A final drop into and out of Sandy Gorge (which can be avoided by a level shortcut) is followed by a pleasant ride to Troutdale through east Multnomah County farmland.

Named Sandy because early explorers in the Vancouver Party discovered quicksand in the vicinity of the town and the river, this area is being steadily developed. Bull Run is an important source of water for the Portland populace. Scenic landscapes and tantalizing scents still reward cyclists venturing through the area.

MILEAGE LOG

0.0 Lewis and Clark State Park. Leave the parking lot and turn left. Follow this road past the Troutdale bridge at 0.3 mile and the Stark Street bridge at 2.9 miles. The entrance to Dabney State Park (day use only; water available) is on the right at 3.3 miles. It offers several paved trails to explore by bicycle.

4.6 Springdale. Bear right along the river, following the sign toward Crown Point.

4.8 Bear right on **Hurlburt Road**, as the Columbia River Highway goes left.

6.8 Turn right on **Gordon Creek Road**. At mile 7.3, the road makes a sudden and steep decline into the Sandy River Gorge. Gordon Creek Road eventually becomes **Bull Run Road**.

15.0 Aims. At the T-intersection, turn right, following Bull Run Road.

15.5 At an intersection with Elsner Road, turn left, following Bull Run Road as it begins another steep descent. At mile 17.5, cross a bridge over the Bull Run River and then begin a steep climb.

18.1 Roslyn Lake. Turn left on **Ten Eyck Road**. (To the right, a dike along the lake offers a place to lunch or rest.) At mile 18.7 is the entrance to Roslyn Lake Park (Thomas Road). Continue on Ten Eyck Road as it descends to the Sandy River at mile 19.8 and then climbs to the town of Sandy. Poor pavement surfaces and quick loss of elevation dictate caution here.

21.7 Sandy. Turn right on **Pleasant Street**, which is one block before an intersection with Highway 26.

22.3 At a T-intersection with **Beers Avenue** (unmarked), turn right and ride one block north.

22.4 Turn left on **Hood Street**.

22.5 At a T-intersection with **Bluff Road**, turn right. Excellent views of Mount Hood and the Sandy River Gorge are available at mile 23.4 (Jonsrud's Viewpoint). Watch for rafters and kayakers in the river below and marvel at where you've been.

25.7 Turn right on **Hudson Road**, which makes a steep descent starting 0.5 mile later. Be careful on this narrow, relatively rough road.
(For those tiring of all the hills, a flat shortcut is available here.
Continue west on Bluff Road and then turn right on Cottrell Road
at mile 27.5, rejoining the main route at its mile 30.0. The shortcut
reduces the length of the ride by 1.2 miles.)

26.9 Turn left at a T-intersection with **Lusted Road**. (Dodge Park,
which features a swimming hole in the river and lots of shade, is
located about 1 mile to the right, down a steep hill.) Lusted Road
is level for 2.5 miles and then climbs out of the gorge.

30.2 Turn right on **Hosner Road**.

30.7 Turn left on **Oxbow Drive**. (To make a side trip into Oxbow Park,
about 1.5 miles each way, continue straight ahead, down another
long hill.) Follow Oxbow Drive as it eventually becomes **Division
Street** (immediately before the intersection with 302nd).

33.2 Turn right on **302nd**, which turns left at mile 34.2 and becomes
Kerslake Road.

35.0 Turn left (uphill) on **Sweetbriar Road** one block before an intersection with Stark Street. Follow Sweetbriar through an intersection with Strebin Road at mile 35.4.

36.1 Turn right on **Troutdale Road** in Troutdale and then right for
one block on **Sandy Avenue**, which becomes **Eighth Street** and
then **Third Street**.

38.3 Turn right on **Harlow Street**.

38.4 Turn right on the historic **Columbia River Highway** at a T-intersection, and follow it to the Troutdale bridge at 39.1 miles. You may wish to visit the depot and historic monument on your left before you begin to descend to the river. It relates a story of busier times in this small community. Troutdale Community Park, at the bottom of the hill, is a good place to watch smelt runs in the springtime.

39.2 Cross the bridge and turn left at a T-intersection onto the **Columbia River Highway** (unmarked).

39.4 Lewis and Clark State Park. Turn right into the parking lot. End of ride.

4 Sauvie Island

Starting point: A gravel parking lot at the east end of the Sauvie Island Bridge, 12 miles north of Portland, just east of Highway 30. To reach the island from I-5 southbound, exit at Lombard Street (Highway 30) and proceed to St. John's Bridge. Turn left toward Scappoose and then right to cross Sauvie Island bridge.
Distance: 12.4 miles
Terrain: Flat

Total cumulative elevation gain: Negligible
Recommended time of year: Any season
Recommended starting time: Any time
Allow: 1 to 2 hours
Points of interest:
Sauvie Island Wildlife Management Area
Walton Beach
Bybee-Howell House

Probably the single most popular backroads bicycle tour in the state, the loop road around the southern end of Sauvie Island also attracts many long-distance runners. The reasons are obvious. The island is only a dozen miles from downtown Portland, yet it is scenic, historic, teeming with wildlife, and (above all else) perfectly level.

One of the largest freshwater islands in the country, Sauvie Island sits in the mouth of the Willamette. The Columbia forms its eastern boundary, while the Multnomah Channel winds past its 20-mile-long western shore. Sailboats populate the Columbia, houseboats line Multnomah Channel, and huge cargo ships steam up and down the Willamette.

The island is only a few feet above sea level, and if the southern end were not diked, the entire island would be under water several times a year. As a result of diking, the southern end is now rich farmland. The northern end remains covered to a large extent with the waters of Sturgeon Lake and the Gilbert River. (Yes, Sauvie Island is large enough to have its own rivers and lakes, and those lakes in turn have their own islands.)

Much of the northern end is a state wildlife management area. A major stopping point on the Pacific Flyway, Sauvie Island is prime birdwatching country. In spring and fall, flocks of sandhill cranes stop by on their way north or south, and great blue herons can be seen year-round. Stop by the management area headquarters on Sauvie Island Road for their brochures on the wildlife of the island. This is a small building that may not be open when you visit. If not, look for their excellent map and other information in an adjacent kiosk.

Sauvie Island has a rich history. Lewis and Clark camped there, but failed to notice a major river, the Willamette, joining the Columbia at the island's southern end. Later the island was used as a dairy farm by the Hudson's Bay Company, and came to be named after a French-Canadian employee of the dairy.

In 1856, a stately home was built on the west side of the island by James Bybee. The last survivor of early farmsteads, the house is open to the public every summer. The Oregon Historical Society opened it after the second owners, the Howells, donated it to Multnomah County in 1959. Each fall, usually on the last Saturday in September, the society holds a "wintering-in" festival at the house to celebrate the island's harvest and the changing seasons.

Also allow time for visiting the wildlife refuge. Unless you're on a bicycle suitable for unpaved roads, you'll need to walk to the best viewing spots. Binoculars would also be helpful.

The main 12.4-mile loop around the southern end of the island is described below, but toward the north end, three side trips can be followed. At mile 6.1, Reeder Road leads north 8 miles to Walton Beach on the Columbia. At mile 9.2, Oak Island Road follows the Gilbert River toward Sturgeon Lake, while at mile 10.5, Sauvie Island Road can be followed north along Multnomah Channel.

One caution: The island's roads are narrow, and the residents are understandably impatient with inconsiderate bikers and joggers. When traffic is present, ride single file. It's just common courtesy.

MILEAGE LOG

0.0 East end of the Sauvie Island Bridge (store). Ride south, under the bridge, on **Gillihan Loop Road**.

6.1 Turn left at an intersection with **Reeder Road**. (For a side trip to Walton Beach, turn right.) At mile 7.3, a set of stairs leads over a dike for watching birds on Sturgeon Lake.

9.2 Keep left at an intersection with Oak Island Road.

10.5 At a T-intersection, turn left on **Gillihan Loop Road**. (For a side trip north along Multnomah Channel, turn right on Sauvie Island Road.)

11.5 The Bybee-Howell House is on the left, down a short driveway.

12.4 East end of the Sauvie Island Bridge. End of ride.

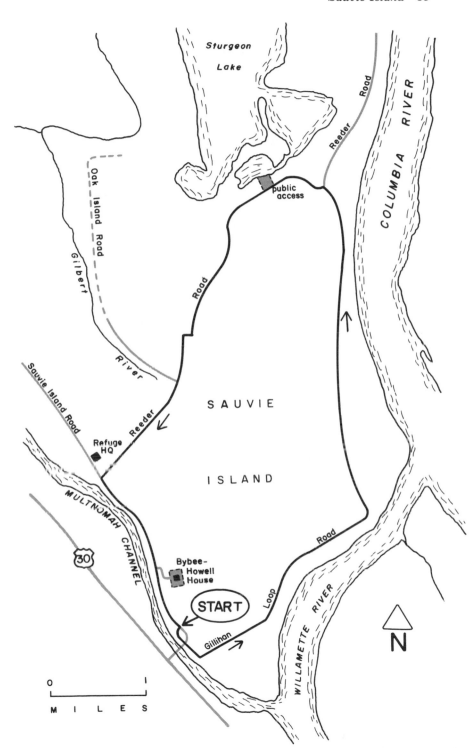

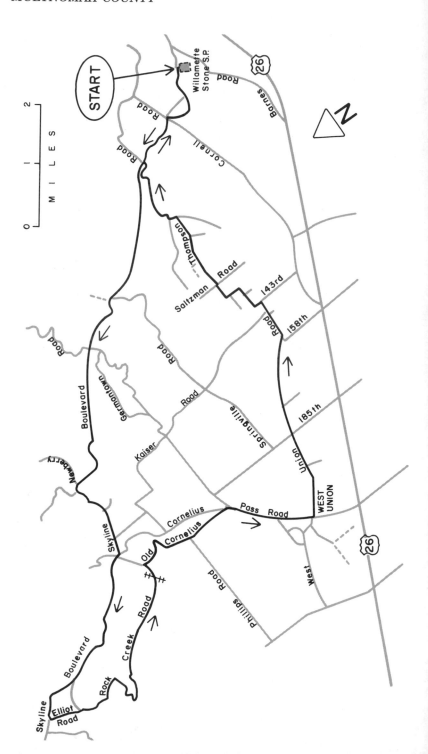

5 Skyline Boulevard

Starting point: Willamette
Stone State Park at 6500 NW
Skyline Boulevard in Portland.
From downtown Portland, drive
west on West Burnside Street,
and then bear right on Skyline
Boulevard.
Distance: 33.2 miles
Terrain: Very hilly
**Total cumulative elevation
gain:** 2900 feet
Recommended time of year:
Any season
Recommended starting time:
Before 11:00 A.M.
Allow: 3 to 4 hours

Points of interest:
Willamette Stone State Park
Forest Park

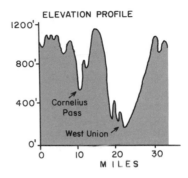

The Tualatin Mountains form a thin ridge that stretches along the
Willamette River from Portland northwest toward Sauvie Island, sepa-
rating the lower Willamette from the Tualatin Valley to the west. For
years the ridge served as an obstacle to Tualatin Valley farmers who
needed to bring their crops to market at shipping ports such as Linnton
and Portland. Eventually, the ridge was crossed by several roads with
colorful names such as Canyon, Logie Trail, and Rocky Point.
   Many road names on the ridge are Teutonic in origin, since the Tualatin
Valley was a popular settling place for German immigrants. While other
Teutonic-named streets in the Portland area were renamed during World
War I, the ridge still boasts Germantown Road, Kaiser Road, and Saltzman
Road.
   One road, appropriately named Skyline Boulevard, was built on the
long crest of the ridge, running 20 miles from Burnside Street to 1609-
foot Dixie Mountain. Following that road for most of its length, this ride
then drops into the Tualatin Valley for the return trip. It is a hilly ride,
since the ridge is more than 1000 feet higher than the valley floor and
is notched by several small passes, but the scenery is unsurpassed. The
road follows the true crest of the ridge, so views in both directions reward
the pedaler's effort. To the southwest, the Chehalem Mountains rise from
the far edge of the flat Tualatin Valley. To the northeast, the Willamette
joins the Columbia and Mount St. Helens stands in the background.
   The ride starts at Willamette Stone State Park near the southern end
of the ridge. (For riders closer to Hillsboro, the route can be initiated at
West Union School; see Trip No. 9 for directions.) Originally marked in
1851, the Willamette Stone is the intersection of the Willamette Meridian

and the Willamette Baseline. It remains the central reference point for surveys of the Pacific Northwest and is a short walk through the woods from Skyline Boulevard.

For the first 9 miles of the ride described here, much of the ridge's northeast side is part of Forest Park, a 4700-acre preserve and probably the country's largest city park. Once platted as a subdivision in the city of Linnton, the wooded hillside became part of Portland in 1915 when Linnton was annexed. Later, the land was turned over to the city due to nonpayment of taxes, and was officially designated a park in 1947. The city has refrained from intensively developing the park, treasuring the urban wilderness it encompasses. There are a few bicycle trails within the park. For details contact the Portland Bureau of Parks and Recreation.

A mixture of wooded hills and small pastures, the ridge itself has an occasional store or grange hall, and a growing number of houses situated to take advantage of the views. Its primary character seems lofty and isolated, as though protected by its steep ramparts.

MILEAGE LOG

0.0 Willamette Stone State Park. Turn left out of the parking area, riding west on **Skyline Boulevard**. Pass through intersections with Cornell Road (1.4 miles), Thompson Road (2.3 miles), Springville Road (5.1 miles), Germantown Road (6.2 miles), and Newberry Road (8.9 miles).

10.6 Cross **Cornelius Pass Road** (store), bearing right and slightly uphill to stay with Skyline Boulevard.

11.5 A good vista point. On a clear day, four mountains and the Columbia River can be seen on the right.

14.1 Turn left on **Elliot Road** as Skyline Drive continues straight ahead. A few feet after this intersection, the ride crosses its highest point (1190 feet) and then starts its rapid drop into the Tualatin Valley.

14.8 Turn right at a T-intersection with **Rock Creek Road**. The road continues to drop rapidly until it crosses Rock Creek at mile 16.4, after which the decline is more gradual.

19.1 Make a hard right turn onto **Old Cornelius Pass Road.**

21.2 Turn right on **Cornelius Pass Road** (historic restaurant).

22.7 West Union (store). Turn left on **West Union Road**. Proceed carefully.

26.7 Turn left at a T-intersection with 143rd Avenue on the right and **Thompson Road** on the left.

27.7 Follow Thompson Road as it jogs right, and then left, at an intersection with Saltzman Road. Thompson Road begins to climb steeply toward Skyline Boulevard, passing through the community of Bonny Slope (store).

30.9 Turn right on **Skyline Boulevard**.

33.2 Willamette Stone State Park on the right. End of ride.

WASHINGTON COUNTY
6 Oregon Coaster

Starting point: Vernonia, 40 miles northwest of Portland. Follow Highway 26 past Hillsboro and Forest Grove, then Highway 47 north into Vernonia. From Washington state, take Highway 432 through Longview, cross into Oregon, and turn right on Highway 30. Follow Old Rainier Road and Apiary Road to Vernonia. Obtain permission in advance for overnight parking at Washington Grade School. The Vernonia School District accepts no liability, but generally grants permission, unless the area is being used for another event.
Distance: Total, 177.6 miles (first day, 68.7 miles; second day, 47.9 miles; third day, 61 miles)
Terrain: Flat to hilly and mountainous

Total cumulative elevation gain: Total, 5450 feet (first day, 1350 feet; second day, 1500 feet; third day, 2600 feet)
Recommended time of year: Late May to September
Recommended starting time: 8:00 A.M.
Allow: 3 days
Points of interest:
Jewell Meadows Wildlife Area
Seaside, Oregon's oldest resort community
Replica of Lewis and Clark saltworks
Oregon Coast beaches, viewpoints, parks
Tillamook Cheese Factory
Oregon's first "Rail to Trail" linear park

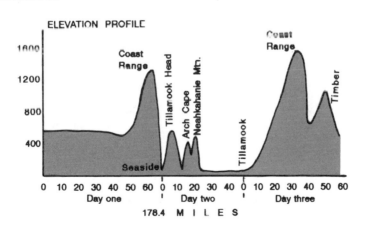

In 1913, the Oregon State Legislature reserved more than 400 miles of seashore "for the people." Today, that strip of land, teeming with cars, buses, recreational vehicles, pedestrians, and bicycles, makes direct deposits into the state's economy. Thanks to the late visionary Oregon governor Oswald West, this land includes Highway 101, which runs along the shoreline from Washington state to California. His contribution was enhanced in 1969, when a court case declared the areas between mean high tide and the visible line of vegetation to be land for public recreation and enjoyment.

In 1991 alone, more than 9000 cyclists enjoyed these public lands, gaining smiles and memories while adding approximately $1.7 million to the area's economy. With the aid of an excellent Oregon Coast bicycling map, available free from the State Bicycling Coordinator, cyclists can ride the shoulder of Highway 101, drink in panoramas and salt air, and discover campgrounds or motels. (See the introduction for details on ordering maps.)

A sampling of the scenic coast, this trip first investigates the forest. Pedaling along quiet backroads, the initial 65 miles sets a serene tone to carry cyclists through the bustle and excitement of the coast. Starting in Vernonia, nestled in a small valley on the east side of the Coast Range, the ride visits Mist, Birkenfeld, and Jewell, and a wildlife reserve. Then it connects with the Sunset Highway from Portland to travel the shoulder up and over the Coast Range to the beach.

To spend the first night in Oregon's oldest resort community, follow the route north about 4 miles to Seaside. Since the majority of cyclists, and many motorists, travel from north to south, this provides a different perspective, but it is no less scenic. In Seaside, where the Lewis and Clark Trail is commemorated, are abundant shops, restaurants, and accommodations, and a spectacular sandy beach to explore. As with this entire tour, this adds to the difficulty of deciding what to try next.

The second day begins with a visit to the Lewis and Clark saltworks replica. After a winter at Fort Clatsop near the Columbia River, the Lewis and Clark party prepared for the long journey back to Missouri. One essential to preserve food on the journey was salt. Since the seawater near the fort was heavily influenced by the freshwater Columbia, three men from the party traveled along the Pacific Ocean to what is now Seaside. Working in shifts around the clock for almost all of December, they boiled 1400 gallons of seawater to obtain 20 pounds of salt.

Leaving Seaside, the route's excitement intensifies. Unpack your smiles and keep the camera handy for the many viewpoints and beaches. An early start is also wise for the day's southbound pedaling. It will end in Tillamook with a special highlight, but all too quickly.

The highlight, a tour of the Tillamook Cheese Factory, which is open daily, offers a look at cheese making and free samples. Also enjoy a huge ice cream cone while you consider the difficulties early dairy farmers in this valley overcame to get their product to market. Blessed with lots of dairy cows feeding well on the lush grasses, the farmers originally sought to sell fresh milk. However, the Tillamook ocean bar was treacherous, even for large ships, and roads through the forest were so arduous and time-consuming the delivery of fresh milk was impossible. They turned to

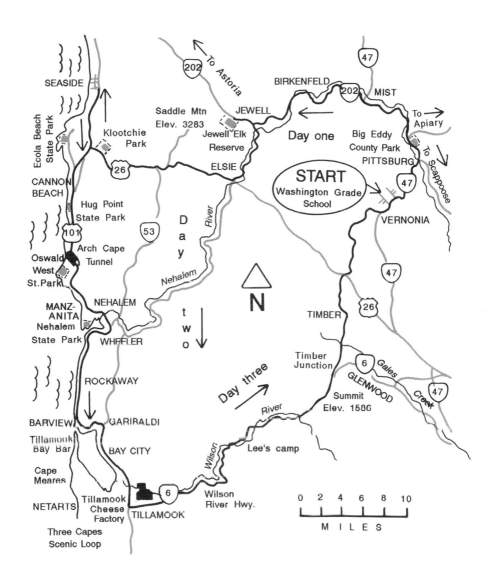

cheese making and turned famous in 1914, when Tillamook cheddar won first place at the St. Louis World's Fair.

After an overnight in Tillamook, the route winds along the Wilson River through the beautiful Tillamook State Forest. The ride is surprisingly easy, despite a climb over the 1586-foot Wilson River Summit. Use the time to enjoy the scenery and to ponder major forest fires (Tillamook Burns), which have wiped out millions of board feet of timber here. A half mile before Glenwood and a return to urban life, the route ducks into the woods again to climb up and down and into the tiny community of Timber. A few miles later, and the last part of the tour is within reach.

Outside of Vernonia, pause to look at Oregon's first "Rail to Trail" conversion. Using an old railroad bed, the trail follows Highway 47 to Banks on the other side of Highway 26. Along the way, the 20-mile trail passes under the 600-foot Buxton trestle, used for a daring train-top fight in the movie *Emperor of the North*. The trail's surface is rough rock, so it possibly won't be your choice for returning to Vernonia.

Cyclists planning this trip should be aware of the popularity of the route. Arrangements for parking in Vernonia and overnights along the way, whether indoors or tents, should be made well in advance. For parking, contact the Vernonia School District. For motels and hotels, take advantage of the many 800 numbers offered by lodging facilities in the area. However, be aware that 3-day weekends bring restrictions on 1-night bookings. Prime cycling time on the coast begins in May and starts to taper off in August, but motorists frequent the area year-round.

MILEAGE LOG

First Day

0.0   Bridge and East streets, Vernonia. Turn right (east) on **Bridge Street**, following **Highway 47** through Vernonia.

0.8   Bear left to continue on Highway 47, now named **Mist Drive** or **Newhalem Highway.**

5.0   Pittsburg Junction. Stay north on Highway 47 as roads to St. Helens and Scappoose split off at this intersection.

8.0   Big Eddy County Park (water, snacks available). Continue toward Mist.

8.9   Apiary Junction. Continue north on Highway 47.

12.5   Old schoolhouse on the right.

13.3   Natal (museum).

16.2   Mist Junction. Bear left onto **Highway 202** toward Birkenfeld.

21.4   Birkenfeld (store, restaurant). Turn right for services. Route continues (southwest) through the intersection. Clatsop County line is crossed at mile 23.4.

33.3   Jewell (tavern). Continue north on Highway 202 to Jewell Meadows Wildlife Area. (Those who do not wish to see the elk herds, deer, coyote, or birds should turn left at this junction (**Highway 103**) and continue south toward Highway 26.)

34.9   Jewell Elk Reserve. Turn left into the park. (Picnic tables, rest rooms; water available.)

35.0   Turn right onto Highway 202 and retrace the route back to Jewell.

36.6   Turn right toward Elsie on **Highway 103** (unmarked).

44.0   Turn right onto **Highway 26**. Ride the shoulder for 21 miles, climbing up and over the Coast Range. Traffic can be busy on this road, so ride carefully.

63.4 To see the world's largest Sitka spruce tree, turn right into Klootchie Park, and then return to this point to continue toward Cannon Beach Junction.

65.2 Cannon Beach Junction. Bear right onto **Highway 101** and pedal north toward Seaside.

68.7 Seaside. There are many accommodations and restaurants here. End of day.

Second Day

0.0 Seaside Turnaround (Pacific Ocean and Promenade). Head eight blocks south down the prom to **Lewis and Clark Way**. One block off the prom is the replica of the Lewis and Clark saltworks.

0.6 Continue away from the beach on Lewis and Clark Way.

0.7 Turn right on **Downing**.

1.0 Turn left on **Avenue U**. Cross the Necanium River.

1.2 Turn right on **Highway 101** toward Cannon Beach.

3.0 Cannon Beach Junction. Continue south, turning right at mile 6.0 toward Cannon Beach. (At mile 6.3 an optional right turn leads to Ecola Beach State Park.) Continue straight ahead.

6.8 Cannon Beach (stores, restaurants, bakeries). After visiting this charming beachfront community, follow **Hemlock Street** south to its end. Several viewpoints and beaches invite stops.

9.4 Turn right onto **Highway 101**, continuing south.

10.7 Hug Point State Park.

13.7 Arch Cape Tunnel. Activate the tunnel's yellow flashing light before entering and be alert to oncoming traffic.

13.9 Begin climbing Neahkahnie Mountain.

17.3 Oswald West State Park. This large park offers shade and nice views of the ocean. It is a great place to rest.

18.5 Viewpoint.

19.1 Summit of Neahkahnie Mountain.

21.2 Manzanita Junction. Turn right for an optional tour of this quiet community (beaches, restaurants, stores).

21.9 Continue south on **Highway 101** as the road to Nehalem Bay State Park comes in on the right. The park is on the point, 2 miles away. The return route offers an option of rejoining Highway 101 in the town of Nehalem.

23.0 Nehalem (stores, galleries, shops).

25.4 Wheeler. Tickets are on sale here for the Oregon Coastline Express, a leisurely train to Tillamook.

31.5 Rockaway Beach (stores, restaurants).

36.1 Barview (store). A right turn here leads to a jetty, a park, and views of Tillamook Bay's bar. Boats must pass over this when going out to or returning from the ocean.

37.8 Garibaldi. This is a departure point for ocean fishermen.

42.3 Bay City (stores).

46.0 Tillamook Cheese Factory (self-guided tours, gift shop).

46.3   Tillamook Chamber of Commerce (Visitor Information Center). In the next 2 miles are overnight facilities, restaurants, and stores.

47.9   Tillamook. Junction of highways 101 and 6 (Wilson River Highway). (An optional tour around all or part of Three Capes Scenic Loop adds 20 or 30 miles to your day. Get detailed information from the Visitor Information Center.) End of day.

Third Day

0.0   Junction of highways 101 and 6 (Third Street) in Tillamook. Turn left (east) on **Third Street**, following the **Wilson River Highway.**

32.5   Rogers Forest Camp, Wilson River Highway summit of 1586 feet is reached.

38.6   Timber Junction. Turn left onto **Timber Road** (unmarked). (If you come to Glenwood Store, you have missed this turn.)

43.0   Start a climb through the woods.

44.8   Summit is reached.

45.4   Timber (tavern).

48.6   Cross **Highway 26** (restaurant). Signs at this intersection indicate 41 miles to Seaside, 35 to Portland, and 11 to Vernonia.

51.4   Enter Columbia County.

59.1   Turn left at a T-intersection onto **Highway 47**. Straight across the highway, paralleling this road, is Oregon's first "Rail to Trail" conversion, a linear park.

60.8   Vernonia.

61.0   Turn right on **Bridge Street** and proceed to Washington Grade School. End of ride.

7 Sherwood–Scholls

Starting point: Sherwood City Hall, Main and First streets in Sherwood, approximately 15 miles southwest of Portland on Highway 99W
Distance: 22 miles
Terrain: Mixed hilly and flat
Total cumulative elevation gain: 625 feet
Recommended time of year: Any season
Recommended starting time: 10:00 A.M.
Allow: 3 hours

Points of interest:
Tualatin River Valley
Chehalem Mountains

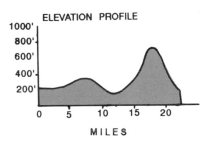

Not so long ago the Tualatin Valley was rich farmland peppered with ferry landings on the river. Oregon's earliest settlers rolled their covered wagons in to settle communities like Scholls, Farmington, and Sherwood.

Now, almost a century and a half later, this area is settled by seekers of a rural escape from Portland. Portland has grown and spilled over into the Tualatin Valley, turning farmland into acreage for housing, shopping centers, and arterial roads. Bridges have replaced ferries and local real estate has taken on a resemblance to patchwork. Main roads bustle, carrying commuters and commerce.

Despite the activity, a pleasant bike ride is possible, mostly on backroads. Wait until commuter traffic slows or choose a summer evening. This ride offers a great escape from the city, aerobic workouts on the hills, high-cadence pedaling on the flats, and a pleasant drop back into the valley.

Beginning in Sherwood, which is celebrating its centennial year in 1992, the ride skirts growing housing developments to the south of Bull Mountain. After a few miles following the busiest part of the route, a brief retreat onto Tile Flat and Clark Hill roads discovers meadows, woods, and farmland. This seems to offer a sampling of what original settlers found in the Lower Tualatin Valley.

Returning to Scholls Ferry Road, the ride crosses the Tualatin near the donation land claim that Peter Scholl first settled in 1847. Like many of the valley pioneers, he used his riverfront property to operate a ferry service. It was a few feet downstream from the present bridge.

Leaving normally quiet North Scholls and Scholls, the ride brushes the edge of the Chehalem Mountains and heads uphill for views, solitude, and greenery. After about 4 miles of ups and downs, the loop takes a few more twists, then coasts back to the bustle of the Tualatin Valley.

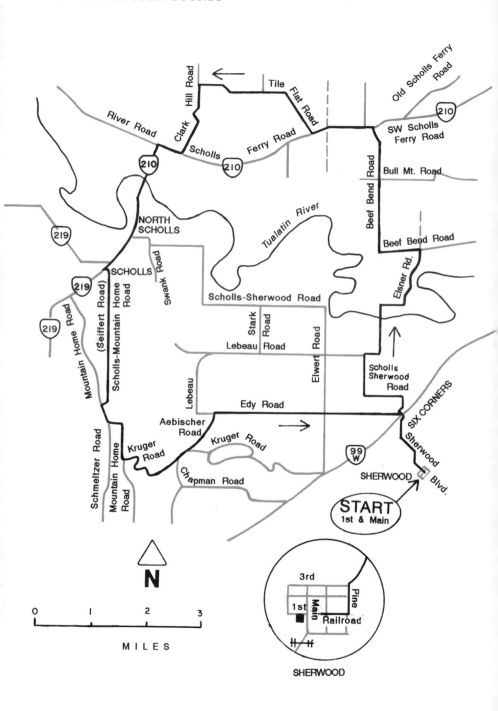

MILEAGE LOG

0.0 Sherwood City Hall, Main Street in old Sherwood. Turn right on **First Street.**

0.1 Turn left on **Pine Street** and bear right as it becomes **Sherwood Boulevard** at mile 0.2.

0.9 Turn left on **Edy Road**, and then immediately cross Highway 99W at a stoplight and turn right onto **Scholls-Sherwood Road.**

2.4 Turn right on **Elsner Road**. Follow it as it bends and finally crosses a bridge over the Tualatin River at mile 3.1.

4.3 Carefully turn left onto **Beef Bend Road** and follow it as it climbs up and down for about 2 miles. (This section can be busy during commute hours.)

6.4 Turn left on **Scholls Ferry Road.**

7.3 Turn right onto **Tile Flat Road** and wind through farmland and meadows.

9.3 Turn left on **Clark Hill Road.**

10.4 Turn right on **Scholls Ferry Road** (Highway 210), which is unmarked at this T-intersection. Follow Highway 210 when it turns left toward Scholls at mile 10.9.

11.5 Cross the Tualatin River and enter North Scholls at mile 12.0 and Scholls at mile 12.8.

13.0 Turn left on **Seiffert Road** (Scholls-Mountain Home Road) and begin climbing.

15.0 Turn left at a T-intersection onto **Mountain Home Road.**

16.3 Turn left on **Kruger Road.**

17.5 Turn left on **Aebischer Road**.

18.3 Turn right on **Edy Road** at a T-intersection. Sail down the hill.

19.9 At a four-way stop with Elwert Road, continue straight on Edy Road.

20.9 Six Corners (stores). Bear right, staying on Edy Road as Scholls-Sherwood Road comes in from the left. Cross Highway 99W at a stop light to Sherwood, then bear right on **Sherwood Boulevard.**

21.8 Bear left as Sherwood Boulevard becomes **Pine Street.**

21.9 Turn right on **First Street.**

22.0 Turn left on **Main Street**. End of ride.

8 North Tualatin Valley

Starting point: Corner of Ninth Avenue and Maple Street in Hillsboro, on the north side of Shute Park
Distance: 35.3 miles
Terrain: Flat with one steep hill
Total cumulative elevation gain: 750 feet
Recommended time of year: Any season
Recommended starting time: Before 11:00 A.M.
Allow: 4 hours

Points of Interest:
Shute Park
Pacific University
Verboort

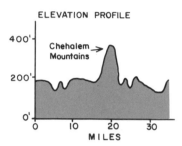

ELEVATION PROFILE

While the Tualatin River itself has a very crooked and meandered course, its valley has shaped a graceful crescent. It flows north from Yamhill County, curves around the north end of the Chehalem Mountains, and then flows south to meet the Willamette near West Linn. The ride described here circles the northernmost section of that crescent, visiting the towns of Hillsboro, Cornelius, and Forest Grove, as well as several smaller communities.

Like the river itself, the ride is flat, with the exception of one short (but steep) detour over the northern toe of the Chehalem Mountains. Since it passes through several towns, the ride has some traffic in places, but relatively lonely farm roads make up the rest of the route.

The tour starts in Hillsboro, the county seat, then proceeds out among the farms northwest of town. After passing through a residential section of Cornelius, the route eventually reaches the tiny community of Verboort. Located well away from any main roads, one cannot imagine travelers passing through Verboort on their way to anywhere else. The home of a sausage festival held in early November, Verboort is a predominantly Catholic community, made up of Dutch immigrants who first settled in Wisconsin. Don't expect the town store to be open on Sunday.

West of Verboort, the route follows Highway 47 south through Forest Grove, a pretty town that grew up around the shady campus of Pacific University. When the school was founded in the 1840s, the area was known as West Tualatin Plains. Hillsboro was referred to as East Tualatin Plains.

The route continues on Highway 47 for 3 miles south of Forest Grove, then turns east and crosses the Tualatin River. The northern toe of the Chehalem Mountains is surmounted by a very steep hill, followed by an equally rapid descent to the valley floor.

The remainder of the ride follows the river south to the Farmington area, and then follows River Road north into Hillsboro. The last few miles have some moderate traffic, so ride carefully.

Local roads offer several opportunities for shortening the 35.9-mile ride described here. The best such opportunity occurs at mile 24.3, where, rather than turning south on Highway 219 toward Farmington, a left turn returns the rider to Hillsboro in about 3 miles, shortening the ride by approximately 6 miles. In addition, for those willing to travel a few gravel sections, a left turn on Long Road at mile 5.3 shortens the route by 2.2 miles.

MILEAGE LOG

0.0 Corner of Ninth and Maple in Hillsboro. Turn left out of the park and proceed north on **Ninth**.

0.1 Turn left on **Walnut Street**.

0.7 Turn right on **Second Avenue**.

1.1 Turn left (west) on **Main Street**. Main Street is one-way west at this point, but becomes two-way one block later.

1.4 Turn right on **Connell Road**. At mile 2.1, Connell Road curves to the west and then becomes **Hornecker Road**.

4.8 Turn left at a T-intersection with **Susbauer Road**.

6.5   Turn right on **Davis Street**.

7.0   At a T-intersection with **10th Avenue,** turn right (north). In a few blocks, 10th Avenue becomes **Cornelius-Schefflin Road**. At mile 9.0, the road turns to the west.

9.1   Cornelius-Schefflin Road turns north. Go straight (west) on **Verboort Road**.

10.0   Verboort. Continue west on Verboort Road.

11.1   Turn left (south) on **Highway 47**. Watch carefully for traffic. At mile 12.3, the highway enters Forest Grove. Lincoln Park is on the right side of the road at mile 12.6.

12.8   Follow Highway 47 as it turns right on **University Avenue** and then left on **College Way**. Pacific University is on the left.

13.2   Turn right on **Pacific Avenue** and then left on **B Street**, following Highway 47.

14.6   Highway 47 joins the **Tualatin Valley Highway** (T.V. Highway). Bear right (south). A bike path starts on the right side of the highway at this intersection, and then ends at mile 15.0. At mile 15.4 the highway passes through the outskirts of the small town of Dilley.

16.3   Carefully cross Highway 47 and turn left on **Springhill Road**. At mile 16.7, the road crosses the Tualatin River.

16.8   Turn left on **Fern Hill Road**. This level road travels northeast along the north end of the Chehalem Mountains.

18.9   Turn right on **Blooming-Fern Hill Road**, which climbs 200 feet in the next 0.4 mile. About 1 mile later, the road drops back down into the valley.

21.1   Turn right (south) at a T-intersection with **Golf Course Road**.

21.4   At a T-intersection with **Tongue Lane**, turn left.

24.3   Turn right at a T-intersection with **Highway 219**. (For those preferring a shorter ride, a left turn at this intersection returns the rider to Hillsboro in about 3 miles.)

27.3   Turn left on **Highway 208** (Farmington Road). At mile 29.2, the road crosses the Tualatin River.

29.3   Farmington. Turn left on **River Road**. At mile 33.2, Witch Hazel Road joins from the right (east). At mile 33.5, at an intersection with Rood Bridge Road, sidewalks begin on both sides of the road, with the sidewalk on the left (southwest) side of the road designated as a bike route. Due to the volume of traffic on this part of River Road, the bike route is the safer approach.

34.7   Intersection with Tualatin Valley Highway (Highway 8). Cross the highway and proceed north on **13th Avenue**.

35.0   Turn left on **Maple Street**. At mile 35.2, follow Maple Street west across Tualatin Valley Highway.

35.3   Corner of Maple Street and Ninth Avenue. End of ride.

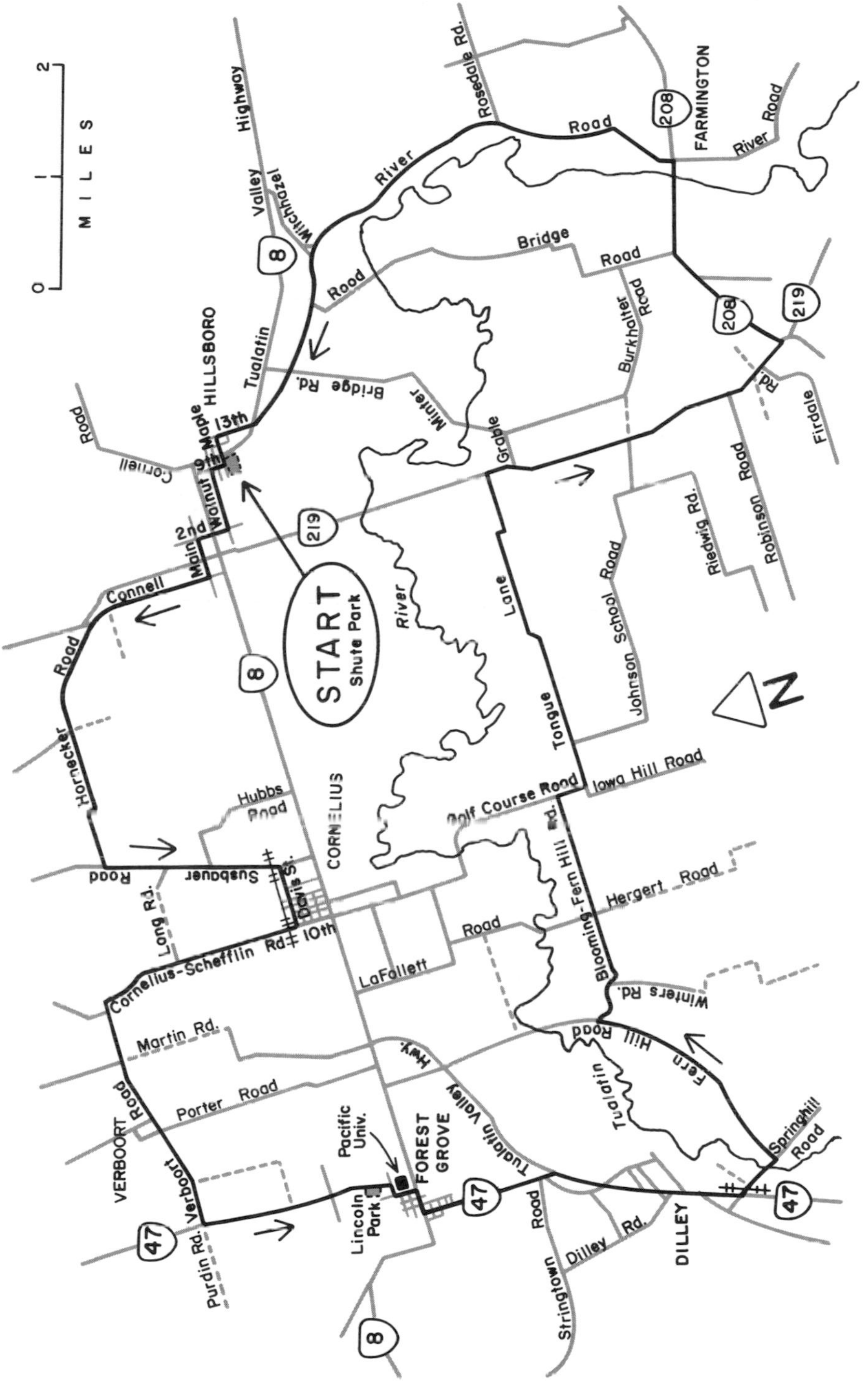
0
1
2
MILES
N
START
Shute Park
HILLSBORO
CORNELIUS
FOREST GROVE
VERBOORT
DILLEY
FARMINGTON
Pacific Univ.
Lincoln Park
Tualatin Valley Highway
Witchhazel
Tualatin
River Road
Rosedale Rd.
River Road
Bridge Road
Burkhalter Road
Bridge Rd.
Minter
Grable
Firdale
Robinson Road
Riedwig Rd.
Johnson School Road
Lane
Tongue
Iowa Hill Road
Golf Course Road
Blooming-Fern Hill Rd.
Hergert Road
Road
LaFollett
Winters Rd.
Fern Hill Road
Springhill Road
Stringtown Road
Dilley Rd.
Tualatin Valley Hwy.
River
Cornell Road
Maple
13th
9th
Walnut
2nd
Main
Connell Road
Hornecker Road
Hubbs Road
Susbauer Road
Long Rd.
Davis St.
10th
Cornelius-Schefflin Rd
Martin Rd.
Porter Road
Verboort Road
Verboort
Purdin Rd.
8
47
208
219

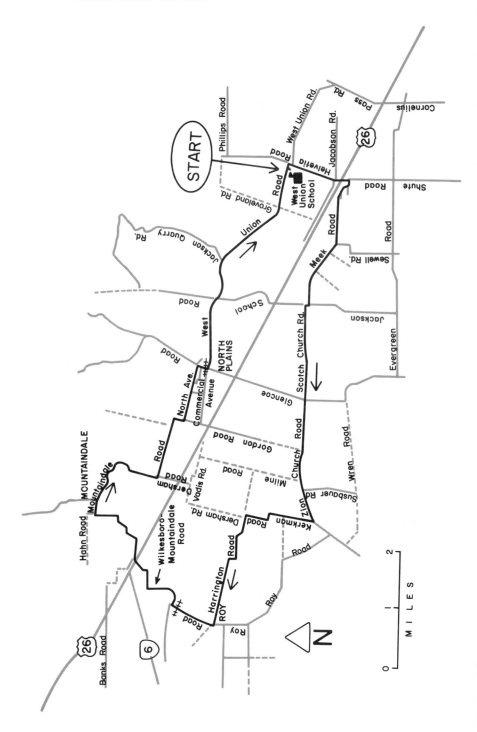

9 Mountaindale

Starting point: West Union School, 12 miles west of Portland. From Highway 26 turn north on Helvetia Road and follow it 1 mile, and then turn left on West Union Road to the school.
Distance: 22.3 miles
Terrain: Flat
Total cumulative elevation gain: 250 feet
Recommended time of year: Any season
Recommended starting time: Before noon
Allow: 2 to 3 hours

Points of interest:
Mountaindale
Glider flights

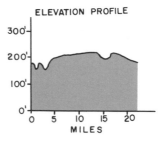

When the Oregon Country's first government was formed in 1843, one of its initial tasks was to divide the region into counties. Of the four counties created that year, the one named Twality stretched from the Willamette River west to the Pacific and from the Yamhill River north into what is now Washington State.

The name Twality was short-lived, as was the sweeping size of the county. Within a year the government created smaller counties, and within six years the name was changed to Washington County. A derivative of the name, however, is still applied to the river that drains nearly all of Washington County.

A bicycle ride through present-day Washington County is normally a leisurely affair. This is particularly true when the route is restricted to level Tualatin Valley farmland in the central part of the county, avoiding hills that make up the outlying areas. This route is such a ride. It starts in Hillsboro, travels northwest to the base of the Tualatin Mountains, and then proceeds southeast, skirting the base of the mountains, being particularly careful not to enter the hills.

Flat doesn't equate with dull, however, for the scenery is superb. The southern half of the ride is pastoral farmland, and the northern half traverses a variety of woods and pastures. Midway through the ride, a lunch stop at the Mountaindale store is most appropriate. The store celebrates its 110th birthday in 1992. Like many small-town businesses (in this case the store is the town), the Mountaindale store sells everything from soup to nuts and from food to feed.

As long as you are watching the scenery, don't forget to watch the skies. With at least four airfields located along the route, the skies are crowded, particularly on sunny days. The busiest of the airfields is Hillsboro

Airport, about 2 miles northeast of Hillsboro. The most interesting of the airfields, located south of the route near mile 16, specializes in glider flights. Take a few minutes to watch the tow plane spiral up into the sky with a glider on the end of its cable, and try to spot the gliders as they swoop in silently to land.

MILEAGE LOG

0.0 West Union School. Leave the parking lot and turn right (east) on **West Union Road**.

0.1 Bear right at an intersection with **Helvetia Road** and follow it south.

1.0 Cross over Highway 26, after which Helvetia Road becomes **Shute Road**.

1.1 Turn right on **Meek Road** and follow it as it bears right and then parallels Highway 26.

3.6 Turn right at a T-intersection with **Jackson School Road.**

3.7 Turn left (west) on **Scotch Church Road**. After passing through an intersection with Glencoe Road at mile 5.4, Scotch Church Road becomes **Zion Church Road**.

7.5 Turn right on **Kerkman Road**.

8.7 At a T-intersection, turn left onto **Harrington Road**.

10.7 Roy. You can't miss St. Francis Church, but note its matching mailbox.

10.8 Turn right on **Roy Road**.

11.6 Turn right at a T-intersection with **Wilkesboro-Mountaindale Road**.

12.8 Carefully cross the busy Sunset Highway (Highway 26), and then turn right on **Mountaindale Road**. At mile 13.9, follow Mountaindale Road as it turns right at an intersection with Hahn Road.

14.4 Mountaindale (store). Continue straight (east) on Mountaindale Road. About 1 mile later, Mountaindale Road turns south.

16.0 Follow Mountaindale Road by turning left (east). Dersham Road continues straight (south).

17.0 Mountaindale Road turns south and becomes **Gordon Road**.

17.2 Turn left on **North Avenue**.

18.2 Turn right on **Glencoe Road**.

18.4 After crossing some railroad tracks, turn left on **Commercial Avenue**, which soon becomes **West Union Road**. Follow this road east, through intersections with Jackson School Road and Jackson Quarry Road.

22.3 West Union School. End of ride.

10 Gales Creek

Starting point: Rogers Park at the corner of Douglas Street and 17th Avenue in Forest Grove (two blocks south of Highway 8 on Douglas Street). Park on the south side of the park (17th Avenue).
Distance: 29.9 miles
Terrain: Moderately flat with some hills
Total cumulative elevation gain: 550 feet
Recommended time of year: Any season
Recommended starting time: Noon

Allow: 3 hours
Points of interest:
Forest Grove
Gales Creek Valley
Vineyards and wineries

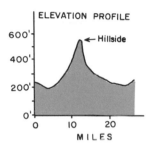

Dairy Creek and Gales Creek are two of the largest tributaries of the Tualatin River. Dairy Creek, named for a Hudson's Bay Company (HBC) dairy that once operated on its banks, is the only Tualatin tributary that has been navigated: In the 1800s steamboats frequently used it to call on a flour mill at the now nonexistent town of Centerville.

Gales Creek, on the other hand, was named for an Oregon pioneer who was no friend of the HBC. In 1842 he drove nearly 5000 head of livestock from California to the Willamette Valley, effectively destroying the HBC's livestock monopoly. He later served as one of three commissioners heading the first Oregon Provisional Government.

This ride visits the valleys of both creeks, and crosses the ridge that separates the two. Beginning at Rogers Park, which occupies a full city block in the center of Forest Grove, a shady little college town, the route heads north into flat farmland. Eventually, the route turns west and begins a gentle climb into the rolling foothills known as David Hill. In the transition, the surroundings change from broad fields to nurseries and small woodlots.

Crossing the ridge near the community of Hillside, the road follows a series of steep curves into the Gales Creek Valley. In contrast to Dairy Creek, Gales Creek is situated in a narrow valley with steep, wooded sides. The valley floor is relatively flat, seeming to make the last few miles of the ride glide by with little effort. Except for a slight detour near Forest Grove, to take advantage of quiet Stringtown Road, the return route follows Gales Creek Road (State Highway 8).

In the hills surrounding Dairy and Gales creeks are at least a half-dozen vineyards, producing wine grapes for a burgeoning Willamette Valley

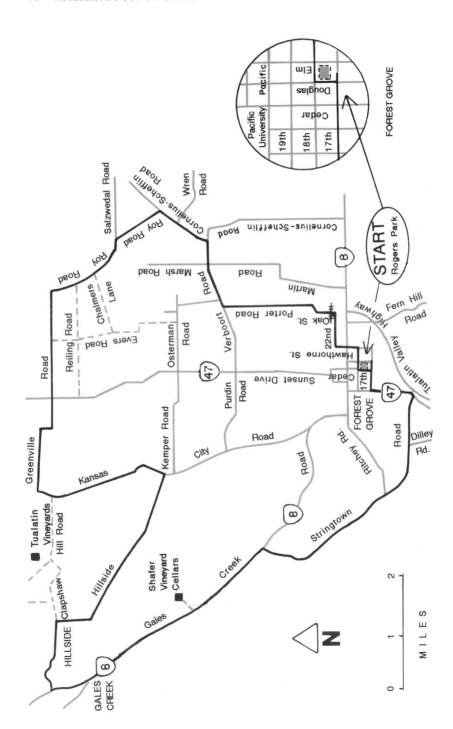

industry. The two closest wineries to this route are indicated on the tour map, but more detailed directions are available from the Hillsboro Chamber of Commerce. All area wineries invite the public to visit their tasting rooms and picnic on their grounds. Cyclists must weigh the delight of these activities against added miles, sometimes over gravel roads, to get there and back. Also, the combination of wine tasting and bike touring should be approached with caution.

MILEAGE LOG

0.0 Rogers Park in Forest Grove, parking lot on the south side.

0.1 Turn right (west) on **17th Avenue**.

0.2 Turn right (north) on **Douglas Street**.

0.3 Turn right on **18th Avenue**.

0.5 Turn left on **Hawthorne Street**.

0.9 Turn right on **22nd Avenue**.

1.5 Turn left on **Oak Street**, which becomes **Porter Road** after it crosses the railroad tracks and leaves the city limits at mile 1.6.

3.4 Turn right on **Verboort Road**.

4.6 Turn left on **Cornelius-Schefflin Road**, watching for traffic.

5.9 Turn left on **Roy Road**. Bear left at a T-intersection with Salzwedal Road at mile 6.9.

8.5 Turn left on **Greenville Road**, which crosses Highway 47 at mile 10.1 and continues toward Kansas City.

11.9 At a T-intersection, turn left on **Kansas City Road**. On clear days, Mount Hood is visible to your left.

14.3 Turn right on **Hillside Road**.

17.9 Hillside. An 1884 church stands just east of this intersection. Turn left on **Clapshaw Hill Road**. Follow it through an intersection with Shearer Road at mile 18.4, after which the road drops steeply into the Gales Creek Valley.

19.3 Turn left at a T-intersection with **State Highway 8** (Gales Creek Road). The road passes through the small town of Gales Creek (store) at mile 20.9.

24.0 Turn right on **Stringtown Road**.

28.5 Intersection with **State Highway 47**. Turn left.

29.3 Turn right on **17th Avenue**.

29.9 Rogers Park. End of ride.

11 Hagg Lake

Starting point: Scoggins Valley Park entrance. From Forest Grove drive south on Highway 47 for 4.5 miles, and then turn right on Scoggins Valley Road. Park just outside the entrance. During summer months this is directly across from the toll booth for collecting from drivers who park near the lake. Cyclists enter the park without a fee.
Distance: 11.6 miles
Terrain: Moderately hilly
Total cumulative elevation gain: 750 feet
Recommended time of year: Any season, but expect heavy traffic during spring and summer

Recommended starting time: Any time
Allow: 1 to 2 hours
Points of interest:
Henry Hagg Lake
Scoggins Dam
Scoggins Valley Park

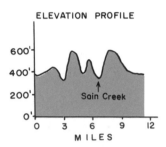

Washington County maps printed as recently as the early 1970s show a secluded valley a few miles northwest of Gaston. Scoggins Valley Road is shown leading west along Scoggins Creek, through a gap in the foothills, and into a small valley of level farmland. In the middle of the valley, where four streams come together, Forest Dale School is shown sitting next to a small church.

Today, Forest Dale School, if it is still there, stands under 50 feet of water. So does most of Scoggins Valley: the result of construction of an earthen dam in 1974 by the Bureau of Reclamation. Houses in the area were purchased and removed, but a small church still stands just outside the park entrance as if in testimony to what once was. The large reservoir formed by the dam, Henry Hagg Lake, holds nearly 60,000 acre-feet of water for flood control, irrigation, and recreation.

The shores of the lake are now a large park, and are circled by a road that makes a fine bike route. The road follows the perimeter of the lake, including a crossing of the 0.5-mile-long dam. Along the way it passes several viewpoints, picnic areas, and short trails. Pack a lunch and let your hunger pangs choose your stopping point.

Although the route is hilly, its length makes the Hagg Lake ride ideal for families or others who prefer shorter trips. During good spring and summer weather, however, the road is heavily traveled by motorists, particularly those with boat trailers. The shoulder is wide, but watch for traffic, especially when riding with children.

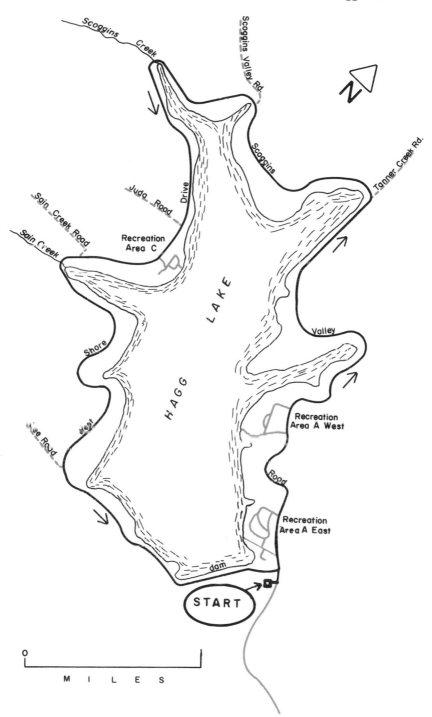

START

MILES

Lunch already? I haven't finished breakfast.

Washington County has few large parks, and even fewer lakes, so Scoggins Valley Park and Hagg Lake see heavy and diverse use. Water skiers dominate the southeastern end of the lake in such numbers that park rules require counter-clockwise travel to avoid collisions, while the upper end of the lake is reserved for "low-wake" activities such as fishing and canoeing. The entire lake is sometimes reserved for boat races, water rescue training, and other uses. In addition to boaters, motorists, and bicyclists, joggers often use the road for training, and triathlons have taken advantage of the lake and road for swimming, cycling, and running.

The only problem with the road is Mother Nature. Perhaps upset at the loss of her pretty valley, she occasionally drops large pieces of the road into the lake. To determine if the road is still there, bicyclists might call the county road department, (503) 648-8715.

Although the road is open all year, the park facilities are closed from October 31 to the opening day of fishing season in late April. The water level also drops late in the fall to make room for winter rains, so the best seasons to visit are spring through early fall. Naturally, those same seasons are popular with boaters and motorists. When facilities are open, a small fee is charged at the park entrance to those wishing to park their cars inside.

MILEAGE LOG

0.0 Parking area outside entrance. Scoggins Valley Park. Ride out of the recreation area and turn left on **Scoggins Valley Road**. The right shoulder of the road is a bike lane.

1.2 On the left is the entrance to Recreation Area A West.

4.7 When Scoggins Valley Road turns right and becomes gravel, continue straight on **West Shore Drive**.
5.1 The bike lane crosses from the right side of the road to the left.
5.5 The road crosses Scoggins Creek on a narrow bridge. Watch carefully for traffic.
6.7 On the left is the entrance to Recreation Area C.
7.4 Bridge over Sain Creek.
10.1 The road starts across Scoggins Dam.
10.9 Turn right at a T-intersection with **Scoggins Valley Road**.
11.6 Parking area. End of ride.

CLACKAMAS COUNTY

12 Lolo Pass

Starting point: Zigzag Ranger Station, 3 miles west of Zigzag, 40 miles east of Portland on Highway 26
Distance: 24.2 miles
Terrain: Very hilly
Total cumulative elevation gain: 2500 feet
Recommended time of year: Spring through fall
Recommended starting time: Before noon
Allow: 3 hours

Points of interest:
Views of Mount Hood
French's Dome

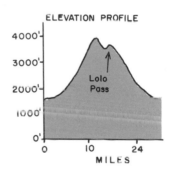

The foothills of Mount Hood offer few backroads suitable for bicycling. Since logging roads are not paved, and the main highways are heavily traveled, bicyclists usually visit the area only when necessary to cross the mountains on their way to central Oregon.

The upper reaches of the Sandy River valley, however, offer an exceptional 25-mile loop ride on paved roads, with relatively little traffic. Long, long hills and close-up views of Mount Hood all contribute to the alpine character of the ride.

Due to that alpine character, a few precautions should be taken. Carry an extra sweater or windbreaker, and maybe even a pair of warm gloves, in case the weather turns chilly. Make sure your legs are up to a relentless climb, and your tires and brakes ready for a long, fast descent.

In late fall and early spring, a phone call to the Zigzag Ranger Station (503-666-0704) is advisable, to check on the weather and to determine if the roads are free of snow. In winter, the roads are normally not plowed more than a few miles from Highway 26. The phone call is advisable any time of year if you plan on riding on a weekday, since a portion of the ride may occasionally be closed to private vehicles, due to heavy logging-truck traffic.

The ride starts at the ranger station on Highway 26. Rest rooms, water, and brochures on the area are available 3 miles west at the information center in the community of Zigzag. After crossing Highway 26, the route follows Lolo Pass Road up the Sandy River for about 4 miles, and then climbs to 3700 feet on a ridge known as Last Chance Mountain. Watch carefully for oncoming vehicles, as the road up the ridge is narrow and twisting. Fine views of the valley of the Clear Fork of the Sandy River also reveal how the valley has been marred by construction of a major power line and extensive clear-cutting.

From the high point near mile 10, the road dips and then climbs slightly to Lolo Pass, where it rejoins the Lolo Pass Road. The final leg of the ride is a 10.6-mile descent to Zigzag—1500 feet of elevation are lost in the first 6 miles. The Lolo Pass Road is a full two lanes wide, but has a bit of loose gravel on it in places, and occasionally has a fair amount of traffic. Ride carefully.

If you're looking for a nice spot to lunch, two places come to mind. For superb views of Mount Hood, stop along the road near mile 10. Lower down, a bridge over the Clear Fork at mile 5.8 offers a pretty streamside setting. In summer come prepared with bug repellent, just in case.

If the ride up to Lolo Pass didn't tire you out, an optional side trip could follow Forest Service Road No. 1825 east past McNeil Campground and Lost Creek Campground toward the Ramona Falls trail.

MILEAGE LOG

0.0 Zigzag Ranger Station on Highway 26 at Zigzag. Leave the parking lot, carefully cross **Highway 26**, turn left, and proceed one block west.

0.1 Turn right on **Lolo Pass Road**.

4.3 Bear right on **Forest Service Road No. 1825**, leaving Lolo Pass Road (F.S. Road No. 18).

5.0 Bear left on **Forest Service Road No. 1828.**

13.6 Lolo Pass. Elevation 3420. Turn left on **Lolo Pass Road** and follow it all the way to Zigzag. At mile 18.0, a dirt road on the left leads a few feet to a view of French's Dome, an unusual rock knob occasionally visited by rock climbers.

24.1 Zigzag. Carefully cross **Highway 26**, turn left, and ride one block east.

24.2 Turn right into the parking lot at Zigzag Ranger Station. End of ride.

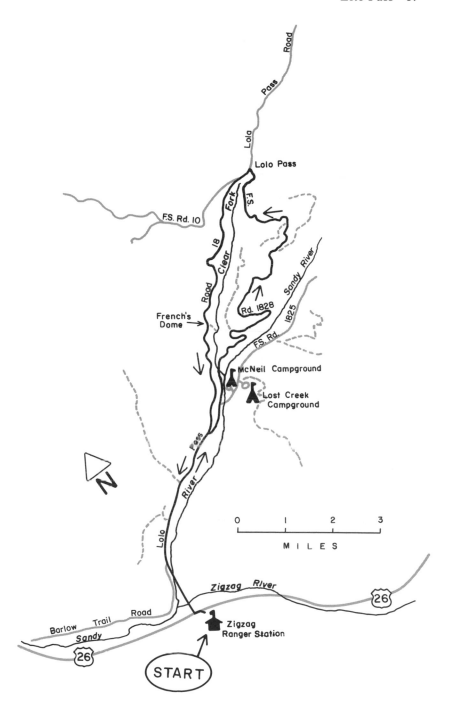

13 Parrett Mountain

Starting point: Boones Ferry
Park in Wilsonville. Take
Wilsonville exit no. 283 from I-5,
turn left onto Boones Ferry Road,
and follow it to Willamette River.
Distance: 33.3 miles
Terrain: Hilly
**Total cumulative elevation
gain**: 2400 feet
Recommended time of year:
Any season
Recommended starting time:
Before 11:00 A.M.
Allow: 4 to 5 hours

Points of interest:
Boones Ferry Park
Parrett Mountain Access
   (Willamette Greenway)
Chehalem Mountains

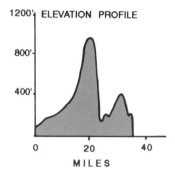

Although named for local postmaster Charles Wilson, Wilsonville was
first settled by Colonel Alphonso Boone, the grandson of the legendary
Daniel Boone, and his family. In 1847 Daniel Boone's great-grandson
began operating a ferry across the Willamette, providing increased commerce and encouraging tourism for those traveling the Portland-Salem
route.

Beginning in Wilsonville at the park named for the Boone Family, this
bike route strikes out along the river and the foot of Parrett Mountain.
Standing along the Willamette north of Champoeg State Park, Parrett
Mountain offers an expansive backdrop to the view from the bluffs over-
looking the park. At 1247 feet, it is one of the highest points in the
Willamette Valley. The mountain also stands near the intersections of
Clackamas, Yamhill, and Washington counties. This ride circles Parrett
Mountain, visiting all three counties while keeping a safe distance from
its steep ramparts.

The road along the river is quite varied, being flat and sunny as it
passes filbert orchards and pastures and then shady as it occasionally
drops into several small ravines. Because of this, the rider should be
especially aware of traffic along the route and avoid swerving out into the
lane. One of the valley's prettiest roads, this one is justifiably popular as
a bike route for heading for Newberg or French Prairie.

In the Newberg area the route crosses Highway 99W and then climbs
up to expansive views of the valley below. If the day is clear, watch for
Mount Hood and Mount Adams in the distance. A quick descent into
Sherwood offers an opportunity to visit restaurants and stores before

passing through an area of rolling farmland known as Pleasant Hill. This last leg of the ride back to Wilsonville has a surprisingly rural flavor.

MILEAGE LOG

0.0 Tauchman Road at Boones Ferry Park, Wilsonville. Turn right onto **Boones Ferry Road** and ride north.

0.6 Turn left on **Wilsonville Road** and stay with it for several miles as it follows the Willamette River. At mile 1.3, the bike lane ends at an intersection with Willamette Way. Continue north on Wilsonville Road toward Newberg. Ride carefully since some sections of this road may be busy.

4.6 Enter Yamhill County.

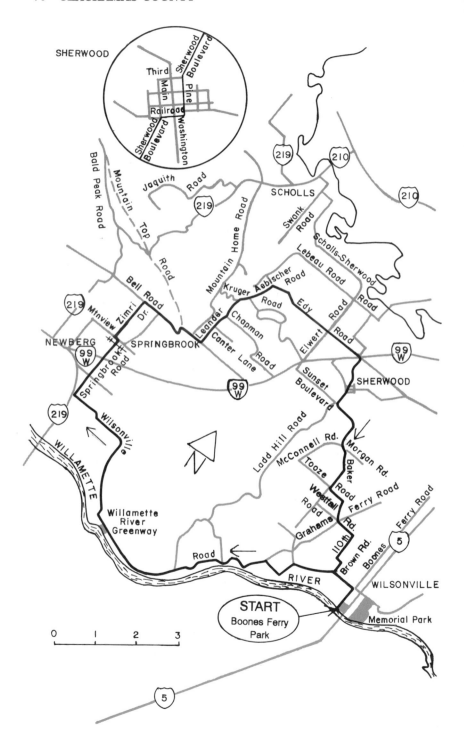

5.0 Willamette River Greenway (Parrett Mountain Access; day use only; water not available). A short trail leads to the Willamette River.

12.8 Turn right (north) on an unmarked road signed as a bike route (**Springbrook Road**) a few feet before an intersection with Highway 219. At mile 13.9 cross Highway 99W and continue north on Springbrook Road.

14.7 Springbrook. After crossing the railroad tracks, bear left on **Mountainview Road**.

14.9 Turn right on **Zimri Drive**.

15.9 Turn right at a T-intersection with **Bell Road** and stay with it through a T-intersection with Springbrook Road at mile 16.3.

17.6 Halfway down a hill, turn left onto **Leander Drive**. Gibbs Cemetery is at the top of the next hill at mile 18.3.

18.7 Turn left at a T-intersection onto **Chapman Road** (unmarked). Enter Washington County and enjoy views of Mount Adams in Washington State and Mount Hood in Oregon.

19.5 Turn right at a Y-intersection with **Kruger Road**, and then almost immediately (mile 19.7) turn left on **Aebischer Road**.

20.5 Turn right at a T-intersection onto **Edy Road** and sail down the hill.

22.1 At a four-way stop with Elwert Road, continue straight on Edy Road.

23.1 Six Corners (stores). Bear right, staying on Edy Road as Scholls-Sherwood Road comes in from the left. Cross Highway 99W at the stop light and then bear right on **Sherwood Boulevard**.

23.2 Sherwood. Sherwood Boulevard bends left and becomes **Pine Street** at mile 24.0. Stay with Pine Street.

24.6 Turn right on **Railroad Street**.

24.7 Turn left on **Sherwood Boulevard** (Main Street).

25.1 Turn left at an intersection with **Sunset Boulevard**. At mile 25.8, Sunset Boulevard veers right (south) at a Y-intersection to become Baker Road.

26.6 Follow Baker Road as it turns left at an intersection with McConnell Road.

27.7 Follow Baker Road as it turns right (south) at an intersection with Morgan Road.

29.7 Turn left at intersection with **Tooze Road**. At mile 30.2, the road turns south.

30.8 Bear left, following the arterial (Tooze Road), at an intersection with Westfall Road. At mile 30.9, continue straight (east) through an intersection with Grahams Ferry Road. At mile 31.3, the arterial turns right (south) and becomes **S.W. 110th**, and then **Brown Road** as it bends left and enters Wilsonville.

32.5 Turn left at a T-intersection onto **Wilsonville Road**, and then use the bike lane on the south side of this busy street.

32.7 Turn right on **Boones Ferry Road**.

33.3 Turn left onto **Tauchman Road** and enter the park. End of ride.

14 Petes Mountain

Starting point: Willamette Park at the foot of 12th Street in the Willamette section of West Linn. This is 2.5 miles south of West Linn on Highway 212 or I-205.
Distance: 19.4 miles
Terrain: Very hilly
Total cumulative elevation gain: 1750 feet
Recommended time of year: Any season
Recommended starting time: Before 1:00 P.M.
Allow: 2 to 3 hours

Points of interest:
Willamette Park
Hebb Park

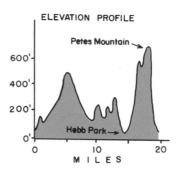

Between Canby and West Linn the Willamette River makes a sharp bend as it turns around the foot of an 800-foot ridge known as Petes Mountain. Of the three roads meeting near the summit of the ridge, the route described here climbs and descends the two steepest. Although it is a short ride, much of it over rolling farmland, it is not for those seeking a leisurely pedal on flat, rural roads.

For some reason, several names shown on the road signs in this area conflict with those on most maps. The names used in this description agree with road signs. For riders who might be using other maps, some of the alternate names are shown in parentheses in the mileage log.

In addition to some confusing names, the route passes through several unusually named communities, or former communities, including Advance, Wankers Corner, Skunk Hollow, and Frog Pond. Perhaps as a result of their names, most of them no longer exist.

The route starts at the mouth of the Tualatin River, only 50 feet above sea level, and follows the Tualatin as it winds its way northwest to Wankers Corner. Following Stafford Road south, the route crosses the northern toe of Petes Mountain and then glides down through the farmland (and spreading suburbia) toward Wilsonville.

Before reaching Wilsonville, the route turns east and, after a few miles of farmland, begins to climb over Petes Mountain. After gaining half of the ridge's 800 feet of elevation, the route drops back down to the Willamette River to visit Hebb Park. The picturesque setting of the park, overlooking the river and the Canby Ferry Landing across the way, makes it worth a rest stop.

You'll be glad you rested when you begin to tackle the ride's last two sections. They are the steepest. From Hebb Park the route climbs from an elevation of 50 to 720 feet in only 3.5 miles. Most of the elevation is

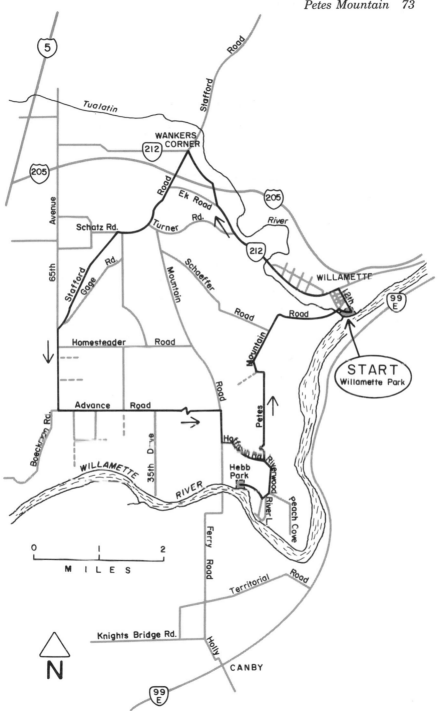

gained in the first 1.5 miles. Effort is rewarded on the last leg, when Petes Mountain Road drops back to the river in 2 miles that seem nearly vertical.

MILEAGE LOG

0.0 Willamette Park in the Willamette section of West Linn. Ride up a steep hill (northwest) on **12th Street**. Follow 12th Street as it joins **Tualatin Avenue** at mile 0.2 and a few blocks later enters "downtown" Willamette.

0.5 Turn left on **Highway 212** (Willamette Falls Drive). After leaving Willamette, Willamette Falls Drive becomes **Borland Road**. At mile 1.8, the road crosses a bridge over the Tualatin River.

3.0 Follow Borland Road as it bears right at a Y-intersection with Ek Road **(Barnes Road)**. The road passes under I-205 at mile 3.3.

4.0 Wankers Corner (stores). Using caution at this busy intersection, turn left on **Stafford Road**, cross I-205 on an overpass, and follow Stafford Road south for several miles. At mile 5.9, follow **Stafford Road** as it bears left at an intersection with Schatz Road (Delker Road).

9.0 Turn left at a T-intersection with Advance Road (Boeckman Road). At mile 9.6, the road drops, with little warning, into a small, but very steep, ravine. In addition to being steep, the road is fairly rough, and not at all suitable for breakneck speeds, so ride carefully. Another such ravine occurs at mile 10.9.

11.7 Turn right at a T-intersection with **Mountain Road**.

12.2 Turn left on **Hoffman Road**.

13.0 Turn right on **Riverwood Drive**.

13.6 At a Y-intersection with Peach Cove Road, bear right, following signs to Hebb Park.

13.7 Bear right at a Y-intersection with River Lane on the left.

13.8 At another Y-intersection, bear right on **Hebb Park Road**.

14.3 Hebb Park. Canby Ferry Landing can be seen across the river. After a break, follow the route back to **Hoffman Road**.

15.6 Intersection of Riverwood Drive, Hoffman Road, and Petes Mountain Road. Turn right on **Petes Mountain Road**, which climbs steeply over the shoulder of Petes Mountain and then drops into the community of Willamette.

19.3 Immediately after crossing the Tualatin River, turn right on **14th Street**.

19.4 Willamette Park. End of ride.

15 Clackamas River

Starting point: Estacada City
Hall, at the corner of Fifth
Avenue and Main Street in
Estacada (one block north of
State Highway 224 on Main
Street)
Distance: 45 miles
Terrain: Very hilly
**Total cumulative elevation
gain**: 2900 feet
Recommended time of year:
Any season
Recommended starting time:
10:00 A.M.
Allow: 5 hours

Points of interest:
Barton Park
Metzler Park

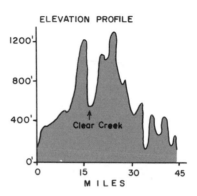

Bicycling near the Clackamas River is similar to riding along the Sandy
River to the north. These rivers have cut deep valleys into the western
foothills of the Cascades, leaving steep, wooded hills interspersed with
high plateaus of farmland. The Clackamas Valley is not as deep as the
Sandy River Gorge, so the riding is not as strenuous, but the Clackamas
area is definitely hilly. This is a fine ride for those looking for a good
workout over varied terrain.

The work getting to the top of the hills is rewarded with great views
of Mount Hood, visits to small farming communities, and long, twisting
descents on shaded roads. A few of the roads, however, have some moderate traffic. Inexperienced riders may want to try a more lonely ride.

The route described is a 45-mile loop between the communities of
Estacada, Beaver Creek, and Barton. The long hills make some of those
45 miles seem very long indeed. For riders who might prefer a shorter
ride, a shortcut can be used to reduce the total length to 36.3 miles and
eliminate some hills.

The route begins in Estacada where it strikes out for the hills and
plateau southwest of the Clackamas River. Estacada, originally a resort
for families of railroad and powerhouse construction workers in Portland,
was named for Estacado, Texas. In the first 4 miles after leaving Estacada,
the route gains 750 feet of elevation and then drops into the Clear Creek
Valley. The highest elevation is reached a few miles later, near the community of Highland, when the route crosses the shoulder of Highland
Butte at mile 12.6.

The route enters few parks, but one a few miles off the route is worth
a visit. Metzler Park is along a secluded stretch of Clear Creek, near the

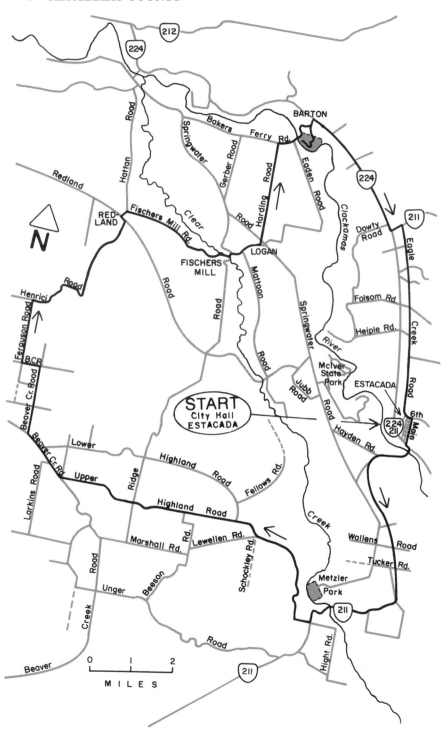

southernmost point of the ride, and would make a fine lunch stop. If the hills on the route might tire you out, however, don't visit Metzler Park. Although only 2.6 miles from the route, the park is at the bottom of a 500-foot hill that must be climbed to continue the ride. An alternate lunch stop may be Barton Park at mile 33.6. A glimpse of its riverfront can be caught from the bridge at mile 32.1. In summer, refreshments are available in the park and, despite parking fees for autos, cyclists enter free. Don't let the drop into Barton Park discourage you. The climb out is gradual and goes quickly.

If you enjoy tackling the hills of the Clackamas River area, try Trip No. 17 also, McIver–Molalla, which is nearly the same length as this ride but hillier. The two routes cross paths at two or three points, and can be combined to truly test your hill-climbing fortitude.

In the summer and fall, several small communities in this area have festivals and events featuring homemade cider, jams, and other fresh farm products, as well as a variety of activities from pioneer days. Check the Oregon Events Calendar, a brochure published quarterly by the Oregon Tourism Division, 1-800-543-8838 (inside Oregon) or 1-800-547-7842 (outside Oregon).

MILEAGE LOG

0.0 Estacada, corner of Main and Fifth. Travel south on Main. Turn left at a T-intersection with **Highway 224** (which for a few blocks is also Highway 211). Be careful on this busy road.

0.1 Turn right on **Highway 211** and then cross a bridge over the Clackamas River. Follow Highway 211 for 7 miles, up over a 1200-foot ridge, and then down into the Clear Creek Valley and up the other side. Ride carefully. Some road sections don't have a shoulder. (To visit Metzler Park, turn right on Tucker Road at mile 4.4 and then turn left on Metzler Park Road 0.6 mile later.)

7.3 Turn right on **Highland Road** (Upper Highland Road) and follow it up onto a plateau, and then down into the Beaver Creek Valley. (An alternate, which shortens the ride by 8.7 miles, is available at mile 13.8 by turning north on Ridge Road and following it to Fischers Mill, which is at mile 29.6 on the regular route.)

15.7 Turn right at a T-intersection with **Beaver Creek Road**. Ride carefully along Beaver Creek Road north, and then west when it turns left at mile 18.8. (This part of the route may be busy.)

19.4 Turn right on **Ferguson Road**.

20.9 Turn right on **Henrici Road**. At mile 21.2, the road turns north and begins to drop steeply to Abernethy Creek. The road eventually climbs back up to the Redland area.

24.8 Turn left on **Redland Road** (cafe).

24.9 Redland (store). Turn right on **Fischers Mill Road**. At mile 25.1, bear right on Fischers Mill Road at an intersection with Hattan Road. A few miles later, the road descends into the Clear Creek Valley.

28.1   Fischers Mill. Turn left, following Fischers Mill Road.

29.0   Logan. Bear left when the road forks, and then cross Springwater Road and ride straight ahead (north) on **Harding Road**.

31.4   Turn right at a T-intersection with **Bakers Ferry Road**. At mile 32.0, the road crosses a bridge over the Clackamas River.

32.6   When the road curves left, turn right toward Barton Park.

33.5   Barton Park (rest rooms; water available; no entry fee for bikes).

34.5   Return to Barton Park entrance and continue straight ahead (north) on **Bakers Ferry Road**.

34.7   Barton (store). Turn right at a T-intersection with **Highway 224**, the route of the Oregon Trail.

38.0   Turn left on **Highway 211**.

38.2   Turn right on an unmarked road **(Eagle Creek Road)**. Pass through the community of Currinsville (store) at mile 41.3. At mile 43.0, the road curves left and becomes **Sixth Avenue** in Estacada.

43.1   Turn right on **Main Street**.

45.0   End of ride.

16 Ripplebrook

Starting point: Estacada City Hall, at the corner of Fifth Avenue and Main Street in Estacada (one block north of Highway 224 on Main Street)
Distance: 54.7 miles
Terrain: Moderate
Total cumulative elevation gain: 1100 feet
Recommended time of year: Any season except midwinter
Recommended starting time: 9:00 A.M.
Allow: 6 hours

Points of interest:
Clackamas River
Cazadero Dam
Faraday Lake
North Fork Dam
Numerous parks and campgrounds

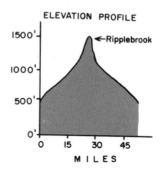

ELEVATION PROFILE

Ripplebrook could hardly be a more descriptive name. The shade from the evergreens is mixed with a patchwork of sunlight filtering through the forest. A few feet away, a stream gurgles as it flows along its bed of

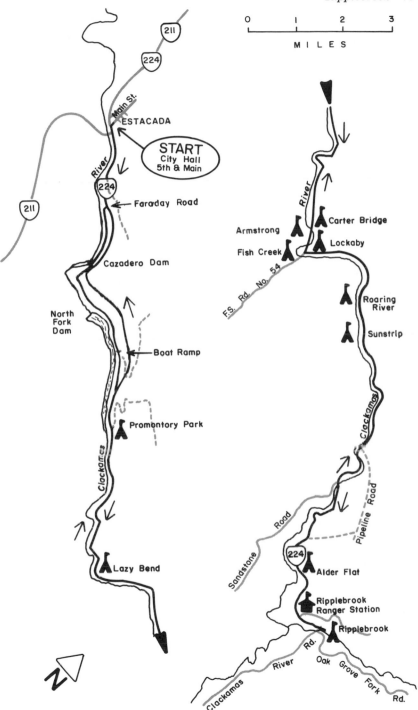

mossy boulders. Located on the Oak Grove Fork of the Clackamas River, this idyllic spot is just 27 miles southeast of Estacada.

The route described here starts in Estacada, follows the Clackamas River for those 27 miles, and then returns to Estacada via an almost identical route. Although uphill nearly all the way to Ripplebrook, the road travels a gentle grade, giving you time to ponder Portlanders of the early 1900s who arrived here in droves on Sundays. Families and employees of railroad and powerhouse construction companies, they came to picnic on the riverbanks.

Today Highway 224 is used by cars and campers headed for the campgrounds that line the route. During busy summer travel times, the route should be chosen only by riders familiar with hazards of narrow mountain roads.

An off-season ride may be the answer for those not willing to risk the summer conditions. Fall can be especially colorful in this canyon and, here at less than 1500 feet in elevation, some years bring little or no snow. Since Ripplebrook is deep in the Cascades, check current road conditions in off-season. Call the Ripplebrook Ranger Station, (503) 630-4256.

Although the upper part of the route is very woodsy and remote, the lower section is hardly wilderness, since the flow of the Clackamas River has been interrupted by two large hydroelectric dams, Cazadero Dam at mile 3.5 and North Fork Dam at mile 4.8.

The Ripplebrook area could also be a layover point for a longer excursion into the mountains. From Ripplebrook, paved roads continue south along the Clackamas and Collawash rivers and east along the Oak Grove Fork of the Clackamas. The large number of campgrounds makes overnight rides fairly easy to plan, and several hot springs in the area can be used to soothe tired muscles.

MILEAGE LOG

0.0 Estacada City Hall, Fifth and Main. Ride south on **Main Street**.

0.1 Turn left (southeast) on **Highway 224** (Clackamas Highway).

0.4 Continue straight on Highway 224 when Highway 211 turns south (right).

1.3 Turn right onto **Faraday Road** (marked dead end) and continue southeast alongside Faraday Lake and the reservoir.

1.7 For a better view of the small lake, enter the parking area, walk your bike across the pedestrian bridge, and peek over the dike. Recross the bridge, turn right, and continue on Faraday Road.

3.3 Go around the car barricade and continue on Faraday Road. (This road belongs to Portland Power & Electric, but is available to cyclists.) Watch for Cazadero Dam to come into view at mile 3.5.

4.8 North Fork Dam and overlook area. Note the fish ladder to your right.

5.3 Exit the barricaded area on Faraday Road and continue straight ahead.

6.2 Public boat ramp and day use area.

6.6 Turn right onto **Highway 224**, continuing toward Ripplebrook.

7.8 Promontory Park Campground and day use area (store only open part of the year).

8.5 Enter Mount Hood National Forest.

11.1 Lazy Bend Campground.

14.4 Big Eddy Picnic Ground.

15.8 Carter Bridge Campground. For a look at the Northwest Rivers Association's color-coded rating system for white-water navigation on the river, cross the bridge and turn right to the sign. Afterward, return to Highway 224, turn right, and continue climbing toward Ripplebrook.

16.0 Lockaby and Armstrong campgrounds.

16.2 Fish Creek Campground.

16.3 Clackamas River Trail; stay with Highway 224.

18.8 Roaring River Campground.

19.3 Sunstrip Campground.

22.9 Clackamas River Trail and Indian Henry Campground are across the river. Continue left to stay on Highway 224.

26.4 Alder Flat Campground.

26.7 Ripplebrook Ranger Station.

27.3 Ripplebrook Campground, the turnaround point of the route. Retrace the highway back to Estacada, staying with Highway 224 all the way. (While the Faraday Lake option is available both ways, it would require crossing the highway twice if taken from this direction.)

54.6 Estacada. Turn right on **Main Street**.

54.7 Estacada City Hall. End of ride.

17 McIver–Molalla

Starting point: Milo McIver State Park west of Estacada on the Clackamas River. Park at the McIver Memorial Viewpoint, 0.5 mile from the park entrance. To reach parking, enter the park and continue straight ahead at the Y-intersection.
Distance: 42.8 miles
Terrain: Very hilly
Total cumulative elevation gain: 3600 feet
Recommended time of year: Any season
Recommended starting time: Before 10:00 A.M.
Allow: 4 or 5 hours

Points of interest:
Milo McIver State Park
Metzler Park
Feyrer Park

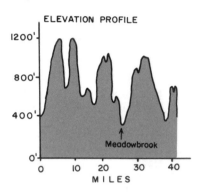

ELEVATION PROFILE

This hilly ride crosses from the upper Clackamas River to the upper Molalla River, and in the process climbs up and down several intervening ridges. It then turns around and follows a hilly route back again.

The hills are numerous and long, but the scenery is superb. Strong riders will have no difficulty, but less ambitious cyclists shouldn't be frightened off. With an early start, a slow but steady pace, and an occasional rest along the way, most cyclists will find the ride to their liking.

Two parks along the route make fine rest stops, but since both are located off the main loop, and at the bottom of hills that must be reclimbed, they are described as optional detours. The first, Metzler Park, involves a 500-foot drop into the Clear Creek Valley. The second, Feyrer Park, requires a 300-foot descent to the Molalla River. If the legs are willing, both parks are worth a visit.

With less-than-willing legs, opt for the two shortcuts to reduce the ride by up to 15 miles. Trip No. 15 covers some of the same territory, and crosses paths with this route at two or three places. It also can be used to shorten or expand the loop described here.

The ride starts at Milo McIver State Park along the Clackamas River. During the summer the park is used heavily by kayakers, rafters, and picnickers. On warm weekends traffic near the park is moderately heavy, but thins out just a few miles away. Also during the summer, a small admission charge is collected. Carry your ticket with you on your bike for free re-admission to the park.

Riders driving from the Salem area might prefer to start the route at its southern end by parking at Feyrer Park, 3 miles east of Molalla.

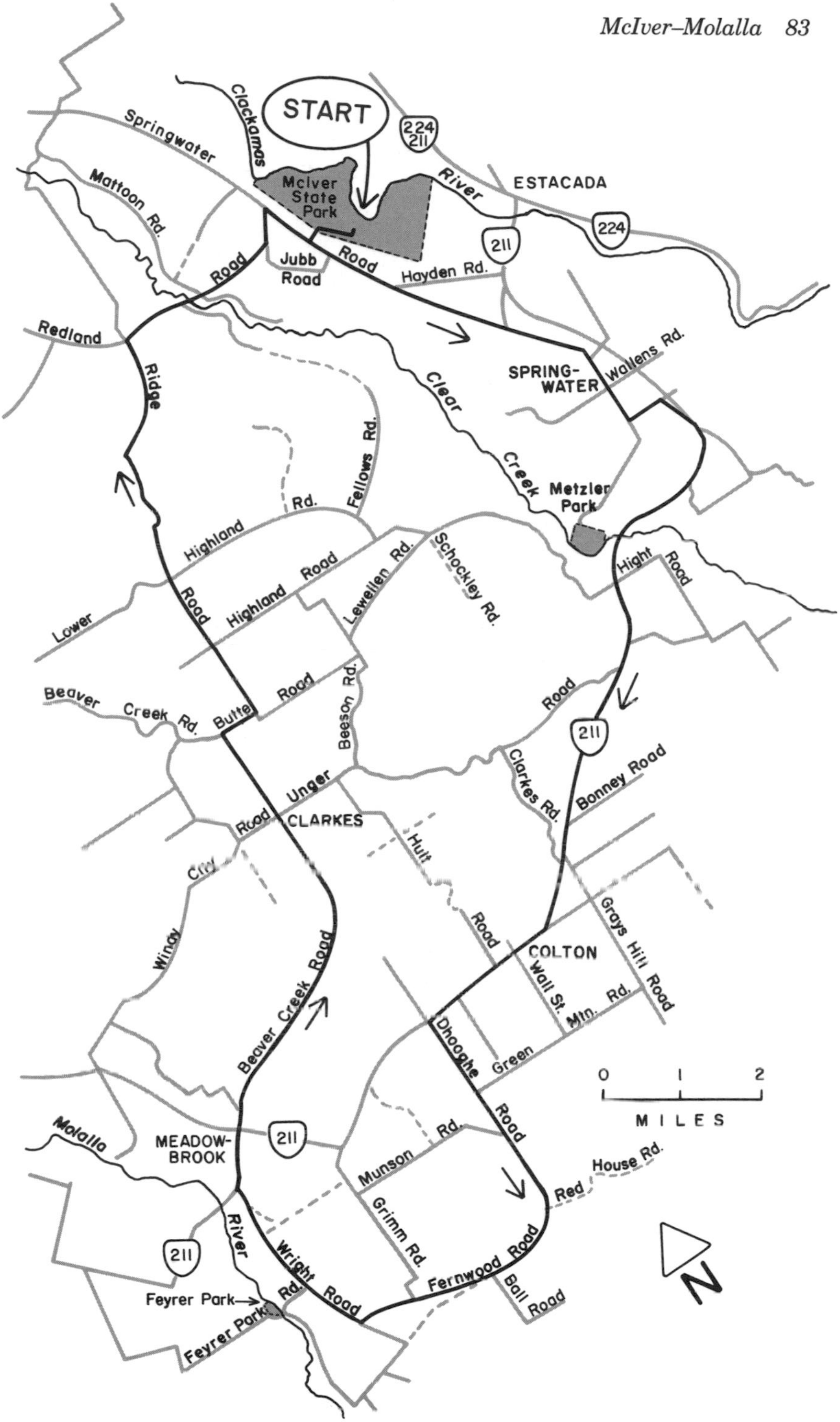

START

McIver State Park

224 211

ESTACADA

211

224

Springwater

Clackamos

Mattoon Rd.

Jubb Road

Road

Hayden Rd.

211

Redland

Ridge

Road

Clear

SPRING-WATER

Wallens Rd.

Creek

Metzler Park

Hight

Road

Highland

Rd.

Fellows Rd.

Lower

Road

Highland Road

Highland Road

Lewellen Rd.

Schockley Rd.

Road

211

Beaver Creek Rd.

Butte

Road

Beeson Rd.

Road

Clarkes Rd.

Bonney Road

Unger

Road

CLARKES

Huit

Road

COLTON

Wall St.

Green

Mtn. Rd.

Grays Hill Road

Ctr.

Windy

Beaver Creek Road

211

MEADOW-BROOK

Molalla

211

River

Dhooghe

Road

Green

Munson Rd.

Red House Rd.

Fernwood Road

Red

Wright Road

Grimm Rd.

Feyrer Park

Feyrer Park Rd.

Fernwood Road

Ball Road

0   1   2

MILES

N

MILEAGE LOG

0.0   Milo McIver Memorial Viewpoint in Milo McIver State Park. Ride out of the viewpoint parking lot, following the road to the park entrance.

0.7   Turn left at a T-intersection with **Springwater Road** and follow it south for 5 miles. At mile 4.9, the road passes through the hamlet of Springwater. At mile 5.5, follow Springwater Road as it turns ninety degrees left (east). To make a side trip to Metzler Park (overnight camping; water available), continue south on Metzler Park Road for 2 miles.

6.0   A few feet before an intersection with Highway 211, follow Springwater Road when it turns south and parallels Highway 211.

6.9   Continue south on **Highway 211** when Springwater Road joins it. Highway 211 drops into the Clear Creek Valley and then climbs over a ridge to the town of Colton at mile 14.7. (For a shortcut, which would shorten the route by 14.8 miles, turn right on Unger Road at mile 10.6. After another 5.3 miles, Unger Road reaches the community of Clarkes, which is located at mile 30.7 of the regular route.)

16.2   Turn left on steep **Dhooghe Road**. (Another shortcut is available by staying on Highway 211 for approximately 3 miles, when it rejoins the regular route at mile 26.0, thus shortening the route by about 7 miles.)

19.7   Dhooghe Road curves to the west and becomes **Fernwood Road**.

22.7   Turn right (north) at a T-intersection with **Wright Road**. At mile 23.5, a side trip to Feyrer Park on the Molalla River (day use only; water available) can be made by turning left on Feyrer Park Road. One-half mile after leaving Wright Road, turn right over a bridge and then turn right into the park.

25.3   Turn right at a T-intersection with **Highway 211**.

26.0   Meadowbrook (store). Continue straight (northeast) on **Beaver Creek Road** when Highway 211 turns right.

32.0   Turn right on **Butte Road** (store).

32.7   Turn left (north) on **Ridge Road**. The road follows the crest of a ridge known as the Hogback and then drops into the Clear Creek Valley.

38.2   Turn right on **Redland Road**, which continues to drop toward Clear Creek. At mile 40.9, follow Redland Road when it turns left at an intersection with Jubb Road.

39.8   Watch for the picturesque Viola School on the left.

41.4   Turn right at a T-intersection with **Springwater Road**.

42.1   Turn left into Milo McIver State Park and follow signs to the Memorial Viewpoint.

42.8   Milo McIver Memorial Viewpoint. End of ride.

18 Molalla–Pudding

Starting point: Molalla River State Park, north of Canby just west of the Canby Ferry landing. Canby is 20 miles south of Portland on State Highway 99E.
Distance: Combined loop, 49.4 miles; Pudding River loop, 29.7 miles; Molalla River loop, 38.9 miles
Terrain: Pudding River loop, rolling farmland; Molalla River loop, flat with a few hills
Total cumulative elevation gain: Combined loop, 1390 feet; Pudding River loop, 650 feet; Molalla River loop, 950 feet
Recommended time of year: Any season
Recommended starting time: Before noon for either loop; before 10:00 A.M. for combined loop
Allow: 3 to 4 hours for either loop; 5 hours for combined loop

Points of interest:
Molalla River State Park
Feyrer Park
Wagon Wheel Park

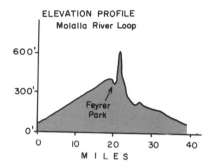

ELEVATION PROFILE
Molalla River Loop

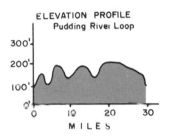

ELEVATION PROFILE
Pudding River Loop

The area south of Canby offers classic Willamette Valley bicycling: rolling farms, meandering rivers, dozens of level backroads, and an infinite number of possible routes. The two routes described here follow the natural triangle formed by the Molalla and Pudding rivers, which join near Canby before entering the Willamette.

The Molalla River is a fast-moving mountain stream, while the Pudding is a farmland slough, twisting and turning on its slow route to Canby from the area east of Salem. It received its name not from its murky waters but from a group of pioneers who made elk-blood pudding on its banks.

While pedaling in this area, watch for teasel along the roads. While this thistle plant now is a quite common Oregon weed, it played a starring role in a thriving industry before the turn of the century. Near Mulino in 1860, Alfred Sawtell established the first teasel farm in the West. Used to finish wool into fabric, teasels complemented area sheep farming and provided jobs to those willing to harvest and/or haul the sticky thistles to drying barns.

Also in Mulino, just north of the Milk Creek Bridge, is Howard's Grist Mill. The oldest industrial building still standing in Oregon, it was the site of much activity, providing flour for pioneers and gold seekers alike.

The Pudding River loop follows this river southwest from Canby. At Hubbard the route turns east toward the Molalla River, a dozen miles away. After only 6 miles, the route turns north and returns to Canby, for a 29.6-mile total. The Molalla River loop completes the crossing to the Molalla, visits two parks, and then returns to Canby via the north bank of the river.

Either loop would provide a pleasant 3 or 4 hours of bicycling. By eliminating the north–south leg they share, the routes can also be combined into a 49.4-mile loop. The resulting ride would follow the full triangle from Canby to Hubbard to Molalla and back to Canby. For cyclists seeking even more miles: They are possible. Follow the several backroads leading west to Champoeg, south to Mount Angel, or east to Estacada.

MILEAGE LOG

Pudding River Loop

0.0   Molalla River State Park (day use only; water available). Ride east toward the park entrance.

0.1   Bear right at the park entrance.

0.2   Turn right at a T-intersection with **Holly Road**.

2.2   Turn right on **Knights Bridge Road** near a small city park. The road crosses Knights Bridge over the Molalla River at mile 2.9 and then turns south at mile 4.1.

4.5   The road bends left and becomes **Arndt Road**, and crosses a bridge over the Pudding River. Arndt Road crosses Airport Road at mile 6.1 and Hubbard Highway at mile 6.4.

6.9   Turn left (south) on **Stoller Road** (Boones Ferry Road).

9.0   Boones Ferry Road eventually parallels Hubbard Highway. Continue south on **Boones Ferry Road**.

9.7   Bear left, following Boones Ferry Road, at an intersection with Donald Road (toward Hubbard).

12.4   Turn left on **Mineral Springs Road**, which becomes **D Street** in Hubbard. A city park is located at mile 13.3 between Fourth and Fifth streets. Cross Highway 99E at mile 13.5.

13.7   Turn right on **Oak Street**.

13.8   Turn left at a T-intersection with **Whiskey Hill Road (J Street)**. Follow it east for several miles, crossing the Pudding River at mile 16.3. Mount Hood can be seen in the distance on clear days. Pass through the community of Whiskey Hill (store) at mile 6.7, where the road name changes to **Barnards Road**.

20.2   Turn left (north) on **Canby-Marquam Road**. (This intersection is mile 9.5 of the Molalla River loop. Continue east from this intersection to ride the 49.4-mile perimeter of both loops.) When Canby-

I wonder why they call it the Pudding River.

	Marquam Road enters Canby, it becomes **Ivy Street**.
26.8	Canby. Cross Highway 99E.
26.9	Turn left on **First Avenue**.
27.0	Turn right (north) on **Holly Street**.
29.5	Turn left at a sign pointing to Molalla River State Park.
29.7	Molalla River State Park. End of ride.

Molalla River Loop

0.0	Molalla River State Park. Ride east toward the park entrance.
0.1	Turn right at the park entrance.
0.2	Turn right at a T-intersection with **Holly Street** in Canby.
2.6	Turn left on **First Avenue**.
2.7	Turn right (south) on **Ivy Street**, cross railroad tracks and Highway 99E, and then follow Ivy Street south for 7 miles. After leaving Canby, Ivy Street becomes **Canby-Marquam Road**.
5.1	Lone Elder (store).
9.5	Turn left on **Barnards Road** and follow it east for 4 miles.
13.7	Turn left at a T-intersection with **Highway 213**.
14.6	Turn right on Molalla Road **(Molalla-Liberal Road)**. (For a shortcut, continue north on Highway 213 for 1.4 miles, where mile 27.2 of the regular route rejoins Highway 213.) At mile 14.9, a building on the left appears to be a former one-room schoolhouse.
16.1	When Molalla-Liberal Road curves to the right and becomes Molalla Avenue, bear left at a Y-intersection to **Vaughn Road**.
17.4	Turn right (south) at a T-intersection with **Highway 211**.
18.2	Turn left on a road **(Lay Road)** marked by a sign pointing to Feyrer Park (store).

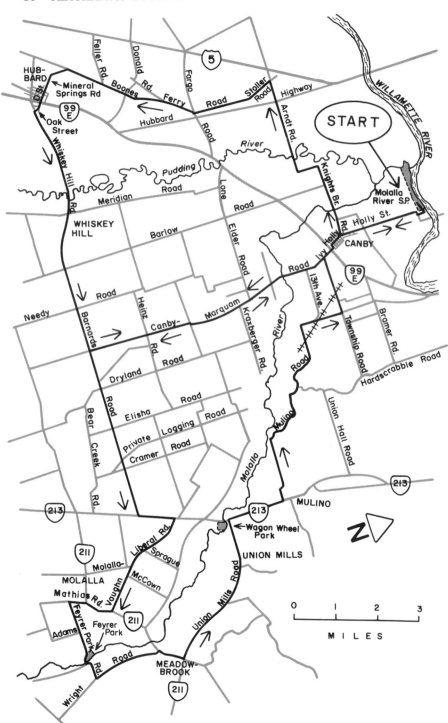

18.5 Follow the arterial by turning left on **Mathias Road (Feyrer Park Road)**.

20.1 Feyrer Park (day use only; water available).

20.2 Immediately after crossing a bridge over the Molalla River, turn left at a T-intersection, following Feyrer Park Road.

20.7 Turn left at a T-intersection with **Wright Road**.

22.5 Turn right at a T-intersection with **Highway 211**.

23.2 Meadowbrook (store). Turn left on **Union Mills Road**. At mile 9.8, pass through the community of Union Mills (store).

27.2 Turn right (north) at a T-intersection with **Highway 213**. Ride carefully on this road, which has no shoulders. (A left turn here, and then another left turn immediately after crossing a bridge, brings you to the entrance of Wagon Wheel Park, an undeveloped county park on the Molalla River.)

28.6 Mulino (store, cafe). Turn left on **Mulino Road** and follow it north and west for 6 miles.

34.1 Follow Mulino Road north, under a railroad trestle, when 13th Avenue (Mundorf Road) curves to the left.

34.7 Turn left on **Township Road**.

36.0 Turn right at a T-intersection with **Ivy Street** and then cross Highway 99E.

36.2 Turn left on **First Avenue**.

36.3 Turn right on **Holly Street**.

38.7 Turn left at a sign pointing to Molalla River State Park.

38.9 Molalla River State Park. End of ride.

YAMHILL COUNTY

19 Chehalem Mountains

Starting point: Herbert Hoover
Memorial Park in Newberg, one
block south of Highway 99W on
River Street
Distance: 51.7 miles (31.5 miles
if a shortcut is used)
Terrain: Extremely steep hills
and moderately flat farmland
**Total cumulative elevation
gain**: 2800 feet
Recommended time of year:
Any season
Recommended starting time:
9:00 A.M.
Allow: 6 hours
Points of interest:
Herbert Hoover Memorial Park
Minthorn House
Laurelwood Academy
Bald Peak State Park

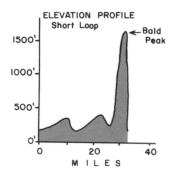

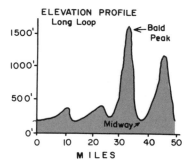

The Chehalem Mountains form a 13-mile-long dorsal fin running from
Forest Grove southeast to Newberg, dividing the Tualatin and Yamhill
valleys. This strenuous trip crosses the Chehalem Mountains not once,
but twice, and visits their highest point, Bald Peak State Park. Be prepared for long hills, probably steeper than you've seen before, but in
return expect rewarding views and delightful descents.

The trip starts in Newberg at a park named for Herbert Hoover, just
across the street from his boyhood home. The house is open to the public
for a small admission fee.

From Newberg the route follows Highway 240 west through the Yamhill

Valley farmland once held by Ewing Young, an Oregon pioneer and reputed horse thief. When Young died in 1841 without known heirs, his neighbors elected Oregon's first judge to decide who would inherit Young's property. The judge probated Young's estate under the laws of New York, since Oregon had none of its own. This initial provisional government used the proceeds of the Young estate to build Oregon's first jail, but later returned the funds when Young's son was located. Today, Young is said to lie under a huge oak near this route.

Small towns dot this ride. Carlton and Yamhill, typical of small Willamette Valley farming communities, have yet to be disturbed by freeways and suburbs. Old churches, grain elevators, cemeteries, and grange halls have thus been spared the bulldozer's wrath.

Laurelwood, on the other hand, is far from typical. Nestled at the very foot of the Chehalem Mountains, Laurelwood consists of a secluded Seventh Day Adventist boarding school and not much else.

From Laurelwood, the road climbs abruptly to the 1629-foot summit of Bald Peak. Few roads in Oregon are as steep, but fortunately the route is well shaded. What little auto traffic there is also moves slowly, due to the steepness of the terrain.

From Bald Peak, the route drops quickly to the Tualatin Valley, then passes through such one-building towns as Laurel, Midway, and Scholls. From Scholls, the route climbs to the trees over the southern end of the Chehalem Mountains, returning to the Yamhill Valley via one of the most pleasant downhill runs anywhere. The steep hills of Bald Mountain are forgotten on this delightful section.

The ride can be shortened, and one of the long climbs eliminated, by continuing south after visiting Bald Peak State Park. After following the road down a 5.4-mile hill from the park, the road rejoins the regular route at mile 47.5, reducing the length of the ride by 20.2 miles.

MILEAGE LOG

0.0 Herbert Hoover Memorial Park, at the corner of River Street and Second Avenue in Newberg. On the northwest corner is the Minthorn House (1881), boyhood home of Herbert Hoover. Proceed west (straight ahead as you face the house) on **Second Avenue**.

0.5 Turn right on **Main Street**. Proceed north, crossing Highway 99W at mile 0.6, where Main Street becomes **Highway 240**. Follow **Highway 240** as it turns left (west) at mile 0.9 and leaves Newberg. On the right at mile 4.3 is the Ewing Young historical marker.

6.5 Turn left on **Kuehne Road**.

8.3 Bear right (west) on **Carlton-Newberg Road**, which soon becomes **Hendricks Road**, and then **Main Street** in Carlton.

12.1 Carlton. Continue straight through the town. On the far side of town Main Street becomes **Meadowlake Road**.

13.5 Turn right on **West Side Road**.

16.7 Intersection with Moores Valley Road. Continue straight on **Moores Valley Road**. At 16.8, cross a bridge over the North Yamhill River.

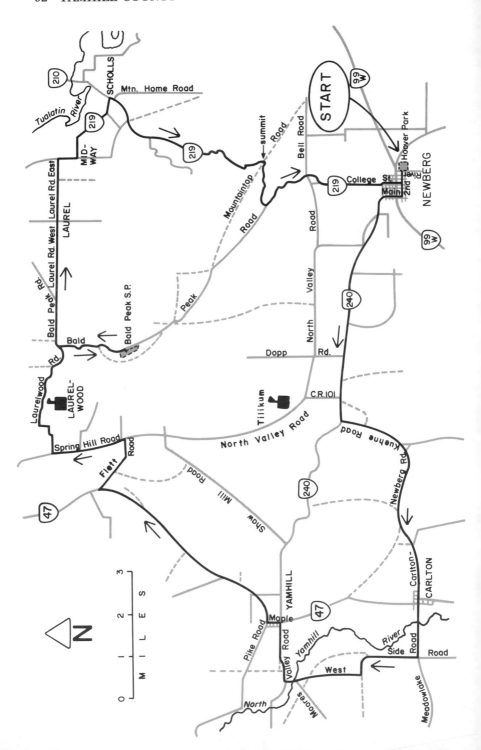

16.9 Turn right, staying on Moores Valley Road.

18.5 Yamhill. Moores Valley Road has become **Main Street**. Turn left on **Maple Street** (Highway 47), and follow it as it turns east a few blocks north of Main Street. At mile 19.2, the road turns north again.

24.1 Turn right on **Flett Road**.

25.6 At a T-intersection, turn left on **Spring Hill Road**.

27.3 Turn right on **Laurelwood Road**. A bike path is available on the right, but it is short, ending at the school. Follow this road as it works its way east and north to Laurelwood at mile 28.8, home of Laurelwood Academy, a Seventh Day Adventist boarding high school. Immediately after leaving Laurelwood, the road climbs up the steep west side of the Chehalem Mountains.

30.6 Turn right at a T-intersection with **Bald Peak Road**.

32.6 Turn right into Bald Peak State Park (day use only; water not available). Elevation 1629 feet. Stop for a rest and enjoy views of Mount Hood, Mount Jefferson, Mount Rainier, and Mount Adams.

32.7 Return to **Bald Peak Road** and turn left (north). (For a shortcut, continue south on Bald Peak Road for 5.4 miles, where the road rejoins the regular route at mile 47.5.)

34.6 At the intersection with Laurelwood Road, bear right, staying on Bald Peak Road.

35.8 Bald Peak Road bears left here. Ride straight on **Laurel Road West** (unmarked) down a very steep hill toward the community of Laurel. Enjoy the vistas as you soar on bicycle wheels.

37.5 Laurel, a town that consists solely of the Laurel Valley Store. Ride straight (east) on **Laurel Road East**.

39.0 At a T-intersection with Highway 219, turn right, following **Highway 219** through the town of Midway (tavern) to Scholls.

41.3 At the intersection of highways 219 and 210 at Scholls (store), turn right (south), following Highway 219 as it climbs up over the southern end of the Chehalem Mountains.

46.0 Yamhill County line, and the summit of the pass over the Chehalem Mountains. The sign showing an elevation of 1272 feet refers to the knoll to the east; the height of the pass is actually 1125 feet. The road then proceeds down a pleasant, long, and steep hill to Newberg where it becomes **College Street**.

50.9 Bear left, following Highway 219 and College Street.

51.5 Turn left on **Second Avenue**.

51.7 Hoover Park, at the corner of Second Avenue and River Street. End of ride.

20 Lafayette

Starting point: Wascher Elementary School in Lafayette, 30 miles west of Portland on Highway 99W. From Highway 99W in Lafayette, drive north on Monroe Street and then turn right on Seventh Avenue.
Distance: 30.4 miles
Terrain: Flat with some gentle hills
Total cumulative elevation gain: 675 feet
Recommended time of year: Any season
Recommended starting time: Before noon
Allow: 3-1/2 hours

Points of interest:
Yamhill County Historical Society Museum
Our Lady of Guadalupe Trappist Abbey
Tilikum Retreat and Conference Center
Valley View School

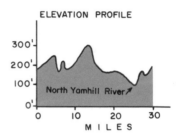

Exploring rolling foothills and farmland north of Lafayette, this pretty ride includes the Chehalem Valley and the valley of the North Yamhill River. While not notable for unusual vistas or spacious parks, the route can be highly recommended as a varied, low-traffic tour for a relaxing day in the country.

The route starts in Lafayette, a small cluster of buildings on Highway 99W. Almost a century and a half ago, Lafayette was a primary commercial center of the territory, shipping a large volume of farm products to the California gold fields via pack trains. Due to the falls on the Yamhill River, just downstream from the town, Lafayette was a poor river port. By the time locks were built on the river in 1900, railroads had usurped much of the shipping business, and Lafayette's commercial importance never recovered.

Before the turn of the century, Lafayette was the home of a successful seminary. Today, a Trappist abbey makes its home in the hills a few miles north of town. A relatively reclusive order, the Trappist monks historically took vows of silence. The vows are no longer taken, and visitors are welcome to tour their modest abbey and book bindery. Fruitcakes made by the monks are available for sale, especially during the holidays.

Beginning at an elementary school in Lafayette, the route immediately passes an 1892 church, now being used as a county historical museum. After leaving the small town, the ride climbs a subtle grade through woodlands and small farms past the Trappist abbey, and then drops

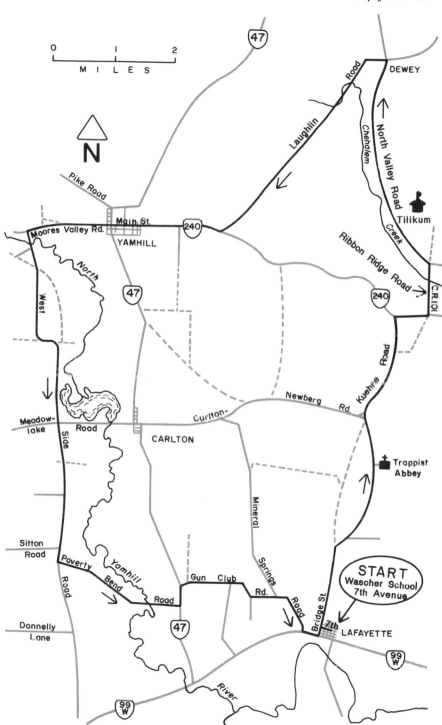

gently down into the Chehalem Creek Valley. The narrow, sparsely populated valley seems isolated. The single road through it runs neither to nor from any place in particular, and the few residents seem to live unhurried lives.

One former resident of this area operated a dairy that was heavily damaged in the 1962 Columbus Day Storm. Vowing to make a significant gift if he recovered from this upheaval, he later donated the land for Tilikum Retreat Center to George Fox College in Newberg. Now the center, which is passed at mile 7.6 of this ride, also is the site of Valley View School (circa 1909). Formerly located at mile 6.6, the tall, one-room schoolhouse, complete with bell and adjacent horseshed, was moved in pieces to avoid the many low power lines along route to Tilikum. Tilikum is private property, often bustling with campers or Elderhostel participants, but permission is usually granted to look inside the schoolhouse (unless it is in use at the time).

After leaving Tilikum, the route proceeds to nonexistent Dewey. Actually just a signed intersection, Dewey is known throughout the valley and appears on most maps, just as if it were a thriving community. From 1898 to 1904 Dewey had a post office named in honor of Admiral George Dewey of Spanish-American War fame.

Leaving the valley behind, the route climbs over a low pass and coasts past farms and dairies to the town of Yamhill. Named for the Indian tribe (Yamhelas) that once roamed Oregon coastal areas in this vicinity, this community is also in the county of Yamhill, one of four original districts of Oregon. It was once the home of film star Mary Pickford of silent picture fame. The remainder of the ride is mostly flat, generally following the North Yamhill River as it winds its way south back to sleepy Lafayette.

MILEAGE LOG

0.0   Wascher Elementary School. Turn right out of the parking lot, traveling west on Seventh Avenue. Yamhill County Historical Society Museum is on the left at mile 0.2.

0.3   Turn right on **Bridge Street** and follow it as it becomes **Kuehne Road** and proceeds through the foothills and farmland north of town. Our Lady of Guadalupe Trappist Abbey is on the right at mile 3.1. At mile 4.2, bear right, staying on **Kuehne Road** as Carlton-Newberg Road (Hendricks Road) comes in on the left.

6.0   At a T-intersection with **Highway 240** (unmarked), turn right.

6.6   Turn left (north) on **Ribbon Ridge Road** (County Road 101).

7.4   Bear left on **North Valley Road**. At mile 7.6, turn right into Tilikum Retreat Center. If historic Valley View School is not in use, request permission to look inside. Afterward, return to North Valley Road and turn right.

11.2   This intersection is on most maps as Dewey, but no buildings are in evidence. Only the road sign with "Dewey" printed vertically on the lower post marks the spot. Turn left on **Laughlin Road** and follow it west and then southwest.

But it is shown on all the maps!

15.4   At a T-intersection with **Highway 240**, turn right and follow it into Yamhill, where it becomes **Main Street**.

17.3   At the intersection with Highway 47 in "downtown" Yamhill, continue straight (west). After leaving Yamhill, Main Street becomes **Moores Valley Road**.

18.8   Turn left, following Moores Valley Road. At mile 18.9, cross the North Yamhill River.

19.0   Moores Valley Road turns right. Ride straight (south) on **West Side Road**. At mile 22.3, go straight through an intersection with Meadowlake Road.

24.6   Turn left on **Poverty Bend Road**. This road is the only paved left turn in the vicinity. Negotiate its rough pavement until it crosses over the North Yamhill River on a narrow bridge.

26.8   At a T-intersection with **Highway 47**, turn left.

27.1   Turn right on **Gun Club Road** and follow it east toward Lafayette. It eventually joins Mineral Springs Road at mile 28.8.

29.6   At a T-intersection with **Highway 99W**, carefully cross the highway and then turn left, using the shoulder.

30.0   Turn left on **Bridge Street** (unmarked), the second street on the left after entering Lafayette. The sign points to Trappist Abbey.

30.2   Turn right on **Seventh Avenue**.

30.4   Wascher School. End of ride.

21 Grand Island

Starting point: City Park in
Dayton, 30 miles west of
Portland, just south of highways
99W and 18. Park on the east
side of the park, near the corner
of Third and Ferry streets.
Distance: 36.3 miles
Terrain: Flat with one
moderately long hill
**Total cumulative elevation
gain**: 550 feet
Recommended time of year:
Any season
Recommended starting time:
Before 11:00 A.M.
Allow: 4 hours

Points of interest:
Historic buildings in Dayton
Grand Island
Maude Williamson State Park

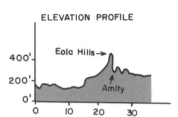

Grand Island lies in the Willamette River about 60 river miles upstream
from Portland, in the heart of a rich agricultural area. Of the islands in
the Williamette, only Sauvie Island appears to be larger. The route described here circles Grand Island and visits several nearby farming communities.

The ride starts in Dayton, a small town with a typical Willamette Valley
history. Founded as a mill town, Dayton's Yamhill River waterfront was
first visited by sternwheelers in 1851. By serving the shipping needs of
area farmers, the town prospered and quickly expanded around its large
central square. Fluctuating water levels, however, made the river an
undependable carrier of freight, and growth of the town slowed after
railroads and highways proved superior to the river and its steamers.

Being bypassed by both the railroad and Highway 99W had certain
advantages. Dayton has a surprising concentration of historic buildings
that might not have survived had the town continued to grow. After your
ride, pedal your bike around Dayton's shady streets and admire some of
the buildings, particularly the churches, that have survived from the last
century.

From Dayton's central square the ride proceeds south through the flat
farmland for several miles and then turns east to Grand Island. Grand
Island is separated from the mainland by Lambert Slough, a brush- and
weed-choked channel of the Willamette. Circling the southern end of the
flat island is a narrow farm road, only a few feet higher than the river
itself.

In late summer and fall, the island's farmers operate several fruit and
vegetable stands to market their produce. The fields may also be teeming

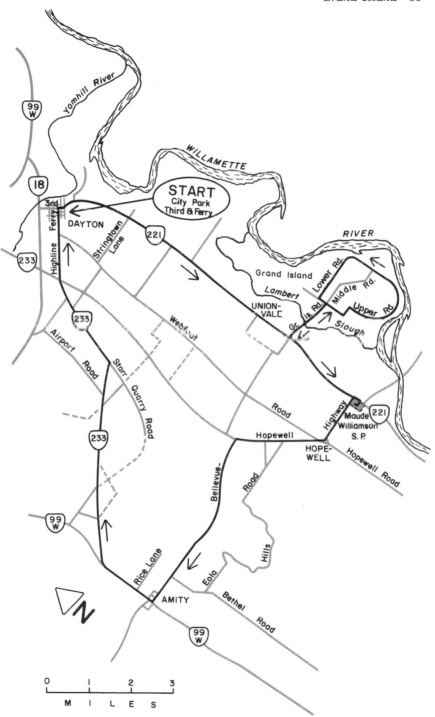

with workers gathering the crops. Prices are low and the produce fresh. If you are planning a fall ride, buy some or all of your lunch at the fruit stands and then bicycle a few miles south to picnic at Maude Williamson State Park. The park consists of a large grove of evergreens that seem out of place in contrast to the surrounding flat farmland.

From the state park the ride proceeds west to Hopewell, a very small town clustered around an interesting church (circa 1880) and a school-house built near the turn of the century. From Hopewell the route turns north and east to eventually cross the Eola Hills. The climb over the hills, about 1.5 miles long, is rewarded by a rapid descent to the town of Amity. From Amity, the ride turns north and then skirts the north end of the Eola Hills on its way northeast to Dayton.

MILEAGE LOG

0.0 City Park in Dayton. From the east side of the park, ride south on **Third Street (Highway 221)**. Follow this road for several miles as it travels through the farmland south of Dayton. At mile 5.7, the road passes through the community of Unionvale.

6.7 Grand Island Junction (store). Turn left on **Grand Island Road**. At mile 7.2, cross Lambert Slough onto Grand Island.

8.0 This intersection, known as Four Corners, is the junction of Upper Island Road, Lower Island Road, and Grand Island Loop (Grand Island Road). Turn right on **Upper Island Road** and follow it around the perimeter of the island. At mile 11.4, do not turn left on Grand Island Loop (which may also be labeled Middle Island Road), but continue north onto **Lower Island Road**.

13.2 At a T-intersection, turn left.

13.4 Four Corners. Turn right (west) and return to the mainland.

14.7 Grand Island Junction (store). Turn left on **Highway 221**. At mile 16.7, go straight, past a road on the right (Bellevue-Hopewell High-way).

17.0 Turn right into Maude Williamson State Park, an excellent lunch stop. Eventually return to the park entrance and turn left (north) on **Highway 221**.

18.0 Turn left on **Bellevue-Hopewell Highway** (a sign points to Hopewell).

19.3 Hopewell. Stay on the main road as it bears right (north).

21.4 Turn left at a sign pointing to Amity, staying on the Bellevue-Hopewell Highway (unmarked). When the road enters Amity at mile 25.5, it becomes **Nursery Avenue**.

26.0 Amity (store). Turn right on **Trade Street** (Highway 99W). (For a short side trip to an Amity city park, turn left on Fourth Street at mile 26.2.)

27.2 Turn right on **Highway 233**. At mile 32.3, follow Highway 233 when it bears left at an intersection with Starr Quarry Road, and stay on Highway 233 through intersections at miles 33.8 and 34.0.

34.6 Ride straight (northeast) through an intersection with Lafayette

Highway, leaving Highway 233, which turns left. You are now on a road known variously as **Highline Road** or **Amity-Dayton Highway**. When it reaches Dayton, it becomes **Ferry Street**.

36.3 Corner of Ferry and Third streets in Dayton. End of ride.

22 Eola Hills

Starting point: Maude Williamson State Park, midway between Salem and Dayton on Highway 221
Distance: 34.7 miles
Terrain: Moderate with one severe hill
Total cumulative elevation gain: 1200 feet
Recommended time of year: Any season
Recommended starting time: Before noon
Allow: 3 to 4 hours

Points of interest:
Maude Williamson State Park
Willamette Greenway Parks
Eola Hills
Hidden Springs Winery

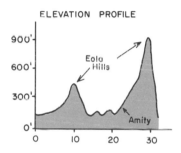

The Willamette Valley is noted for flat farm roads but, tucked away in a few of the valley's corners, long, steep hills can be found by energetic riders. Oddly enough, some of these are not in the Cascade foothills or the Coast Range, but in the heart of the valley only a few miles from the river. Two examples are the Chehalem Mountains near Newberg (Trip No. 19) and the Eola Hills west of Salem.

The Eola Hills form a 13-mile-long ridge from Salem north almost to McMinnville. The 1000-foot crest of the ridge is breached by two 450-foot passes, one at Spring Valley between the communities of Lincoln and Bethel, and the other between Grand Island and Amity.

The route described here starts near Grand Island, follows the Willamette upstream to Lincoln, and then crosses the pass at Spring Valley. Once on the west side of the ridge, the route continues north through rolling farmland to Amity.

At Amity the rider has the choice of crossing the second 450-foot pass or climbing to a crest twice as high. The choice is easy, right? Wrong. Waiting at the top of that 1000-foot ridge are some of the finest views

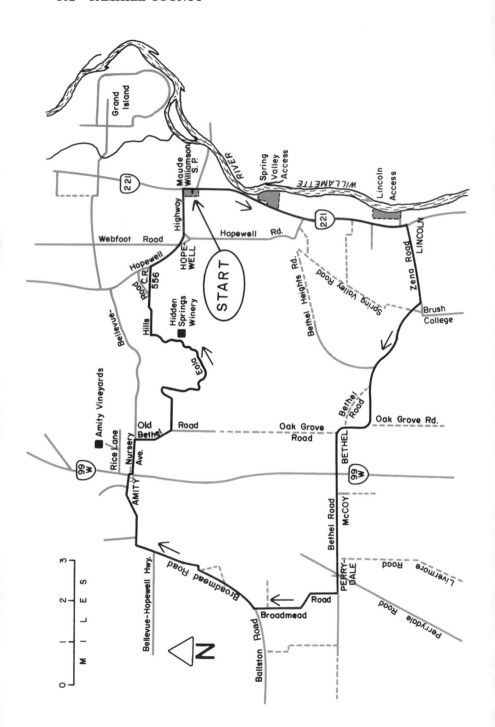

around. The entire Willamette Valley is spread before you, with Grand Island at your feet and the Cascades shimmering in the distance. Not enough, huh? How about an exhilarating descent down a narrow farm road? Still not enough? How about wine tasting at a vineyard near the summit? What more could you ask?

Alas, if you still are not interested, follow detours described below around both the 1000-foot ridge and the 450-foot pass. Be aware, however, that on the Bellevue-Hopewell Highway, car traffic may be busier than on the more scenic route.

If the climbs over the Eola Hills don't wear you out, several side trips are available. Just north of the route, Amity Vineyards offer wine tasting, and you won't have to climb a 1000-foot ridge to get there. From Amity, turn north 0.4 mile on Trade Street (Highway 99W) and then turn right on Rice Lane.

Another diversion is just 1 mile east of the route, where the Wheatland Ferry crosses the Willamette. The ferry boat, the *Daniel Matheny IV*, is named after the founder of Wheatland who originated the ferry service in 1844. Although motorists are charged a small toll, bicyclists and pedestrians ride free.

MILEAGE LOG

0.0 Maude Williamson State Park. Ride toward the park entrance and then turn south on **Highway 221**.

2.4 Spring Valley access (Willamette River Greenway) is on the left, at the end of a 0.4-mile road (day use only; water not available).

5.6 Lincoln Access (Willamette River Greenway) is on the left, at the end of 0.4-mile Lincoln Road (day use only; water not available).

5.7 Lincoln (store). Turn right on **Zena Road**. At mile 7.7, follow Zena Road when it curves right (northwest) at an intersection with Brush College Road and Spring Valley Road. Cross Highway 99W at mile 13.1, where Zena Road becomes **Bethel Road**.

13.6 McCoy.

15.6 Perrydale. Continue straight (west) on **West Perrydale Road** (Byerley Corner Road).

16.0 Turn right (north) on **Broadmead Road**.

18.3 At a T-intersection, turn right, staying with Broadmead Road.

21.4 Broadmead Road joins **Bellevue-Hopewell Highway**. Continue straight (north) at a stop sign, following signs pointing to Amity.

23.7 Amity (store). Turn right (south) on **Highway 99W** (Trade Street).

23.8 Turn left on **Nursery Avenue**, which regains the name **Bellevue-Hopewell Highway** after leaving Amity.

24.6 Turn right (south) on **Old Bethel Road**. (For an alternate route with a less severe hill, but more car traffic, continue straight, climb over a 450-foot pass, and then follow Bellevue-Hopewell Highway when it turns right at a T-intersection at mile 28.4).

25.6 Turn left on **Eola Hills Road**, which climbs 800 feet in the next 3.5 miles. The crest of the hill is reached at mile 29.1, and Hidden

Springs Winery is on the right at mile 30.0. The road begins a
steep descent at mile 30.8.

31.3   When Eola Hills Road bears left, bear right on **County Road 556**.

32.0   Turn right at a T-intersection with **Bellevue-Hopewell Highway**
and ride carefully on the road shoulder. At mile 33.0, the road
curves left and passes through the town of Hopewell, which consists almost entirely of an 1880 church and a turn-of-the-century
schoolhouse.

34.4   Turn right (south) at a T-intersection with **Highway 221**.

34.6   Turn right into Maude Williamson State Park.

34.7   Maude Williamson State Park. End of ride.

23 Upper Yamhill Valley

Starting point: Grenfell Park,
2 miles west of Sheridan on
Highway 18. Turn south on
Harmony Road and then turn
west into the park.

Points of interest:
Grenfell Park
Buell Park
Ballston Park

Distance: 32.1 miles
Terrain: Mixed hilly and flat
**Total cumulative elevation
gain:** 1100 feet
Recommended time of year:
Any season
Recommended starting time:
Before noon
Allow: 3 hours

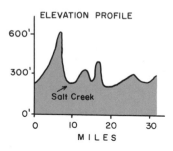

The South Yamhill River has its source in the Coast Range, barely 10
miles from the Pacific. It is a mountain stream for its first few miles, but
after it passes the town of Sheridan, it meanders its way through a broad
valley of flat farmland. The ride starts in the valley near Sheridan and
circles through the foothills south of the river. Much of the ride is level,
but crossing a 600-foot ridge between Mill Creek and Salt Creek requires
some extra effort.

The ride starts in Yamhill County, just outside of Sheridan, and then
crosses into Polk County for most of its distance. Three small parks are
visited along the way. The starting point, Grenfell Park, is on Mill Creek,
as is Buell Park, 5 miles later. The third park, in the tiny town of Ballston,
boasts an equally tiny, yet well-preserved, 1865 schoolhouse.

The route passes other historic buildings, including several grange halls,

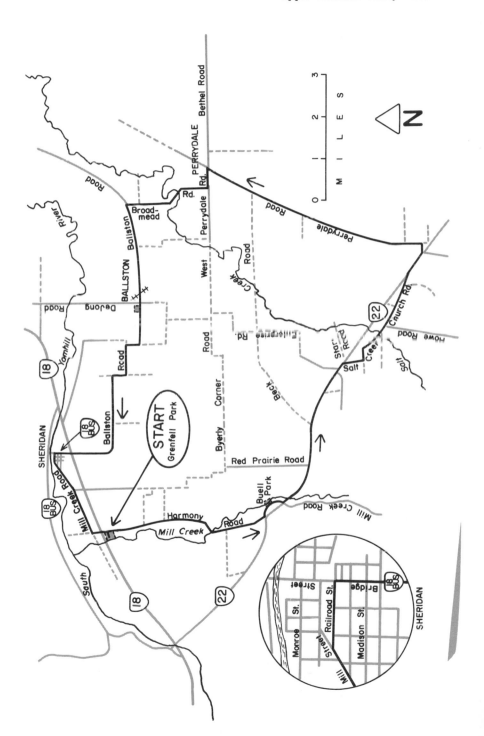

schoolhouses, and churches, at least one of which is complete with a churchyard cemetery. Particularly near Perrydale, the route also passes several Victorian houses in various states of repair.

Several miles of the route follow Highway 22, a major auto route and an officially designated bike route to the coast from the Salem area. Although traffic can be heavy on summer weekends, the shoulders are wide and the experience not at all unpleasant. At mile 9.2, a 3-mile detour parallels Highway 22 on Salt Creek Church Road. Hurried riders can stay on Highway 22 if they prefer the fast and straight to the slow and winding.

For other diversions, Perrydale is visited by two other routes described in this guidebook. Eola Hills (Trip No. 22) circles the farmland (and steep hills) northeast of Perrydale, while Rickreall (Trip No. 29) circles the area southeast of Perrydale. Another possible side trip would be to visit Basket Slough National Wildlife Refuge, 3 miles southeast of this route on Highway 22. But the best diversion is west, up over the mountains on highways 22 and 18 and then down to the coast.

MILEAGE LOG

0.0 Grenfell Park (camping permitted; water available). Ride east to the park entrance and then turn right (south) on **Harmony Road**.

4.6 One block before an intersection with Highway 22 (store), turn left on **Mill Creek Road** (unmarked). At mile 5.0, Buell Park is on the left (day use only; water available).

5.3 Turn left on **Highway 22**. The highway climbs a 1-mile-long hill, is level for a short section, and then descends a long hill.

9.2 Turn right on **Salt Creek Church Road** (store).

12.1 Turn right (east) when Salt Creek Church Road rejoins **Highway 22**.

12.7 Turn left (north) on **Perrydale Road**.

18.6 Perrydale. Turn left on **West Perrydale Road** (Byerley Corner Road).

19.1 Turn right on **Broadmead Road**.

21.3 Turn left at a T-intersection with Ballston Road.

23.8 Ballston (store). Continue westbound.

23.9 Ballston Park (day use only; water not available) is on the right.

24.7 Follow Ballston Road through the first of several ninety-degree turns. Eventually the road curves north toward Sheridan.

28.8 Ballston Road joins **Highway 18-Business**. Continue north on an overpass across Highway 18, where Ballston Road (Highway 18-Business) becomes **Bridge Street** in Sheridan.

29.4 Turn left on **Mill Street**. After leaving Sheridan, Mill Street becomes **Mill Creek Road**.

30.5 Bear right on Mill Creek Road.

31.5 Follow Mill Creek Road when it turns left (south) at an intersection with two gravel roads, and becomes **Harmony Road**.

31.9 After crossing Highway 18, turn right into Grenfell Park.

32.1 Grenfell Park. End of ride.

MARION COUNTY

24 French Prairie

Starting point: Champoeg State Park, west of I-5 via exit no. 278 or 282. Drive into the park to the day use area.
Distance: 52.2 miles
Terrain: Flat
Total cumulative elevation gain: 500 feet
Recommended time of year: Any season
Recommended starting time: 10:00 A.M.
Allow: 5 hours

Points of interest:
Champoeg State Park
Numerous historic houses
St. Paul Catholic Church
St. Louis Catholic Church
Aurora Colony Historic District

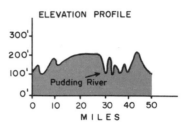

Although traveling in a generally northerly direction, the Willamette River, when it reaches Newberg, makes a pronounced turn east to the Canby area for about a dozen miles. In so turning, the Willamette cradles a broad plain of approximately 150 square miles known as the French Prairie.

In many ways one of the most historic areas of the valley, French Prairie first was inhabited by Calapooya Indians, who recognized its fine hunting, pasture, and fishing opportunities. Later, French-Canadians, who came to Oregon with the Hudson's Bay Company, settled there. The first French-Canadians settled in 1829, and by 1845 the population numbered nearly 700. Their agricultural successes resulted in construction of a grain warehouse on the river at an Indian camp called Champoeg.

A sizable town grew up. In 1843, it was the site of a series of meetings, resulting in a narrow vote of 52-50 that created a provisional government for the territory. The territory progressed toward statehood and prosperity, but the town was destroyed by the floods of 1861 and 1890. If you are interested in the early life here, consider attending a historical pageant in the park, Thursday through Sunday evenings in July. (Call 503-245-3922 for information.)

The former townsite is now a huge (and hugely popular) state park, with extensive camping and picnic grounds, three small museums, and broad pastures complete with grazing sheep. This ride starts in the park near the bicycle trail and winds its way out into the surrounding countryside.

French Prairie has retained much historic character. The area is still mainly agricultural and many of the farmhouses are well over a century old. The most imposing building in the vicinity is St. Paul Catholic Church, a towering brick structure built in 1846 to replace a log chapel that had been used for ten years. This brick church building is the oldest west of the Rocky Mountains.

On the east side of the prairie, the town of Aurora also offers several historic buildings, many dating from the 1850s and 1860s. At that time Aurora was a Christian communal colony under the strict leadership of Dr. William Keil. This experiment in communal living essentially died before 1900 with Dr. Keil and today Aurora is a bustling village frequented by antique shoppers and history buffs.

Slightly over 50 miles long, this route can be shortened by dissecting its general grid pattern at almost any point. Flat terrain of the French Prairie and multiple roads carrying light auto traffic give the rider many route options.

The shortest route of all is the bike path within Champoeg State Park. Winding through the trees and alongside the river to Butteville and returning to the day use area by the same route provides about 8 miles of pedaling. This can be an educational event if the museums in the park are included. Check museum hours in advance; times for opening and closing vary with the season.

MILEAGE LOG

0.0 Champoeg State Park, day use area. Ride east on the road toward the park entrance.

0.9 Turn right toward the park entrance and then turn right again on **Champoeg Road**. A bike path along the right side of the road extends 0.1 mile to the Robert Newell House (1852), now a Daughters of the American Revolution (D.A.R.) museum.

1.1 Turn right at a T-intersection, following **Champoeg Road** north and then west. Ride straight ahead (west) at an intersection with Highway 219 at mile 3.6.

3.7 Bear right at an intersection with Ray Bell Road. Stay with **Champoeg Road** for several miles as it follows the Willamette River toward St. Paul.

7.3 Champoeg Road becomes Riverside Drive. On clear days Mount Hood can be seen from here and in the fall the pungent smell of drying hops fills the air.

10.6 Turn left at a T-intersection with **Blanchet Avenue**. At mile 11.6, St. Paul Church (1846) is on the left.

11.7 Turn right at an intersection with **Main Street** in St. Paul. After leaving St. Paul, Main Street becomes **River Road**.

19.6 Turn left (north) at a T-intersection with **Highway 219** (French Prairie Road). The Nusom House (1904) stands on the south side of this intersection.

20.3 Turn right on **St. Louis Road** and follow it through the town of St. Louis at mile 21.3. Located a half-block north of this intersection is St. Louis Catholic Church (circa 1880). On the right at mile

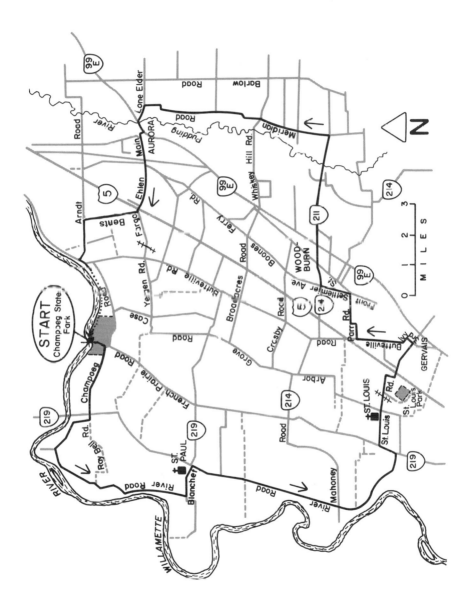

22, Tesch Road leads to public fishing ponds at St. Louis County Park. (The road is partially gravel.)

22.9 Cross I-5 on an overpass.

23.9 Gervais. St. Louis Road becomes **Douglas Avenue**. Turn left (north) on **Third Street**.

24.2 Follow the arterial as it turns left (west) on **Ivy Avenue**. A few blocks later, Ivy turns north and becomes **Butteville Road**.

25.9 Just before an overpass with I-5, turn right on **Parr Road** and follow it into Woodburn.

27.7 Turn left on **Settlemier Avenue** one block before an intersection with Front Street. Settlemier City Park is on the right at 28.0 miles.

28.7 Turn right on **Highway 214**, using a bike path and then a lane on the right side of the highway.

30.1 At an intersection with Highway 99E, ride straight (east) on **Highway 211**. At mile 32.0, cross a bridge over the Pudding River.

33.9 Turn left on **Meridian Road** and carefully follow it north for several miles through a section of busy road. At mile 35.3, cross Whiskey Hill (store) and continue straight on Meridian.

40.4 Turn left on **Lone Elder Road** at a T-intersection.

40.9 Turn left on **Highway 99E**, cross the Pudding River, and enter Aurora.

41.3 Turn right on **Main Street**. After leaving Aurora, the road eventually becomes **Ehlen Road**.

44.0 Turn right on **Bents Road**, just after crossing under I-5.

45.7 Turn left on **Arndt Road**.

47.0 Butteville (store). Turn left on Butteville Road. A bike lane begins on the right one block later.

47.2 Turn right onto **Schuler Road**, following the bike route into the park.

47.6 Turn left onto the bike path in Champoeg Park. If it is wet, take care crossing the wooden bridge at mile 48.4.

49.5 Continue on the bike path past the exit to the campground. Pass the exit to the visitors center at mile 50.2. Pioneer Mothers Cabin at mile 51.9, where the story of Champoeg is told, requires an exit from the path and re-entry across the parking area.

52.2 Exit the bike path in the day use parking area. End of ride.

25 South French Prairie

Starting point: Wheatland Park in Marion County on the east side of the Willamette River at the Wheatland Ferry. From I-5 exit no. 263, drive west through Hopmere, turn north on Wheatland Road, and then turn west on Matheny Road.
Distance: 33.5 miles
Terrain: Flat
Total cumulative elevation gain: 575 feet
Recommended time of year: Any season
Recommended starting time: Before noon
Allow: 3 to 4 hours

Points of interest:
Wheatland Ferry
St. Louis Catholic Church
St. Louis fish ponds
Mount Angel
Willamette Mission State Park

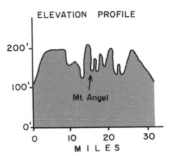

Meandering through farmland northeast of Salem, this 32-mile loop offers fine riding, little traffic, and a variety of diversions. For those who like to ride hard and fast, the route provides relatively flat roads with occasional small hills, but without much traffic. For those who prefer to take their time, the route presents numerous parks, small towns, and old cemeteries to distract riders looking for distractions.

The route visits several parks, two of which are quite large. The ride begins and ends at Wheatland County Park, little more than a gravel parking lot along the river, adjacent to Willamette Mission State Park. Although Wheatland was once a sizable community, all that remains is the Wheatland Ferry, named for founder Daniel Matheny. It has been operating since 1844. Today the ferry is a critical commuter link between Yamhill and Marion counties. The ferry was established to carry loads of wheat and other farm products, which now seem almost forgotten.

Farther east on the ride, St. Louis County Park features seven man-made fishing ponds that have been stocked with catfish, bass, bluegill, and crappies. The Willamette Valley has relatively few lakes and ponds, making these seem completely out of place in the midst of farms and freeways.

The ride is completed on the bike paths snaking through Willamette Mission State Park. The park includes sprawling wheatfields, filbert orchards, and the site of Jason Lee's 1834 Methodist mission. Today, the lowlands between Wheatland and Salem are still known as Mission Bottom. While winding through the park, be sure to stop near the pond for

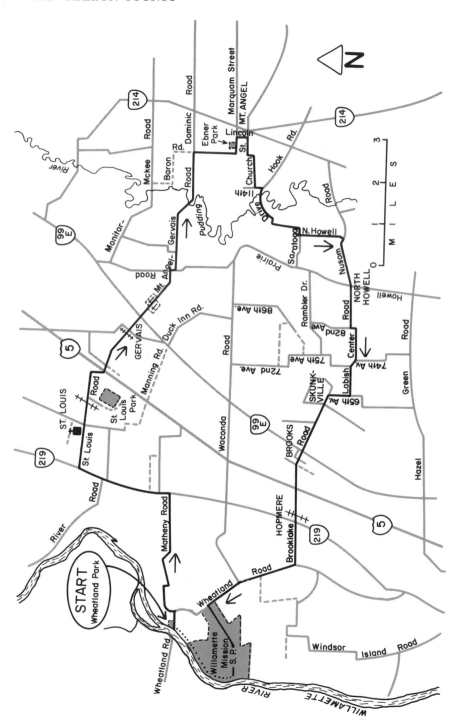

Wow, isn't that a neat building?

a look at the world's oldest (250 years) black cottonwood tree and the monument to Jason Lee. You may also hear the occasional mechanical sounds meant to scare the birds away from the filberts.

Several interesting old cemeteries can be visited along the cycling route. The St. Louis cemetery, which lies a few blocks north of the loop, is one of the oldest in the state. Its residents include Madame Marie Dorion, the first pioneer woman to settle in the Oregon Territory.

Just east of Gervais, two small cemeteries straddle the route. Both contain a variety of tombstones from this century and the last. On the south side of the road, the Masonic Cemetery includes two sections of Russian graves, several of which are marked with the distinctive cross of the Russian Orthodox Christian Church.

Farther east, the route passes through the western edge of Mount Angel. Visible from more than 1 mile away, the town presents a picturesque scene of a small farm community centered around a towering church steeple, with a beautiful wooded knoll in the background.

MILEAGE LOG

0.0 Wheatland Park. Ride east on **Matheny Road**.

0.4 At a T-intersection, turn left, staying on Matheny Road. Wheatland Road is on the right.

3.6 Turn left at a T-intersection with **Highway 219** (River Road).

5.8 Turn right on **St. Louis Road**. At mile 6.7, the St. Louis cemetery is visible off to the left. At mile 6.9, pass through the town of St. Louis at an intersection with Manning Road. A half-block north on Manning Road is the St. Louis Catholic Church (circa 1880). At mile 8.4, cross I-5 on an overpass. (To leave the route to visit St. Louis County Park, turn right at mile 7.4 on Tesch Lane, immediately after crossing the railroad tracks. This road into the fish ponds is about 1 mile long, the first half of which is paved.)

9.3 St. Louis Road enters Gervais, a town named for one of the earliest

Willamette Valley pioneers, Joseph Gervais, and becomes **Douglas Street**. Continue straight through Gervais. After crossing Highway 99E at mile 9.9, the road becomes **Mount Angel-Gervais Road**. At mile 10.3, small cemeteries lie on both sides of the road.

11.3   Turn right (south) at a T-intersection with **Howell Prairie Road**.

11.4   Turn left on **Mount Angel-Gervais Road**. At mile 13.1, cross a bridge over the Pudding River.

14.5   Bear right on **Baron Road** at an intersection with Dominic Road. At mile 15.5, the road turns left toward Mount Angel and becomes **Marquam Street**. At mile 15.7, Ebner County Park is on the left at the end of a short side street.

15.9   Turn right on **Lincoln Street**.

16.1   Turn right on **Church Street**. Mount Angel city center (stores, cafe) is one block east of this intersection. (To visit it, turn left here.)

17.5   Turn left at a T-intersection with **114th Avenue**.

17.6   Turn right at an intersection with **Saratoga Drive** on the right and Hook Road on the left.

19.4   Turn left on **North Howell Road**.

20.5   Turn right at a T-intersection with **Nusom Road**. At mile 21.7, pass through an intersection known as North Howell (store) where Nusom Road becomes **Labish Center Road**.

22.7   Turn left at a T-intersection with **82nd Avenue**. A block later, the road turns west again and regains the name **Labish Center Road**.

23.5   Follow Labish Center Road when it turns right at an intersection with 74th Avenue. Cross a bridge over the Little Pudding River a block later.

23.7   Labish Center. Bear left at a stop sign, following Labish Center Road as it heads west.

24.5   Turn right toward Brooks and Woodburn at a T-intersection with **65th Avenue**.

25.0   Turn left at **Brooklake Road**. This intersection has the distinction of being known as Skunkville. Follow Brooklake Road for the next several miles, through the town of Brooks at mile 26.4 and Hopmere at mile 28.1.

29.2   Turn right at a T-intersection with **Wheatland Road**. At mile 31.6, turn left into the entrance of Willamette Mission State Park and follow bike paths along the river to your car.

33.5   Wheatland County Park. End of ride.

26 Mount Angel Foothills

Starting point: St. Mary's
Church on Church Street
between Oak and Elm streets in
Mount Angel. Park along the
south side of Church Street.
Distance: 38.5 miles
Terrain: Mixed hilly and flat
**Total cumulative elevation
gain:** 1750 feet
Recommended time of year:
Any season
Recommended starting time:
10:00 A.M.
Allow: 4 to 5 hours

Points of interest:
Mount Angel Abbey

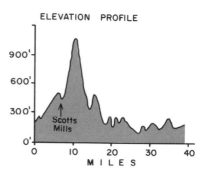

Foothills and farmland around Mount Angel offer fine bicycling over
varied terrain. The farmland offers bicycling on typical Willamette Valley
rural roads, and the foothills offer pleasant views of the valley. Roughly
one-third of this ride is in foothills; the rest travels flat farm roads.
Except for a few connectors, roads are nearly devoid of traffic.

Farms are as varied as the terrain: Look for hop fields and filbert
orchards in the flatlands, Christmas tree farms in the hills, and berry
and pumpkin patches in between.

The population of the Mount Angel area is equally varied. Many residents are Catholic, descended from the French-Canadians who settled
the area in the 1830s. Another segment of the population consists of
Russian Old Believers, who fled religious persecution by traveling to
Brazil and New Jersey and then to the Willamette Valley. Still another
group is of Mexican descent, as evidenced by the many bilingual signs in
Mount Angel.

Adding to the cultural hodgepodge is the town's effort to create the
atmosphere of a Bavarian village, complete with ersatz chalet architecture, German signs, and an "Oktoberfest" in mid-September. The festival,
by the way, attracts throngs of high-spirited celebrants. It is not a recommended time for bicyclists to visit the area, even though fall colors make
this a fine autumn ride.

The starting point for the ride is not hard to find: Just look for the huge
steeple a few blocks east of the center of Mount Angel. The ride then
proceeds east, over a shoulder of the knoll on which Mount Angel Abbey
sits. A side trip to the top of the knoll offers excellent views of the valley
and a look at a Benedictine monastery. Established in 1884, the monastery has a fine collection of neo-Romanesque architecture, but the most
notable exception—their library designed by the Finnish architect Alvar

Aalto and completed in 1970—is alone worth the trip. Another feature is a small museum devoted to the history of the Russian Old Believers.

After a few miles of flat farmland, the route climbs the end of a small ridge, and then drops into a sleepy little hollow and the town of Scotts Mills. After crossing Butte Creek, the grade steepens considerably as the route climbs "Missouri Ridge" and then drops into the Rock Creek Valley. Rock Creek is followed north several miles into farmland that steadily grows flatter and flatter. Several nonexistent "towns" are visited, with curious names like Needy, Ninety One, and Whiskey Hill.

Since the roads in the farmland are basically in a grid pattern, several shortcuts are available for those who might not want to pedal the full 38.5 miles. For example, from the Yoder area, a rider could easily cut south and west to return to Mount Angel.

MILEAGE LOG

0.0 St. Mary's Church in Mount Angel. Ride east on **Church Street**, which soon becomes **College Street** and later **College Road**. At mile 1.6, the entrance to Mount Angel Abbey is on the right.

2.7 Turn right on **Meridian Road** and then a block later turn left on Mount Angel-Scotts Mills Road. Ride straight (east) through Lone Pine Corner at mile 4.3.

6.9 Scotts Mills (store), founded in 1893. **Mount Angel-Scotts Mills Road** becomes **Third Street**. Scotts Mills Area Historical Society Museum (an old church) is located one block north on Grandview

You say your orange helmet blew off here?

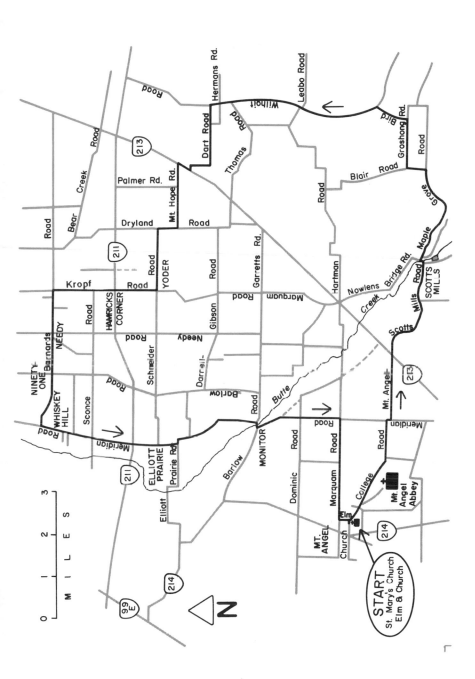

Avenue. Scotts Mills County Park is located 0.25 mile south of town on Crooked Finger Road. Continue east on Third Street and cross Nowlens Bridge on the east edge of town, where Third Street becomes **Nowlens Bridge Road**.

7.1 Turn right on **Maple Grove Road** (Scotts Mills Road) and follow it as it climbs Missouri Ridge.

9.6 Turn left on **Blair Road**.

10.1 Bear right (east) on **Groshong Road**.

11.2 Turn left on **Bird Road**, which makes a rapid drop into the Rock Creek Valley. Beware of tight corners and wet leaves.

12.1 Turn left at a T-intersection with **Wilhoit Road** and follow it as it glides down the Rock Creek Valley. Watch for the next turn to appear on this downhill run.

16.3 Turn left on **Dart Road** and follow it through farmland west and north to Highway 213.

18.3 Turn right on **Highway 213**. Watch for moderate traffic.

18.6 Turn left on **Mount Hope Road**.

20.1 At a T-intersection with **Dryland Road**, turn right.

20.6 Turn left on **Schneider Road**.

22.1 Yoder (store). Turn right on **Kropf Road**, and follow it north through Hamricks Corner at mile 23.1. At mile 23.5, Smyrna Church (1891) stands on the left.

24.6 Turn left on **Barnards Road** and follow it west through the communities of Needy and Ninety One.

28.0 Whiskey Hill (store). Turn left on **Meridian Road**. At mile 30.9, pass through the community of Elliot Prairie. At mile 31.4, stay on Meridian Road when it jogs left at an intersection with Elliot Prairie Road.

33.5 At a T-intersection with **Barlow Road**, turn right, cross a bridge over Butte Creek, and enter the town of Monitor.

33.6 Turn left on **Meridian Road**. Continue through an intersection with Dominic Road at mile 34.7.

35.7 Turn right on **Marquam Road** and follow it into Mount Angel.

38.1 Turn left on **Elm Street**.

38.4 At a T-intersection, Church Street is on the right and College Street is on the left. Turn right on **Church Street**.

38.5 St. Mary's Church. End of ride.

27 Silver Creek

Starting point: Coolidge and McClaine Park at the corner of Charles Avenue and Coolidge Street in Silverton. From Highway 214 in downtown Silverton, turn west on Main Street and then left on Coolidge Street.
Distance: 34.7 miles
Terrain: Hilly
Total cumulative elevation gain: 2500 feet
Recommended time of year: Any season except during snowy conditions
Recommended starting time: 10:00 A.M.
Allow: 4 to 5 hours

Points of interest:
Silver Falls State Park
Gallon House Covered Bridge

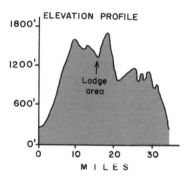

ELEVATION PROFILE

Silver Falls State Park is Oregon's largest, and probably prettiest, state park. Noted for more than a dozen waterfalls, the park is justifiably popular, particularly in summer when the cool, mossy forests attract refugees from Willamette Valley's heat. Its most popular attraction is the "Trail of the Ten Falls," a 7-mile hike meandering through second-growth Douglas fir and western hemlock.

The park is open all year, and thus the ride can be made in any season, but spring and fall are probably best. In summer, the park can often be crowded, and in winter many of the facilities are closed, including some of the park's footpaths and bike trails. During cold weather the roads may also be icy or covered with snow. However, cold-weather visitors enjoy the roaring fire in the park's main lodge, generally tended on weekends by volunteers. Volunteers also provide interpretative information, and a concession sells snacks. The lodge is located in the park on the south fork of Silver Creek.

The ride starts in Coolidge and McClaine Park, a shady grove of trees just across Silver Creek from downtown Silverton. After crossing a pedestrian bridge, the route proceeds south along Silver Creek for about 2 miles, and then begins to climb steeply up the side of the wooded valley, offering views of Silver Creek Reservoir. The winding road has no shoulders, so ride carefully.

After 1 or 2 miles of climbing, the road begins to level out and then traverses southeast along a ridge known as the Silverton Hills. Gently rolling tree farms and fine views to the south and west characterize this part of the ride. Gently undulating hills seem to disguise the several

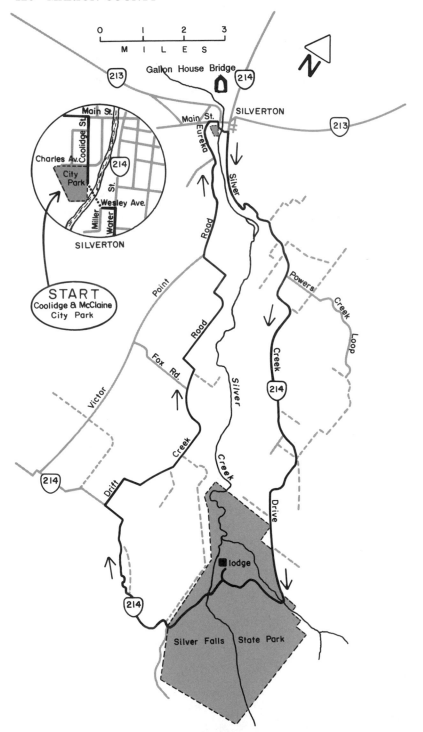

hundred feet of elevation gained as the highway climbs the ridge.

Near mile 13.0, the route enters the heavily wooded state park, leaving behind the openness of sprawling tree farms. The park offers a variety of activities, the two most popular being picnicking and hiking. Most of the picnic sites are in the central area of the park near the lodge. A swimming hole is also nearby. Trails to the waterfalls are generally short and well graded, although a few involve some stairs. Either walk your bike along the trails, or carry a lock and leave your bike at the trailhead. The highest waterfall in the park, South Falls (177 feet), is less than a 0.5-mile walk from the lodge area.

From the park the route continues to climb to 1750 feet and then sweeps down through the woods to farmland at the head of Drift Creek. The final leg of the journey is perhaps the most scenic: The road runs north on a ridge between Drift Creek on the west and Silver Creek on the east, with dramatic views into the steeply sided Silver Creek Valley. Silver Creek disappears around a bend to the south, giving no hint of the dozen waterfalls hidden at the head of its valley.

Upon returning to town, continue by bike or car through Silverton to visit Marion County's only remaining covered bridge. Approximately 1.5 miles north of Silverton on Highway 214, turn left toward the cemetery on Hobart Road. The next right turn is Arbiqua Road, which crosses the bridge to return to the highway.

Gallon House Bridge was named for its use long before prohibition days. Silverton's "Good Templars" made sure no one sold liquor in their town, but it could be purchased in Mount Angel. Since the bridge was the boundary between the two counties at that time, moonshine in gallon jugs was left or exchanged there for dollars.

MILEAGE LOG

0.0 Coolidge and McClaine Park in Silverton. Proceed south on **Coolidge Street** through the park.

0.1 Turn left and cross a footbridge over Silver Creek. At the far end of the footbridge, bear right (southeast) and cross a parking lot.

0.2 Turn left (east) on **Wesley Avenue**.

0.3 At a T-intersection with **Water Street** (Highway 214), turn right (south). Follow this road for several miles. After leaving Silverton, Water Street becomes **Silver Creek Drive**, but retains the Highway 214 designation.

12.9 Highway 214 enters Silver Falls State Park. A road on the right leads to a group campground. Continue southeast on Highway 214.

13.0 Bridge over the North Fork of Silver Creek. From the parking lot at this bridge, trails lead to North Falls and Upper North Falls. At mile 13.6, a short walk to the right gives a good view of North Falls. At mile 14.8, the road crosses a bike path. For an alternate route to the lodge and picnic area, turn right on the bike path.

15.7 Turn right into the central area of the park, including the lodge and picnic area. After lunch and/or exploring the area, return to this intersection and turn right (south).

22.4 Turn right (north) on **Drift Creek Road**. At mile 30.4, Drift Creek Road joins **Victor Point Road**, which eventually becomes **Eureka Avenue** after entering Silverton.

34.3 Turn right at a T-intersection with **Main Street**.

34.6 At the bottom of a hill, turn right on **Coolidge Street**.

34.7 Coolidge and McClaine Park. End of ride.

28 North Santiam

Starting point: Jefferson Middle School, 1 mile north of Jefferson at the intersection of Talbot Road and Jefferson Highway

Distance: Combined loop, 49 miles; east loop, 36.7 miles; west loop, 34.5 miles

Terrain: East loop, gentle; west loop, mixed hilly and flat

Total cumulative elevation gain: Combined loop, 1275 feet; east loop, 775 feet; west loop, 1500 feet

Recommended time of year: Any season

Recommended starting time: Before noon for either loop; 10:00 A.M. for combined loop

Allow: 3 to 4 hours for either loop; 5 hours for combined loop

Points of interest:
Jordan Covered Bridge
Pioneer Park
Mill Creek
Turner Tabernacle
Ankeny National Wildlife Refuge
Buena Vista Ferry

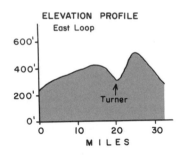

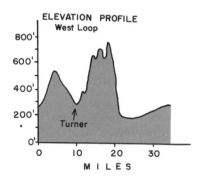

Southwestern Marion County is a mixture of flat farm country and steep hills. The hills, which run from Jefferson north toward Salem, divide the farmland. The eastern section borders on the twisting North

Santiam River, while the western section, known as Ankeny Bottom, is surrounded by the Willamette and Santiam rivers.

When steamboats were plying the Willamette River prior to the turn of the century, Ankeny Bottom was an important source of fuel. Boats could pull in at landings such as Sidney to load a fresh supply of cordwood. Today, Sidney is a cluster of houses nearly 1 mile from the river and Ankeny Bottom is noted not for its woodlots but for a national wildlife refuge.

Two routes, one flat and one hilly, are described here. The gentle east loop follows the North Santiam River upstream through corn and mint fields to Stayton, where it visits Jordan Bridge. Now in Pioneer Park, Jordan Bridge formerly spanned Thomas Creek in neighboring Linn County. It was built in 1937 and in 1985 was saved from destruction. After a brief time in storage, it was restored and proudly dedicated in Stayton.

After visiting the bridge, the route turns around and follows Mill Creek downstream. Along the way, it crosses Mill Creek at least eight times before turning south for the ride back to Jefferson. It also passes through several small towns, including Marion, Aumsville, and Turner.

According to *Oregon Geographic Names*, Marion and Turner have a common history. When a railroad worker was instructed to build a station and a warehouse at a site on Mill Creek to be called Marion, the materials were delivered by mistake to another site 6 miles farther down the line. The railroad realized the mistake, but went ahead and used the new site and the name Marion, later building a station at the original site under the name of Turner. Turner is now a sizable community, despite its early difficulties, while Marion, like Sidney, is just a sleepy little cluster of houses. Turner is also the location of a sizable church, the huge Turner Tabernacle, on the east edge of town.

The hilly west loop also visits Turner, and then rides west across the Salem Hills before turning south to Ankeny Bottom and the Buena Vista Ferry landing. A level route is then followed along the Santiam River back to Jefferson. Along the way, watch for a long row of black walnut trees and, in season, the road covered with walnuts. It's also possible to combine the two loops by simply riding the 49-mile perimeter.

MILEAGE LOG

East Loop

0.0   Jefferson Middle School 1 mile north of Jefferson. Turn right out of the parking lot to ride south on **Jefferson Highway**. A bike lane is available on the west side of the road.

0.5   Turn left, following the sign pointing to Marion and Stayton. This unmarked street (**North Avenue**) turns north at mile 0.7 and becomes Marion Road (**Jefferson-Marion Road**).

5.4   Marion (store). Turn right on **Stayton Road**.

10.9   At a Y-intersection where Stayton Road merges with **West Stayton Road** (store), continue straight ahead (east).

Next stop—Pacific Ocean!

Note: Refer to map inset for mile 12.8 through 16.8.

12.8 **Wilco Road** (store, services). Bear right onto **Ida Street**.

13.8 Cross First Avenue in Stayton, continuing on Ida Street.

13.9 Turn left on **Third Avenue** and enjoy a pedal through the old town section of Stayton. Stayton was chartered in 1891.

14.0 Turn right on **Marion Street**.

14.2 Pioneer Park. Jordan Bridge stands across a stream here. This was the first full-size covered bridge to be dismantled and moved to another site. Dedicated here in 1987, it formerly spanned Thomas Creek near Scio.

14.4 After a rest and a visit at the bridge, exit to a stop sign on nearby **Seventh Avenue** and turn right.

14.6 Turn right on **Jefferson Street**, and bear left as the road name changes to 10th.

15.4 Turn left onto **Fern Ridge Road** at a T-intersection.

15.8 Cross over **Cascade Highway**, continuing straight as Fern Ridge Road becomes **Shaff Road**.

16.8 Turn right on **Golf Club Road** (truck route).

18.3 Immediately before an intersection with Highway 22, turn left on **Mill Creek Road**.

20.9 Mill Creek Road is named **Main Street** as it passes through Aumsville, a community named in honor of a man called Aumus. It was the site of a pioneer farm and flour mill. At mile 21.2, a pretty city park (water available) is on the north side of the road in a grove of alders along Mill Creek. At mile 24.3, Mill Creek Road becomes **Marion Road**. The route passes the Turner Tabernacle at mile 24.8, and then becomes **Denver Street** in Turner.

25.0 Follow the arterial as it turns right on **Second Street**.

25.1 Follow the arterial as it turns left on **Chicago Street** one block later (store), and then follow Chicago Street west out of town (store).

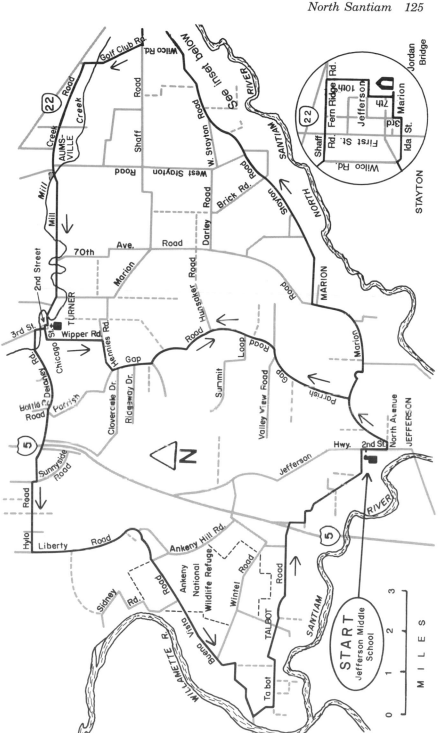

At mile 25.4, Chicago Street turns south, crosses a small bridge, and becomes **Wipper Road**.

26.8 Turn right on **Hennies Road**.

27.5 Turn left (south) on **Parrish Gap Road** and follow it south for 7 miles.

34.5 Turn right at a T-intersection with **Marion Road (Jefferson-Marion Road)**.

36.0 Marion Road curves right (west) and becomes **North Avenue** in Jefferson.

36.2 Turn right (north) on **Jefferson Highway** (Second Street).

36.7 Jefferson Middle School. End of ride.

West Loop

0.0 Jefferson Middle School 1 mile north of Jefferson. Turn right out of the parking area and ride south on **Jefferson Highway**. A bike lane is available on the west side of the road.

0.5 Turn left, following the sign pointing to Marion and Stayton. This unmarked street (**North Avenue**) turns north at mile 0.7 and becomes **Marion Road (Jefferson-Marion Road)**.

2.2 Turn left (north) on **Parrish Gap Road** and follow it north for 7 miles.

9.2 Turn right on **Hennies Road**.

9.9 Turn left (north) on **Wipper Road**. At mile 11.3, Wipper Road turns east, enters Turner, and becomes **Chicago Street**.

11.6 Turner (store). Turn left (north) on **Third Street**.

11.8 Turn left on **Delaney Road**. At mile 13.9, follow Delaney Road when it turns left across a bridge at an intersection with Battle Creek Road. At mile 14.8, pass under I-5.

15.7 Turn right (north) at an intersection with **Sunnyside Road**.

15.8 Turn left on **Hylo Road**.

17.6 Turn left (south) at a T-intersection on **Liberty Road**. At mile 21.3, the road enters Ankeny National Wildlife Refuge and becomes **Buena Vista Road**.

26.2 Turn left on **Talbot Road**. The Buena Vista Ferry landing is 0.3 mile west of this intersection. (The ferry does not run November through March, or on Monday and Tuesday during its season.)

31.3 Cross I-5 on an overpass and then bear right, following Talbot Road.

34.4 Turn right (south) at a T-intersection with **Jefferson Highway**.

34.5 Jefferson Middle School. End of ride.

POLK COUNTY
29 Rickreall

Starting point: Holman
Wayside, 4 miles west of Salem
on Highway 22
Distance: 44.3 miles
Terrain: Mixed hilly and flat
**Total cumulative elevation
gain:** 2200 feet
Recommended time of year:
Any season
Recommended starting time:
Before 10:00 A.M.
Allow: 5 hours
Points of interest:
Eola Park
Brush College Park
Spring Valley
Historic churches
Dallas City Park
Polk County Courthouse
Polk Marine Park
Historic soda fountain

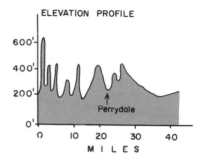

Rickreall Creek is a small stream flowing through the towns of Dallas
and Rickreall. It enters the Willamette near Salem. Although the Dallas-
Rickreall area is flat farmland, the area north of the Rickreall Valley is
quite hilly. This route starts out by climbing those hills, and then settles
into the valley for the return leg.

The route comes within a short distance of two county and two city
parks. The distance between the parks and the route varies from a few
feet to 0.5 mile. Take your pick of the ones you'd like to visit, but none
of the side trips to the parks are included in the mileage of the loop
described below.

The first park, Eola Park, is a large wooded tract near the start of the
route. A narrow blacktop lane leads through the park in a 1-mile horse-
shoe. A picnic area is located three-fourths of the way around the loop.

Brush College Park, a Salem city park, is near mile 3.9. The park was
named for a local school, which in turn was named for the vegetation still
dominating the area.

Dallas City Park, the prettiest park on the ride, straddles Rickreall
Creek just west of downtown Dallas. In Independence, Polk Marine Park
gives access to the Willamette River. The park is on the east side of

Independence, along Highway 51. While in Independence, you may also seek out the local soda fountain—a relic of yesteryear—on Main Street.

The route passes several interesting old buildings. Three churches of note can be seen at Zena, Bethel, and Perrydale. The Bethel church appears to be unusual architecture for a church. Older maps show it was once a schoolhouse. Both Bethel and Zena are located in Spring Valley, surrounded by the Eola Hills. While the area seems isolated today, Spring Valley was once bustling, when Doaks Ferry (now Lincoln) was the largest grain port on the upper Willamette.

Dallas also shows some interesting architecture. The route passes in the shadow of the Polk County Courthouse, or rather in the shadow of its ivy-covered clock tower, built in 1900 of limestone from a nearby quarry.

MILEAGE LOG

0.0   Holman Wayside (day use only; water available). Leave the wayside and turn right (north) on **Doaks Ferry Road**. At mile 0.5, Eola Park (day use only; water available) is on the left. A 1-mile-long blacktop road winds through the park and then returns to Doaks Ferry Road.

2.1   Turn right to stay with Doaks Ferry Road at a T-intersection. The sign points to Glen Creek.

2.4   At a fork in the road, bear left on **Doaks Ferry Road**.

3.9   Turn left on **Brush College Road**. Brush College Park (day use only; water available) is immediately northeast of this intersection.

8.1   Follow Brush College Road when it turns right at an intersection with 4-H Road.

8.7   Turn left on **Spring Valley Road** and then turn left on **Zena Road**. At mile 14.0, cross Highway 99W and continue straight as Zena Road becomes **Bethel Road**.

14.5   McCoy.

16.4   Perrydale. Turn left (south) on **Perrydale Road**. Cross Highway 22 at mile 22.3. Perrydale Road eventually becomes **Orchard Drive** in Dallas.

25.2   After entering Dallas, turn right toward the city center at a T-intersection with **Highway 223** (Kings Valley Highway).

25.3   Carefully cross Ellendale Avenue at a major five-way intersection by bearing slightly to the right, following Highway 223 (Main Street) south. To visit Dallas City Park (day use only; water available), turn right either on Walnut Avenue at mile 25.5 or on Academy Avenue at mile 25.7.

26.1   Turn left on **Washington Street**.

26.5   Turn right at a T-intersection with **Uglow Street**, and then immediately turn left on **Miller Avenue**.

30.4   Turn right (south) on **Riddell Road**. Continue straight at mile 31.3 as Clow Corner Road is crossed.

34.0   Turn left on **Hoffman Road** and then cross Highway 99W at mile

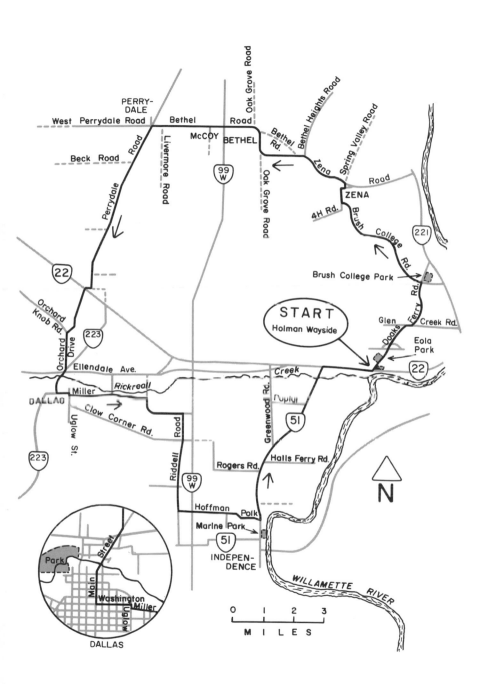

34.4. Hoffman Road becomes **Polk Street** when it enters Independence.

36.8   Turn left (north) on **Main Street** (Highway 51). (To visit Polk Marine Park in Independence, ride south 0.5 mile on Main Street and then turn left on B Street.)

42.7   Turn right (east) on **Highway 22**, using either the shoulder on the south side of the highway or the bike path on the north side.

44.2   Turn left on **Doaks Ferry Road**.

44.3   Turn right into Holman Wayside. End of ride.

30 Luckiamute Loops

Starting point: Monmouth City Park, at the corner of Main Street (Highway 51) and Warren Street in Monmouth

Distance: Combined loop, 42 miles; west loop, 28.7 miles; east loop, 28.5 miles

Terrain: West loop, moderate; east loop, flat

Total cumulative elevation gain: Combined loop, 965 feet; west loop, 950 feet; east loop, 550 feet

Recommended time of year: Any season

Recommended starting time: Before noon for either loop; 10:00 A.M. for combined loop

Allow: 3 hours for either loop; 5 hours for combined loop

Points of interest:
Helmick State Park
Buena Vista Park and Ferry
Polk Marine Park

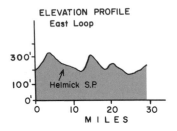

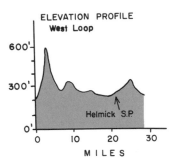

The Luckiamute River and its northern fork, the Little Luckiamute River, drain the southern half of Polk County, flowing from the Coast Range down to flat farmland near Buena Vista and American Bottom. In the hills of the Coast Range the two streams are clear and fast. By the

time they join and then cross the farmland south of Monmouth, the waters are muddy and the riverbed meandered.

Described below are two 28-mile loops that explore the lower Luckiamute Valley. The western loop skirts the edge of the Coast Range, but the few hills encountered are gentle. The eastern half is relatively flat.

Both loops start in Monmouth, and each uses the 7-mile Helmick Road running south from Monmouth to Suver Junction. Either loop can be ridden by itself, but both combined are a manageable day. Omit Helmick Road for a pleasant 42-mile ride around the perimeter of the two loops.

Helmick Road, however, is one of the better parts of the two loops. Apparently an old section of Pacific Highway, it closely parallels Highway 99W. The transcontinental Bikecentennial route follows Highway 99W through this area, but Helmick Road has much less traffic. In places its width was obviously designed for Model A's, but the lack of traffic makes the width immaterial.

Helmick Road also visits Sarah Helmick State Park, one of three riverfront parks along the route. Another is Buena Vista Park, a day use area on the Willamette just south of the Buena Vista Ferry landing. The farmland just across the Willamette from Buena Vista is fine for biking, but the ferry doesn't run on Monday and Tuesday, and is closed between the last Sunday in October until the first Wednesday in April.

The third park is Polk Marine Park along the Willamette, a block north of the main light in Independence on the east loop.

MILEAGE LOG

West Loop

0.0 Monmouth City Park at the corner of Warren and Main streets in Monmouth. Ride west on **Main Street** (Highway 51).

0.3 Turn left on **Whitman Street**, following the arterial (Monmouth Highway). About 2 miles later, the road climbs up over Fishback Hill and then drops down to the Little Luckiamute River.

7.4 Turn left on **Highway 223**.

8.5 Turn left on **Airlie Road**. At mile 14.9, pass through the town of Airlie (store).

21.0 Suver Junction. Turn left (north) on **Highway 99W**.

21.1 Bear left on an unmarked road (**Helmick Road**) that parallels Highway 99W.

23.8 Helmick State Park (day use only; water available).

28.5 In Monmouth, bear left at a Y-intersection, following **Warren Street**.

28.7 Monmouth City Park at corner of Warren and Main streets. End of ride.

East Loop

0.0 Monmouth City Park at corner of Warren and Main streets. Ride south on **Warren Street**. After leaving Monmouth, Warren Street becomes **Helmick Road**.

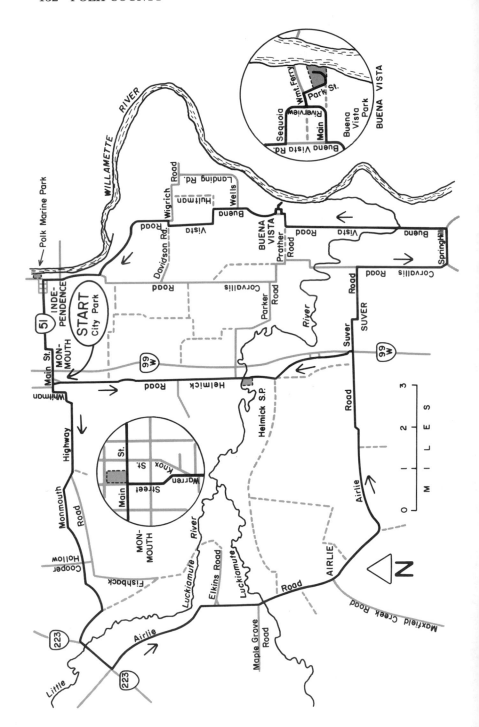

4.9 Helmick State Park (day use only; water available).

7.6 Continue south when Helmick Road joins **Highway 99W**.

7.7 Suver Junction. Turn left on **Suver Road**. At mile 8.5, the road passes through the tiny town of Suver.

9.9 Turn right (south) at a T-intersection with **Corvallis Road**. (For a shortcut, turn left and follow Corvallis Road 8.6 miles north to Independence.)

12.1 Turn left on **Spring Hill Drive**.

13.0 Turn left (north) on **Buena Vista Road** (Buena Vista Street). At mile 16.9, follow Buena Vista Road when it turns right at an intersection with Prather Road.

17.3 The road turns north at the town of Buena Vista.

17.4 Turn right (east) on **Main Street**, and then follow it when it turns north two blocks later.

17.6 Turn right on **Willamette Ferry Street**. The Buena Vista Ferry landing is at the foot of this street.

17.7 Turn right on **Park Street**.

17.8 Buena Vista Park (day use only; water available). Return to **Willamette Ferry Street** and turn left (west).

18.0 Turn right (north) on **Riverview**, and then follow the arterial when it turns north on **Sequoia Street**.

18.2 Turn right (north) on **Buena Vista Road**.

20.1 Follow Buena Vista Road when it turns left at an intersection with Hultman Road.

21.5 Follow Buena Vista Road when it turns right at an intersection with Davidson Road.

21.7 Follow Buena Vista Road when it turns left at an intersection with Wigrich Road.

24.3 Turn right (north) at a T-intersection with **Corvallis Road**, which soon becomes **Main Street** in Independence.

25.8 Independence, at the intersection of Main Street and Highway 51. Polk Marine Park (day use only; water available) can be visited by riding one block north on Main Street and then turning right on C Street. The route turns left on **Monmouth Street** (Highway 51) and follows it to Monmouth, where it becomes **Main Street**.

28.5 Monmouth City Park at the corner of Main and Warren streets in Monmouth. End of ride.

LINN COUNTY
31 Linn County Covered Bridges

Starting point: Chapin Park,
First and Ash streets in Scio.
From I-5, use exit no. 242 or 244,
and then travel about 8 miles
east on Jefferson-Scio Road.
Distance: 47.2 miles
Terrain: Flat with two optional
hills
**Total cumulative elevation
gain:** 1400 feet
Recommended time of year:
Any season
Recommended starting time:
9:00 A.M.
Allow: 6 hours

Points of interest:
Five covered bridges
Larwood County Wayside

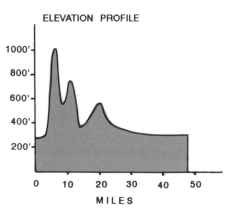

Long before the days of reinforced concrete and steel I-beams, Oregon's bridges were made of wood. Those days were also before chemical preservatives, so bridges didn't last long in the rainy weather of the Willamette Valley. The problem was solved by building roofs over the bridges and installing siding on their trusses. More than 300 covered bridges once stood in Oregon, but eventually most were demolished in the face of severe floods, increased traffic volumes, heavier loads, and modern technology. Today, fewer than fifty-five survive and some of those have been relocated.

In northwestern Linn County, not far from Albany, five covered bridges stand within a few miles of each other. Of these, three span Thomas Creek and three more cross Crabtree Creek. Follow this gerrymandered loop to yesteryear, traveling nearly 48 miles over all five bridges, or select one of the loops within the route to shorten the ride.

For example, the southeastern loop, a flat 9.9 miles, visits both the community and the bridge of Larwood, as well as a quaint park. The northeastern loop climbs two steep hills, but includes two bridges and some fine scenery along its 16.1 miles. For riders who may prefer to avoid the two hills, the mileage log describes level alternate routes to shorten the loop by about 3 miles, but still visit both bridges.

Like most covered bridges built in Oregon, the five crossed on this ride were built using Howe trusses, a design incorporating diagonal timbers and vertical steel rods with adjustable tension. Unlike most other counties, however, Linn County adopted bridge designs employing large windows or merely leaving trusses exposed, shedding light where darkness normally reigns.

For more information on Oregon's covered bridges, get a copy of *Roofs over Rivers* (second edition, Oregon Sentinel Publishing, 1990), a well-researched guide to the remaining covered bridges, or *Oregon Covered Bridges* (Webb Research Group, 1991). Although not true for these five bridges, many are closed to motorized traffic, making a bicycle the best vehicle for touring them. Covered bridges are also great sites for protection from two seasonal enemies, cold rain and (somewhat less frequently) hot sun. Don't linger too long, since all the bridges are narrow and offer little protection from oncoming traffic.

Designed for Model A's, not modern logging trucks, the bridges are popular destinations for group outings of local antique car clubs. In Linn County, especially, don't be surprised if you see a few dozen horseless carriages near the bridges.

No bridge on this ride is closed to motor vehicles, but all should be considered threatened by progress. In the last twenty-five years, perhaps two dozen of Oregon's covered bridges have been destroyed. During the same period only four new ones have been built, and two of the four new ones were non-truss bridges that were covered with purely ornamental roofs. One of the other two, Shimanek Bridge, was built in 1966. It is crossed twice on this ride, at miles 3.2 and 16.3.

One other bridge near this route deserves mention. On your drive to Scio, divert a block east at Jefferson's south end. There stands an example of engineering ruined to an art form, a grand bridge erected in 1933 and dedicated to Jacob Conser, who founded Jefferson in 1851 and operated a ferry there for many years. The bridge, which consists of three 200-foot reinforced-concrete through-arch spans, was designed by Conde B. McCullough. During his tenure as state bridge engineer from 1919 to 1938, McCullough supervised the design and construction of hundreds of bridges, large and small, but he is best remembered for his magnificent arch bridges on the Oregon Coast.

P.S. Drinking water is available infrequently on this ride. Be sure to carry enough.

MILEAGE LOG

0.0 Chapin Park in Scio. Ride west on First Street, out of the park, turning left on Main Street at mile 0.1.

0.9 Turn left on Highway 226, after crossing a bridge over Thomas Creek.

2.4 Turn left (north) on **Richardson's Gap Road**.

3.2 Shimanek Bridge. The fifth covered bridge to stand over Thomas Creek, this one succeeded the victim of the 1962 Columbus Day storm. The original Shimanek Bridge was built in 1891.

3.4 Continue straight past an intersection with County Road 639 (Shimanek Bridge Drive). (To shorten the ride and avoid an up-coming hill, turn right and follow County Road 639—Shimanek Drive—east 2.2 miles to Highway 226, and then follow Highway 226 east and north to Hannah Bridge at mile 13.9.)

4.4 At the top of a long, steep hill, turn right (east) on **Ridge Drive** (County Road 609).

4.5 Continue bearing right (east) on Ridge Drive at an intersection with Cole School Road.

8.3 Turn right on **Spring Valley Drive**.

8.8 Turn right at a T-intersection with **Valley View Drive**. At mile 9.1, the road curves left (east) and begins to descend back into the Thomas Creek Valley.

10.6 Turn right at a T-intersection with **Kingston-Jordan Drive**.

11.2 Bear right on **Highway 226**.

11.8 Turn left (south) on **Jordan Road** and climb a steep hill. The Jordan Covered Bridge, now in Pioneer Park in Stayton, once stood here. (To avoid the hill, continue west 1.7 miles on Highway 226 to Hannah Bridge, described below at mile 13.9.)

12.4 Jordan. Turn right at a T-intersection with **Camp Morrison Drive**.

13.9 Hannah Bridge. This bridge honors John Joseph Hannah, who built one of the first sawmills in this area.

14.0 Turn left (west) at a T-intersection with **Highway 226**.

16.3 Turn right onto **Shimanek Drive** (County Road 639).

18.5 Turn left at a T-intersection with **Richardson's Gap Road** and again cross the Shimanek Bridge.

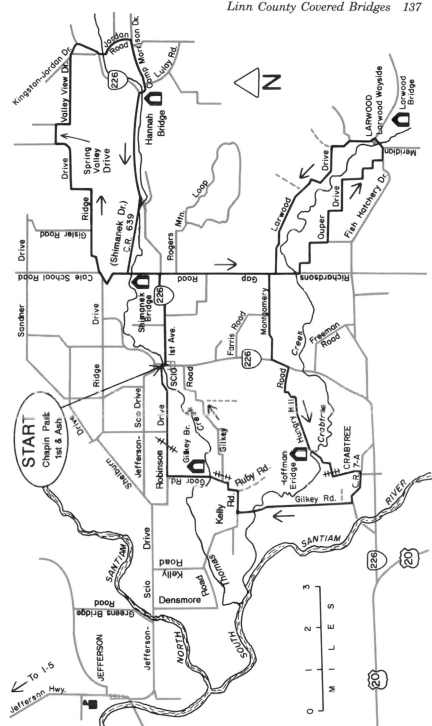

19.2 Cross **Highway 226**, continuing straight ahead on **Richardson's Gap Road**.

22.1 Turn left on **Ouper Drive** (County Road 644) and follow it east and south through several ninety-degree turns. (At the Crabtree Creek crossing the Bohemian Hall Covered Bridge once stood. It was replaced in 1987, but remains in storage.)

26.5 Turn left at a T-intersection with **Fish Hatchery Drive**. Bear left at an intersection with Meridian Road at mile 26.6.

26.8 Larwood Bridge over Crabtree Creek. This is the bridge of *Ripley's Believe It or Not* fame. The Roaring River flows into Crabtree Creek here—an oddity in U.S. geography.

26.9 Larwood. Turn left on **Larwood Drive** (County Road 643). Larwood County Wayside (water not available) is on the left, at the junction of Crabtree Creek and Roaring River. Follow Larwood Drive as it winds north and west for several miles.

31.8 Turn right (north) at a T-intersection with **Richardson's Gap Road**.

32.0 Turn left on **Montgomery Drive**.

34.0 Turn left (south) at a T-intersection on **Highway 226**.

34.5 Turn right on **Hungry Hill Road**.

36.8 Hoffman Bridge over Crabtree Creek. Built by Lee Hoffman, it was constructed in 1936 to state specifications. It has been reinforced recently.

38.3 Crabtree (store). Turn right (west) at a T-intersection with **County Road 7-A** (Crabtree Drive). (The town, named for John Crabtree, who settled here in 1845, is one block to the left.)

39.2 Turn right (north) on **Gilkey Road** (County Road 7-A).

42.0 At a T-intersection, turn right to continue on Gilkey Road as Kelly Road comes in from the left. (Weddle Covered Bridge once stood near here over Thomas Creek, but is now in Sankey Park in Sweet Home.)

42.4 Bear left, continuing on Gilkey Road, as Ruby Road comes in from the right.

42.9 Continue straight ahead on **Goar Road** as Gilkey Road turns right.

43.2 Gilkey Bridge. This bridge was named for Allen and William Gilkey. Until 1960, a covered railroad bridge also spanned Thomas Creek here.

44.3 Turn right on **Robinson Drive** at a T-intersection. At mile 45.0 cross the rail tracks carefully.

46.9 Robinson Drive becomes First Avenue in Scio as it passes Centennial School.

47.0 Cross Main Street into the park.

47.2 Chapin Park. End of ride.

32 South Santiam

Starting point: River Park in Lebanon. From Highway 20 in Lebanon, drive 0.7 mile east on Grant Street and then turn north into the park.
Distance: Short loop, 34.3 miles; long loop, 45 miles
Terrain: Mainly level with some hills
Total cumulative elevation gain: Short loop, 675 feet; long loop, 725 feet
Recommended time of year: Any season
Recommended starting time: Before 11:00 A.M.
Allow: Short loop, 4 hours; long loop, 5 hours
Points of interest:
River Park
Larwood Covered Bridge and Wayside

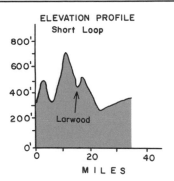

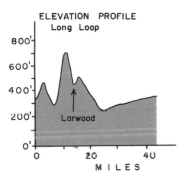

Situated on the South Santiam River, the area surrounding Lebanon is noted for strawberries and timber, two crops on opposite ends of the agricultural spectrum. The routes described below venture up toward the timber-growing foothills and then return to the flat, berry-producing valley of the lower South Santiam River.

Two routes are described. Both share a 29-mile section that visits the Larwood Covered Bridge. Built in 1939, the bridge spans Crabtree Creek adjacent to the mouth of the Roaring River. Since this site is the only place in the U.S. where a river flows into a creek, it has been featured in *Ripley's Believe It or Not.*

Near the bridge is a decaying waterwheel, used in 1900 to create electricity for area residents and for the grist mill farther downstream. Linn County has established a perfect little park at the site, an excellent place to enjoy a streamside lunch. A short distance from the park is a fish hatchery, which may still be home to Herman, an aging sturgeon often displayed at the state fair.

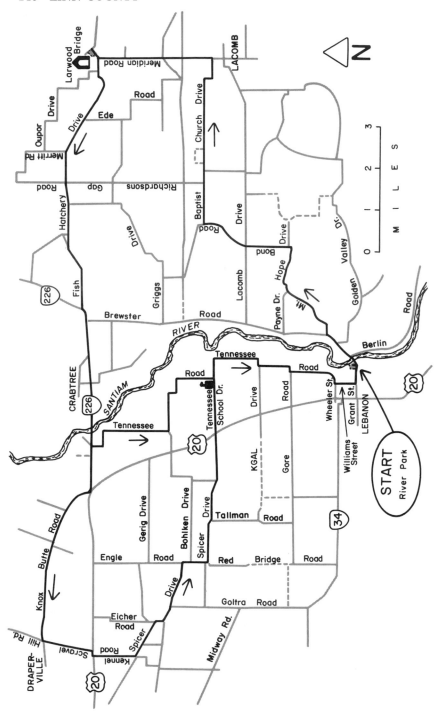

The area north of this ride contains five covered bridges. All of those are visited by Trip No. 31, but several could also be stopovers on short detours from this route.

Only the very first section of these loops is hilly. Eleven miles after leaving Lebanon, the routes cross a shoulder of Mount Hope, reaching an elevation of 700 feet before dropping back down to the 300-foot floor of the valley.

When the routes return to the South Santiam from the foothills, the shorter of the two routes turns south and follows the river back to Lebanon. Before returning to the river, the longer route continues west, out into the flat berry country. It has a couple of short sections of busy road, one of which also involves narrow shoulders, so if you choose the longer route, be cautious on those parts.

MILEAGE LOG

Short Loop

0.0 River Park in Lebanon. Follow the mileage log for the long loop through mile 24.3.

24.3 Turn left on **Tennessee Road**. At mile 26.6, follow Tennessee Road when it turns left (east) at an intersection with Honey Sign Drive.

29.0 Turn left at a T-intersection, following **Tennessee Road**. Tennessee School Road is on the right. This is mile 39.8 of the long loop. Follow the remainder of the long loop back into Lebanon.

34.3 River Park in Lebanon. End of ride.

Long Loop

0.0 River Park in Lebanon. Ride toward the park entrance and then turn left (east) on **Grant Street** and cross a bridge over the South Santiam River (a sidewalk is available on the north side of the bridge).

1.3 Turn right on **Mount Hope Drive**.

4.1 Shortly after Mount Hope Drive turns north, continue north on **Bond Road** when Mount Hope Drive turns east. At mile 5.2 cross Lacomb Drive.

6.5 Turn right on **Baptist Church Drive**.

10.8 Turn left (north) on **Meridian Road** at a T-intersection.

13.7 At a Y-intersection with **Fish Hatchery Drive**, turn right (east).

13.9 Larwood Bridge. Just past the bridge is Larwood Wayside (day use only; water not available), at the junction of Crabtree Creek and the Roaring River. After stopping at the park, recross the bridge and ride west on Fish Hatchery Drive.

14.3 Continue straight ahead, bearing right (west) on Fish Hatchery Drive past the Y-intersection with Meridian Road.

20.9 Turn left at a T-intersection onto **Highway 226**. At mile 23.9, the highway crosses the South Santiam River. (The short loop turns left on Tennessee Road at mile 24.3.) The shoulder is very narrow from mile 24.3 to mile 25.3. Ride carefully.

25.3   Turn right on **Highway 20**.

25.4   Turn right on **Knox Butte Road** (store).

29.6   Draperville. Turn left on **Scravel Hill Road**.

30.8   Turn right on **Highway 20**, and then immediately turn left on **Kennel Road**.

31.9   Turn left on **Spicer Drive** and follow it east through several turns and intersections. At mile 38.5, Spicer Drive crosses Highway 20 and becomes **Tennessee School Drive**. After passing Tennessee School at mile 39.8, Tennessee School Drive becomes **Tennessee Road**. The road eventually turns south and then west.

41.6   Turn south, following Tennessee Road, at an intersection with KGAL Drive.

42.5   Turn south, following Tennessee Road, at an intersection with Gore Road. At mile 43.5, Tennessee Road curves right (west) and becomes **Wheeler Street** in Lebanon.

43.9   Turn left on **Williams Street**.

44.4   Turn left on **Grant Street**.

44.9   Turn left at the entrance to River Park.

45.0   River Park. End of ride.

33 Calapooia River

Starting point: Periwinkle School in Albany, at 2200 21st Avenue (turn east on 21st Avenue from Geary Street)

Distance: 52.2 miles

Terrain: Almost all flat

Total cumulative elevation gain: 450 feet

Recommended time of year: Any season

Recommended starting time: 10:00 A.M.

Allow: 5 hours

Points of interest:
Periwinkle Creek Bike Path
Bryant Park
Thompson Rolling Mill
Brownsville
Freeway Lakes Park

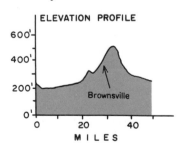

The sleepy little town of Brownsville was once an important trade center for Linn County. But "once" was more than 100 years ago, when Brownsville was the county seat, the site of a major woolen mill, a Calapooia River ferry crossing, and on the Oregon Railroad line.

Today Brownsville is well off the beaten path. The ferry, a critical link between Fort Vancouver (Oregon Territory) and Fort Sutter (California) across a roaring river, has been replaced by a steel truss bridge that doesn't seem to go anywhere in particular. The river doesn't appear capable of floating a large boat, the woolen mill has burned down, the county seat has moved downstream to Albany, and Interstate 5 is about 5 miles to the west. While other towns have been hurtled into the progress and prosperity of the twentieth century, Brownsville has retained its nineteenth-century character. As a result, it now boasts one of the most concentrated collections of historic architecture in the state, and attracts visitors who want to see "the way it was."

Brownsville may be off the beaten path, but it's worth pedaling a path to for a visit. Plan to see the extensive collection of artifacts from pioneer times and silent movies in the Linn County Historical Museum, walk around town, and visit Moyer House. Donations are welcomed, but no admission fees are asked. If you like big festivals, plan to visit Brownsville the third weekend in June when Oregon's oldest continous celebration, the Pioneer Picnic, is in full swing.

This ride starts in Albany, at a modern elementary school, and then follows a bike path and downtown streets to Bryant Park at the mouth of the Calapooia River. The route then turns south and proceeds across flat farmland to Brownsville. This first half of the ride makes nearly two dozen ninety-degree turns, and the road names and county road numbers are often confusing. Use the map and mileage log carefully to avoid unexpected detours. A compass would also be helpful. The second half of the ride, on the other hand, has few turns to miss, since much of the route follows Sevenmile (Seven Mile) Lane due north toward Albany.

Due to the grid nature of the roads between Albany and Brownsville, several shortcuts are available to shorten the 50-mile ride. Gravel roads abound, however, so choose carefully. One good shortcut crosses the Calapooia near the community of Shedd, and rides past the Thompson Rolling Mill, one of two nineteenth-century water-powered mills still operating in Oregon. The shortcut, which reduces the length of the ride from 52.2 to 37.4 miles, is described in the mileage log.

Even if you don't take the shortcut, look at the mill. Today the mill produces animal food such as rabbit pellets, and signs that once announced its history are as faded as its past. Still, the mill's picturesque setting next to its millrace and award-winning, well-kept farms nearby will add to the enjoyment of your tour.

MILEAGE LOG

0.0 Periwinkle School, on 21st Avenue east of Geary Street in Albany. Ride west on **21st Avenue**.

0.2 Turn right (north) on a **bike path** along Periwinkle Creek.

0.5 At the intersection of the bike path, Geary Street, and Queen Avenue, ride west on the sidewalk on the north side of **Queen**, and then turn north on the **bike path** at mile 0.6.

1.0 When the bike path ends, turn right (north) on **Oak Street**.

1.2 Turn left at a T-intersection with **Ninth Avenue**.

1.4 Turn right (north) on **Madison Street** and follow it across Pacific Boulevard (Highway 99E).

1.8 Turn left on **Third Avenue**.

2.7 Follow Third Avenue across a bridge over the Calapooia River, after which Third Avenue becomes **Bryant Way**. Bryant Park, at the confluence of the Calapooia and Willamette rivers, is on the right at mile 2.8.

3.9 Follow the arterial when it bears left on **Bryant Drive**.

4.8 Follow Bryant Drive when it turns left (south) at an intersection with Lone Oak Lane.

5.3 Turn left (east) at a T-intersection with **Riverside Drive** (County Road 1).

5.9 Turn right on **Oakville Road** (County Road 32). At mile 9.8, carefully cross Highway 34 and then follow **Oakville Road** south through several ninety-degree turns to Oakville.

14.6 Oakville, which consists primarily of an old church. Turn left on **Church Drive** (County Road 12).

15.1 Follow the arterial as it turns right (south) on **Green Valley Road** and follow it south through several turns.

20.6 Turn left (east) at a T-intersection with **Fayetteville Drive**. Cross Highway 99E at mile 22.0, where Fayetteville Drive becomes **Boston Mill Drive** (County Road 13).

23.3 Turn right on **Roberts Road** (County Road 420). The Thompson Mill is visible to the east. (For those looking for a shortcut, continue straight at this intersection, turn left on Saddle Butte Road at a T-intersection at mile 24.6, and then, at mile 26.7, rejoin the longer route at its mile 41.5, thus reducing the length of the ride by 14.8 miles.)

26.4 Turn left at a T-intersection with **Linn-West Drive** (County Road 26).

28.6 Linn-West Drive joins **Sevenmile Lane**. Follow it as it continues east and then curves to the southeast. It eventually enters Brownsville, where it becomes **Linn Way**.

31.2 Brownsville. Follow the arterial when it bears left on **Depot Avenue**.

31.3 Turn right on **Main Street** and follow it as it turns left and then right in downtown Brownsville.

31.7 Corner of Main Street and Kirk Avenue. On the left is a small city park (water not available), and on the right is the Moyer House (1881), property of the Linn County Historical Society. A second city park (camping permitted; water available) is located at the foot of Park Avenue (turn west one block north of this intersection). After lunch or a break, retrace the town route by riding north on **Main Street**. Bypass Depot Avenue, continuing straight instead, on **Main Street**, which becomes **Brownsville Road** out-

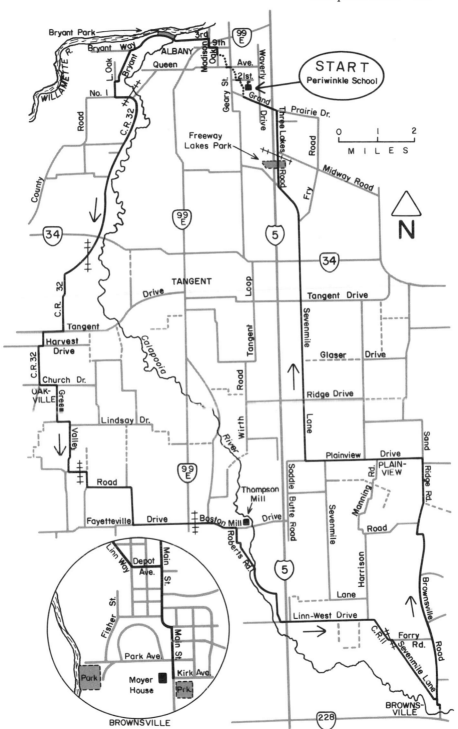

side the city limits. At mile 37.3, the name of the road changes to **Sand Ridge Road**.

38.4   Turn left on **Plainview Drive** and pass through Plainview at mile 39.7.

41.5   Follow the arterial as it turns right on **Sevenmile Lane** (County Road 11) and follow it north for several miles.

48.8   Immediately before an overpass over I-5, turn right on **Three Lakes Road**.

49.3   Freeway Lakes County Park (day use only; water not available).

50.7   Turn left on **Grand Prairie Drive** and then cross I-5 on an overpass.

51.7   About two blocks after passing through an intersection with Waverly Drive, turn right (north) on a **bike path** along Periwinkle Creek.

52.1   Shortly after crossing a bridge over Periwinkle Creek, turn right on a bike path to Periwinkle School.

52.2   Periwinkle School. End of ride.

34 Santiam–Calapooia

Starting point: River Park in Lebanon. From Highway 20 in Lebanon, drive 0.7 mile east on Grant Street, and then turn left into the park.
Distance: 54 miles
Terrain: Mixed flat and hilly
Total cumulative elevation gain: 1450 feet
Recommended time of year: Any season
Recommended starting time: 10:00 A.M.
Allow: 5 hours

Points of interest:
River Park
Brownsville
McKercher Park
Crawfordsville Covered Bridge
Weddle Covered Bridge
Sankey Park

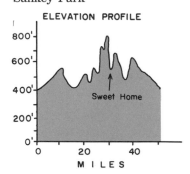

The logging country of the western slopes of the Cascades keeps the mills of Lebanon and Sweet Home humming. Surrounded by mountain roads and logging trucks, the South Santiam Valley is an unlikely place for cyclists to find good bicycling routes, but they are there.

This route circles between the South Santiam and Calapooia valleys. Both have enough backroads to enable a loop ride almost totally avoiding main highways that follow the two rivers. The ride starts in Lebanon, at River Park on the South Santiam, and then rolls along farm roads to one of Oregon's most historic communities—Brownsville. Few Oregon towns contain the concentration of early architecture found in Brownsville.

From Brownsville, backroads on the north bank of the Calapooia are followed to a 1932 covered bridge at Crawfordsville. Then another backroad is traced through Holley and the South Santiam is reached by crossing a 900-foot pass between Holley and Sweet Home. The last leg of the ride tracks backroads back to Lebanon along the east bank of the South Santiam.

Surprisingly level, considering the mountainous country through which it travels, the route follows the gentle gradient of the rivers, except for the pass between Holley and Sweet Home. Traffic levels are low, because an old rule for bike route planners is employed: Between any two points, find the main highway that attracts most of the traffic, and then follow a backroad paralleling that arterial. In this case, Northern Drive, Crawfordsville Drive, and Old Holley Road parallel Highway 228 between Brownsville and Sweet Home, but have only a fraction of the traffic. Along the South Santiam, Pleasant Valley Road and Berlin Road provide a quiet return from Sweet Home to Lebanon, while most of the traffic follows Highway 20 on the opposite bank of the river.

MILEAGE LOG

0.0   River Park at the east end of Grant Street in Lebanon. From the park, turn right (west) on **Grant Street**. At mile 0.8, follow Grant Street when it jogs a few feet south at an intersection with Main Street (Highway 20).

0.9   Turn left (south) on **Second Street**, which soon becomes South Main. Follow it south for 2 miles, using the bike path on the right side of the highway.

4.1   Turn right at a T-intersection with **Rock Hill Drive**. (Notice the road straight ahead that seems to climb into the sky.)

5.1   Follow Rock Hill Drive when it turns left at an intersection with Stoltz Hill Road.

8.7   Turn left at a T-intersection with **Sand Ridge Road** (County Road No. 412). Its name will change to Brownsville Road, but continue to follow it south about 6 miles to Brownsville, where it becomes **Main Street**.

15.1   Brownsville. Follow Main Street when it turns left and then turns right a few feet later. Brownsville has two primitive city parks. One is Pioneer Park, located on the Calapooia River, two blocks west of the route at the foot of Park Avenue (camping permitted; water available). It can be reached by turning right on Park Avenue at mile 15.2. The third weekend in June every year, this is the site of Oregon's oldest continuous celebration. Pioneer Picnic

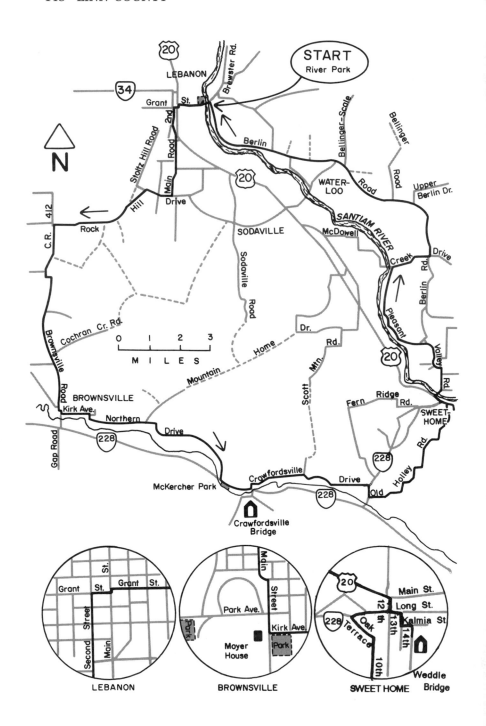

was celebrated for the hundredth time in 1987.

15.3 Turn left (east) on **Kirk Avenue**. The second city park is located on the south side of this intersection (day use only; water not available).

16.3 Turn right on **Northern Drive** at a Y-intersection.

22.2 Turn left (east) at a T-intersection with **Highway 228**.

22.4 McKercher Park along the banks of the Calapooia River (day use only; water not available).

23.3 Just before a modern bridge over the Calapooia, turn right to a covered bridge that is now closed to auto traffic (Crawfordsville Bridge). After visiting the bridge, return to its northern end and cross the highway to proceed on **Crawfordsville Drive**. At mile 25.5, bear right at an unmarked Y-intersection.

27.6 Turn right (south) at a T-intersection with **Highway 228**.

28.0 Turn left onto **Old Holley Road** and follow it into Sweet Home, where it becomes **Oak Terrace (10th Avenue)**.

33.5 Sweet Home. At a T-intersection, turn right on **Long Street**.

33.9 Turn right on **13th Avenue**, left onto **Kalmia Street** at mile 34.0, and right on **14th Street**, and in one block enter Sankey Park. Weddle Covered Bridge, originally on Crabtree Creek near Scio, was dedicated here over Thomas Creek in July 1990. The bridge was in storage from 1987 to 1989.

34.2 After visiting the bridge, retrace the route, turning right on **13th Avenue** and then jogging left and right to proceed north on **12th Avenue**.

34.7 Turn left on **Main Street** (Highway 20), which is a busy four-lane highway. Use the sidewalk on the north side of the highway.

35.7 Turn right on **Pleasant Valley Road** and cross a bridge over the Santiam River.

36.7 Follow Pleasant Valley Road when it turns left (west) at an intersection near Pleasant Valley School.

37.7 Stay left with Pleasant Valley Road at a Y-intersection with Berlin Road.

41.5 Turn right at a T-intersection with **McDowell Creek Drive**.

42.9 Turn left on **Berlin Road**.

53.7 At a T-intersection with **Brewster Road** (unmarked), turn left and cross a bridge over the South Santiam River. A sidewalk is available on the north side of the bridge.

54.0 Turn right into River Park. End of ride.

35 Harrisburg–Coburg Hills

Starting point: Harrisburg City Park, at the corner of Fourth and Smith streets in Harrisburg, one block east of Highway 99E on Smith Street
Distance: 38 miles
Terrain: Generally flat
Total cumulative elevation gain: 500 feet
Recommended time of year: Any season
Recommended starting time: 11:00 A.M.
Allow: 4 hours

Points of interest: Coburg Hills

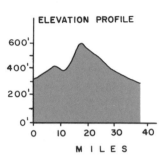

When the first white settlers came to Oregon, they chose their farm sites carefully. Rather than settling along the banks of the Willamette, they chose the edges of the valley instead. These were at the base of the first foothills where the valley grasses met the wooded hillsides. The forests provided fuel and building materials, while the distance from the river protected the settlers from frequent floods.

The area south of Brownsville fits the above description perfectly. The line between the flat valley floor and the wooded foothills is distinct. In this case the foothills are the Coburg Hills, a steep 2900-foot ridge running from the Calapooia River southwest toward Eugene.

The Coburg Hills form a dramatic backdrop to this rectangular route. From Harrisburg the route proceeds due east to the base of the ridge and then follows the line between farms and trees north nearly to Brownsville. The third side follows Lake Creek Drive almost to the Willamette, and the fourth side returns to Harrisburg on a 6-mile section of the Bikecentennial transcontinental bike route.

Like much of the Willamette Valley, the grid nature of the farm roads permits numerous shortcuts and variations. Several different roads could be used to halve the rectangle and others could be ridden to expand the route to the north or south. From the route's northeast corner, historic Brownsville is only 1.5 miles away, although it is not shown on this map. Detours to the west end on the banks of the Willamette, while routes east are stopped by the Coburg Hills.

MILEAGE LOG

0.0 Harrisburg City Park, at the corner of Fourth and Smith streets in Harrisburg. Ride east on **Smith Street**, heading away from the river.

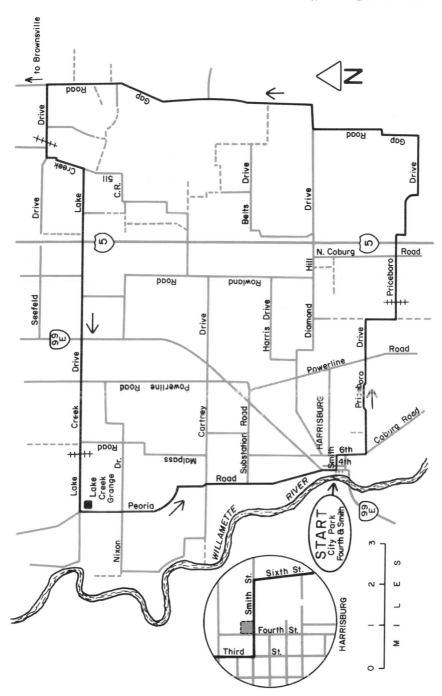

0.2   Turn right (south) on **Sixth Street**. At mile 0.5, cross LaSalle Street and continue south on **Sixth Avenue** (Coburg Road).

1.0   Turn left on **Priceboro Drive** and follow it east for 9 miles. At mile 4.4, stay on Priceboro Drive when it turns right (south) at an intersection with a gravel road, and at mile 5.1, follow it left at an intersection with another gravel road. At miles 6.6 and 7.0, Priceboro Drive crosses North Coburg Road and I-5, respectively.

10.0   Priceboro Drive turns left (north) and becomes **Gap Road**.

12.8   At a T-intersection, turn right, following Gap Road (Diamond Hill Road). At mile 13.5, Gap Road turns north again.

20.1   Turn left on **Lake Creek Drive**.

21.8   Follow Lake Creek Drive as it turns left (south) at an intersection with Seefeld Drive.

22.8   Follow Lake Creek Drive as it turns right (west) at an intersection with Center School Road (County Road 511). Continue west on Lake Creek Drive for the next 8.5 miles.

31.3   Lake Creek Grange. Turn left (south) on **Peoria Road** and follow it south for 6.3 miles.

37.6   Turn right (south) on **Highway 99E**.

37.9   Harrisburg. Turn left on **Smith Street**.

38.0   Harrisburg City Park, Fourth and Smith streets. End of ride.

BENTON COUNTY
36 Kings Valley

Starting point: Aquathusiasts Park in Corvallis at the foot of Tyler Avenue, one block north of the Highway 34 bridges. (This park lies next to the river, but is not signed.)
Distance: 57.5 miles
Terrain: Mixed hilly and flat
Total cumulative elevation gain: 2300 feet
Recommended time of year: Any season
Recommended starting time: 9:00 A.M. or earlier
Allow: 6 hours

Points of interest:
Corvallis-Philomath Bike Path
Corvallis riverfront parks
Ritner Covered Bridge

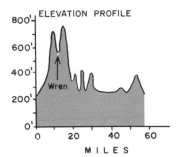

Like many towns that grew up dependent on the Willamette River for their livelihood, Corvallis was once centered around a waterfront of warehouses and loading docks serving a busy steamboat trade. Railroads and highways have stolen the river's importance, but Corvallis has found other uses for the Willamette and its tributary, Marys River. Both are now lined with parks, boat ramps, and bike paths serving cyclists, joggers, and boaters.

This ride explores the countryside northwest of Corvallis. It starts on the waterfront and follows a scenic bike path from Corvallis to Philomath before striking out for the hillsides and farmland. The bike path follows the west bank of the Willamette and the north bank of the Marys, visiting a half-dozen parks along its 7-mile length.

Unfortunately, the 7 miles of bike path are followed by 4 miles of Highway 20, a busy road without a bike lane or path. To avoid some of the traffic on Highway 20, get an early start in Corvallis.

The remainder of the ride makes up for the short Highway 20 section. The west half follows rolling backroads through wooded valleys, hills planted with tree farms, and microscopic towns like Wren, Kings Valley, Ritner, Pedee, and Airlie. The east half is flat farmland, dotted with small communities such as Suver and Lewisburg.

The best place to stop for lunch is inside a covered bridge at Ritner (mile 22.7). The only remaining covered bridge in Polk County, Ritner preceded the county ban on construction of the spans. In the early 1900s, nearly every major bridge in the county had been a roofed structure. In

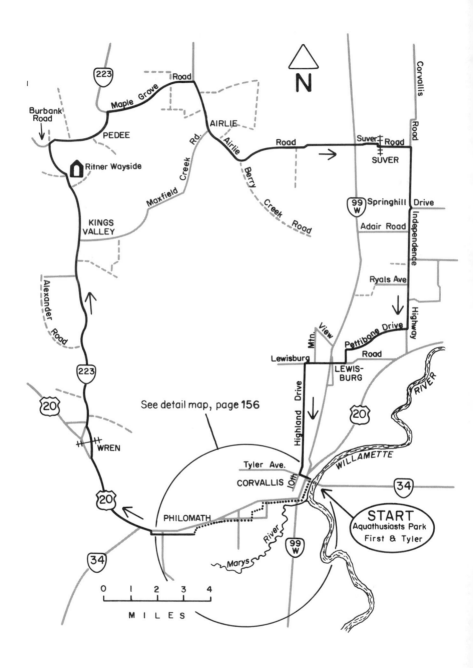

the 1930s, a county judge, who considered covered bridges unsafe and a hazard to speedy traffic, outlawed them. Ritner survives the Pumping Station Bridge that stood on private property near Dallas. Winter winds swept it away in 1987. When the 1927 Ritner bridge was threatened with destruction a few years ago, local residents raised money to move it a few feet downstream, out of the path of progress. A small wayside park has since been established, complete with picnic tables, one of which is inside the bridge.

Just north of Ritner, the hillsides have been taken over by scotch broom. In late spring the entire valley seems afire with their yellow blooms.

MILEAGE LOG

0.0 Corner of First Street and Tyler Avenue in Corvallis. Ride south on the bike path along the Willamette River. Follow the bike path all the way to Philomath.

0.7 Take either fork in the bike path, since the two rejoin a short distance later. The path then passes under Highway 99W and proceeds west along Marys River through Pioneer Park. Eventually the path parallels Highway 20 and then turns south, away from the highway, at mile 2.5.

2.8 Turn right (west) at a Y-intersection in the path. Continue west on the path, disregarding any opportunities to turn right (north).

3.3 At Bruce Starker Arts Park and Sunset Park, the path turns south and then turns east along the shoulder of **Country Club Drive**. At mile 4.6, Country Club Drive joins Highway 20. Continue west on the bike path along **Highway 20**.

5.4 Follow the bike path when it turns south away from the highway and follows a stream through a residential area.

5.7 Turn right on **Applegate Street**. When it ends, use a bike bridge to continue west to rejoin Applegate, and then follow it west through Philomath. A Philomath City Park (water available) is located on 23rd Street, a block south of the bike bridge.

7.4 Turn right on **Seventh Street**.

7.5 Turn left on **Main Street** (highways 20 and 34). This is a busy road. Ride carefully.

7.9 Continue west on Highway 20 when Highway 34 turns south.

11.7 Turn right on an unnamed road with a sign pointing to Wren.

12.3 After passing through Wren, turn right at a T-intersection with **Highway 223** and follow it north for 15 miles.

20.6 Kings Valley (store).

22.7 Ritner Wayside and Covered Bridge.

24.2 Follow Highway 223 when it turns right at an intersection with Burbank Road.

26.4 Pedee.

27.1 When Highway 223 turns left, turn right on **Maple Grove Road**.

30.8 Turn right (south) at a T-intersection with **Airlie Road**.

32.9 Airlie (store).

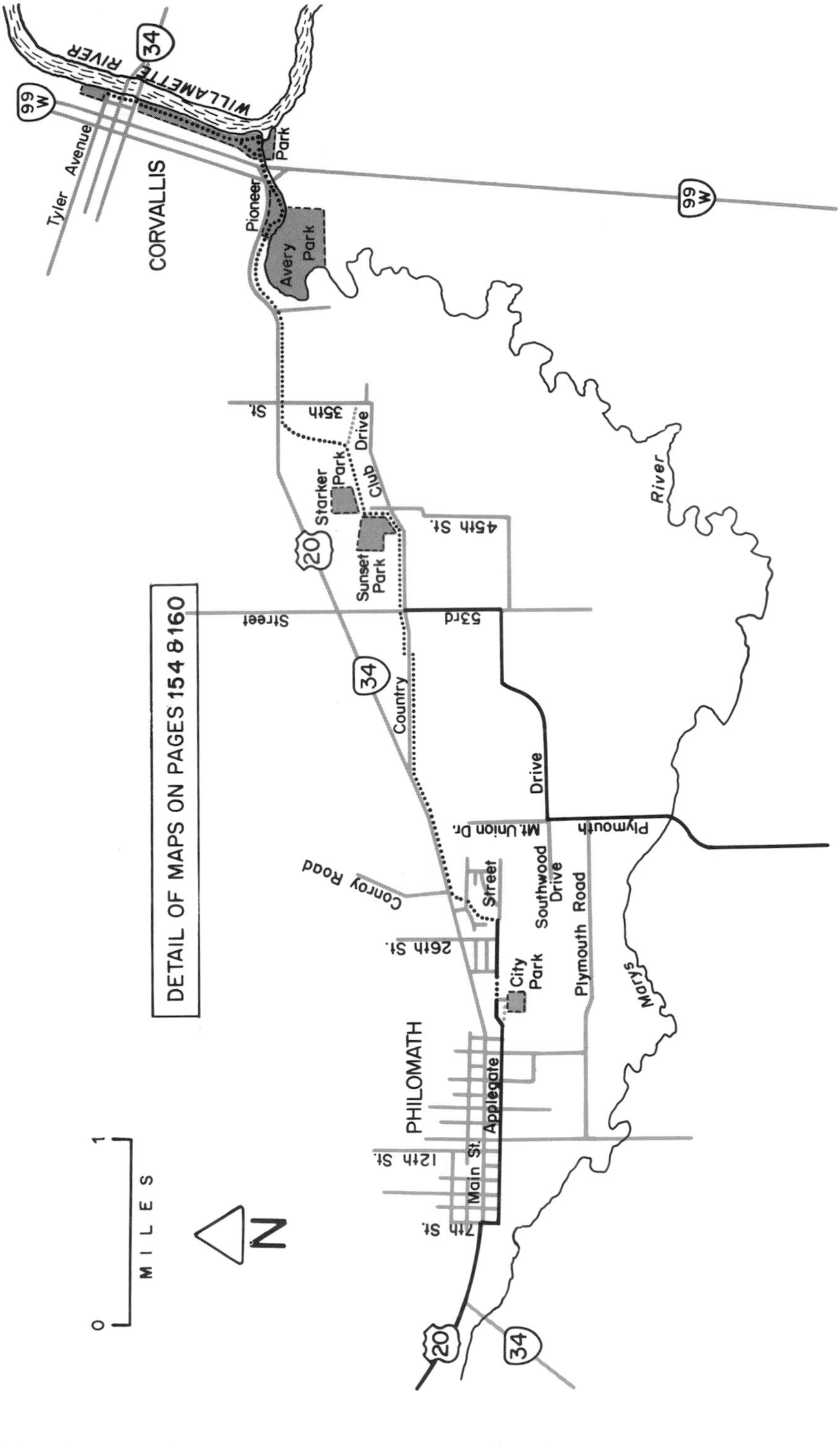

DETAIL OF MAPS ON PAGES 154 & 160

CORVALLIS

WILLAMETTE RIVER

Tyler Avenue

Pioneer Park

Avery Park

PHILOMATH

City Park

Starker Park

Sunset Park

35th St.

45th St.

53rd

Club Drive

Street

Country

Conroy Road

26th St.

Street

Mt. Union Dr.

Plymouth Drive

Southwood Drive

Plymouth Road

Marys River

12th St.

7th St.

Main St.

Applegate

N

MILES
0   1

38.9 Cross Highway 99W (store) and continue east on **Suver Road**.

39.8 Suver.

41.1 Turn right (south) at a T-intersection with **Corvallis Road**, which later becomes Independence Highway. At mile 43.4, bear right (south) on **Independence Highway** at an intersection with Springhill Drive.

48.0 Turn right (west) on **Pettibone Drive**.

51.1 Turn right (west) at a T-intersection with **Granger Avenue**.

51.7 Lewisburg (store). Cross 99W and continue west.

52.7 Turn left on **Highland Drive**. Although the road has no shoulder on the right, a wide bike lane is provided on the left. After about 2 miles, bike lanes are provided on both sides of the road as it enters Corvallis. Eventually, Highland Drive becomes **10th Street**.

57.0 Turn left on **Tyler Avenue**.

57.5 Foot of Tyler Avenue. End of ride.

37 Corvallis–Harrisburg

Starting point: Aquathusiasts Park at the foot of Tyler Avenue in Corvallis, just north of the Highway 34 bridges. (The park lies next to the river, but is not signed.)

Distance: 58.2 miles

Terrain: Flat with some hills

Total cumulative elevation gain: 1000 feet

Recommended time of year: Any season

Recommended starting time: 9:00 A.M.

Allow: 6 hours

Points of interest:
Peoria Park
Finley National Wildlife Refuge
Philomath-Corvallis Bikepath
Corvallis riverfront parks

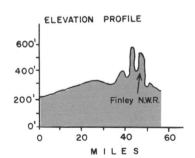

Straight and flat for 22 miles as it follows Peoria Road from the Corvallis area to Harrisburg, the east half of this ride happens to be part of the Bikecentennial transcontinental route. Along the way it also passes miles and miles of "certified grass" that will eventually seed lawns, golf courses, or wildlife range areas all over the world. In the meantime, it can be a major irritant to riders prone to hay fever. Also, the fields are burned after harvest to eradicate straw and kill diseases. Avoid this ride in early June or late July if you're sensitive to pollen or smoke.

Nearly 60 miles in length, this ride deserves an early start, particularly in hot weather, since many of the farm roads are not shaded. It won't be easy to short cut the ride, since bridges or ferries no longer cross the Willamette between Corvallis and Harrisburg. Cyclists looking for a shorter ride might prefer to ride south from Corvallis for a few miles and then return via the same route. On the west side, a good turnaround point might be William L. Finley National Wildlife Area, 15 miles south of Corvallis. Although the roads within that area are gravel, good views of the refuge are available from the route, which follows paved Bellfountain Road.

On the west side of the Willamette, this ride provides sharp contrast to the area pedaled across the river. The roads are serpentine and, in places, hilly. The crops are many and varied, bearing testimony to where the river has dumped the richer soils. Research indicates there are more different types of soil in the Willamette Valley than anywhere else in the world. Area farmers on the east side of the Willamette also tell of several different types of clay, some so sticky they will pull a plow under during all but a few days a year.

On the east side, Peoria Park, 10 miles south of Corvallis, would be a good turnaround point for either a return ride on Peoria Road or exploration of the many farm roads east of Peoria. Some of the roads are shown on this map, and others are shown on the map accompanying Trip No. 33 (Calapooia River).

For riders looking for an even longer route, either the west or east halves of this ride can be combined with Trip No. 38 (Eugene–Harrisburg) for a one-way ride from Corvallis to Eugene of 40 to 50 miles, or a round trip of about 95 miles.

One interesting feature of the eastside ride is the Mennonite Church. The modest cluster of unadorned white buildings reflects the simple ways of the Mennonites. The Mennonite sect, which includes the Amish church, originated among the Swiss Anabaptists in the 1500s.

Whatever route you choose, allow time to explore Harrisburg. Its quiet waterfront park once stirred with activity created by the flatbed ferry crossing the Willamette. Photos in the old mercantile show the historic town and ferry. According to locals, the bridge opened in 1926. With a bridge to cross, the ferry was no longer needed, so the cables were cut. The ferry's fate was left to the swift waters of the Willamette.

MILEAGE LOG

0.0 Aquathusiasts Park in Corvallis at the foot of Tyler Avenue. Ride south on **First Street** (do not use the bike path on the left side of First). At mile 0.1, cross under the Harrison Boulevard Bridge (westbound lanes of Highway 34).

0.2 Cross Van Buren Boulevard and then turn left on the bike path/ sidewalk on the south side of **Van Buren** and cross the bridge over

the Willamette (eastbound lanes of Highway 34). At the far end of the bridge, the bike path ends, but the shoulder is quite adequate.

1.3   Turn right (south) on **Peoria Road**. Follow this road south for 22 miles to Harrisburg. At mile 10.0, Peoria Park (rest rooms; water available) is on the right between Peoria Road and the Willamette River. At mile 16.8, Lake Creek Mennonite School stands on the east side of the road.

23.3   Bear right (south) on **Highway 99E** as Peoria Road merges with it. Follow this road through Harrisburg, where there are two small city parks. The first is on the Willamette, and is reached by riding two blocks west on Monroe Street through the city center. The second has drinking water and rest rooms, and is located one block east of the route on Smith Street.

23.9   At the south end of Harrisburg, follow Highway 99E as it curves right and crosses a bridge over the Willamette. On the bridge the sidewalk is the safer route.

24.6   Turn right on **McMullin Lane** and follow it north and then west.

26.1   Turn right at a T-intersection with **Noraton Road** and stay with it, even after the name changes to Old River Road. At mile 30.4, continue north on Noraton Road through an intersection with Ingram Island Road. At mile 32.5, follow Noraton Road when it turns right (north) at an intersection with Stow Pit Road.

34.1   Turn left (west) on **Hubbard Road**. At mile 35.8, cross Highway 99W, after which Hubbard Road becomes **Dawson Road**.

39.3   Bellfountain (store). Turn right (north) on **Bellfountain Road**.

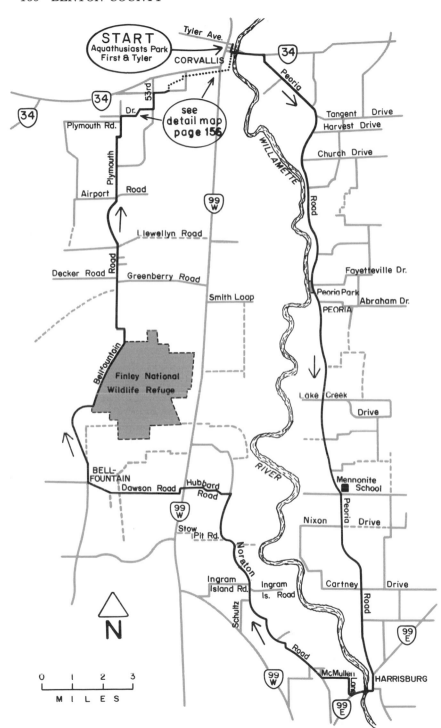

START
Aquathusiasts Park
First & Tyler

Tyler Ave.

CORVALLIS

34

Peoria

34

34

53rd

Dr.

see
detail map
page 156

Plymouth Rd.

Tangent   Drive

Harvest Drive

Church Drive

Plymouth

Airport   Road

Road

99
W

Llewellyn Road

Road

Decker Road

Greenberry Road

Smith Loop

Fayetteville Dr.

Peoria Park

Abraham Dr.

PEORIA

WILLAMETTE

Road

Belfountain

Finley National
Wildlife Refuge

Lake Creek

Drive

BELL-
FOUNTAIN

Dawson Road

Hubbard
Road

RIVER

Mennonite
School

99
W

Stow
Pit Rd.

Nixon   Drive

Peoria

Noraton

Ingram
Island Rd.

Ingram
Is. Road

Cartney   Drive

Road

Schultz

99
E

N

0   1   2   3

M I L E S

Road

99
W

McMullen

HARRISBURG

Ford

99
E

Continue north past the entrance to William L. Finley National Wildlife Refuge at mile 43.3. When Bellfountain Road approaches the Corvallis area, it becomes **Plymouth Drive**.

52.6 Follow Plymouth Drive as it turns ninety degrees right (east) at an intersection with Southwood Drive and Mount Union Drive.

53.9 Turn left (north) at a T-intersection with **53rd Street**.

54.4 Turn right on **Country Club Drive**, using the bike path on the north side of the road. Follow this bike path all the way into downtown Corvallis.

54.7 Follow the bike path as it turns left at the entrance to Sunset Park and then turns right at the entrance to Starker Art Park. Ignore any opportunities to turn left on paths near a small pond.

55.4 Bear left at a fork in the bike path.

57.1 Pass under Highway 99W and then take either fork in the bike path. The two paths rejoin shortly.

58.1 Follow the bike path under the two bridges of Highway 34.

58.2 Foot of Tyler Avenue. End of ride.

LANE COUNTY

38 Eugene–Harrisburg

Starting point: In Eugene at the Skinner Butte Park parking lot at the north end of High Street, where High Street becomes Cheshire Avenue
Distance: 39.9 miles
Terrain: Flat
Total cumulative elevation gain: 190 feet
Recommended time of year: Any season, except when the Willamette is flooding
Recommended starting time: 10:00 A.M.

Allow: 4 to 5 hours
Points of interest:
Eugene bike paths
Armitage State Park

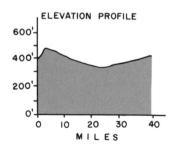

Eugene has done a model job of preserving the Willamette River's shoreline. In contrast to other communities where the river is lined with industrial sites, Eugene has developed linear parks along the Willamette. Perhaps poor navigability of the Willamette in Eugene contributed to keeping industry off the river. Early steamboats could reach the town only during periods of high water.

Eugene also may have the finest system of bike paths and bike lanes in the valley, if not in the Northwest. Not surprisingly, many of the bike paths are along the river. What is surprising is that the number of bike/pedestrian bridges over the river in Eugene continues to equal those for automobiles. Currently, there are four bike/pedestrian crossings and four auto bridges within the city limits.

Starting just a few blocks from downtown Eugene, this ride follows the river's bike paths. Since the scenery is superb, and the paths heavily used by joggers, children, and pets, this is not the place to set speed records.

This route departs town via 4 miles of bike paths and then passes through a 2-mile section of commercial development. Although bike lanes are present much of the way, and traffic only moderate, ride carefully.

After you cross the McKenzie River at Armitage State Park, the traffic volume decreases considerably and the horizon is broken by only occasional barns and silos.

The few towns encountered hardly seem to intrude upon the landscape. In Coburg, a small community named for a black stallion, look for several nineteenth-century houses. One small house along the route is thought to have been built as early as 1848, and another larger house, built in 1877, is now a well-known restaurant. Farther north, Harrisburg looks as if it were lifted off a model railroad set, complete with a water tower proudly painted HARRISBURG.

From Harrisburg, the route crosses the Willamette River and follows Highway 99E south for about 2 miles, and then returns to farm roads. A low point in the road at mile 25.4 is likely to be under water if the Willamette is near flood stage, as it occasionally is during winter or early spring.

Most of the return leg of this trip follows River Road, which was a major thoroughfare prior to construction of Interstate 5. Most evidence of the earlier days is gone, but watch for a faded sign painted on a barn advertising a hotel in Ashland, 210 miles distant.

Shortly after re-entering suburban Eugene, the route returns to the wonderful greenway bike paths for the last few miles to Skinner Butte Park.

MILEAGE LOG

0.0 Parking lot at Skinner Butte Park, at the north end of High Street. From the northwest end of the parking lot, follow a short bike path toward the river, and then turn right and follow the bike path southeast along the river. Ignore the many opportunities to turn right (away from the river).

0.3 Pass under the Ferry Street Bridge and continue following the river.

1.3 Turn left and cross the **Autzen Footbridge**. At the north end of the bridge, turn right, then left, and continue following the river upstream (southeast).

1.7 The bike path joins **Day Island Road**. Pass through automobile

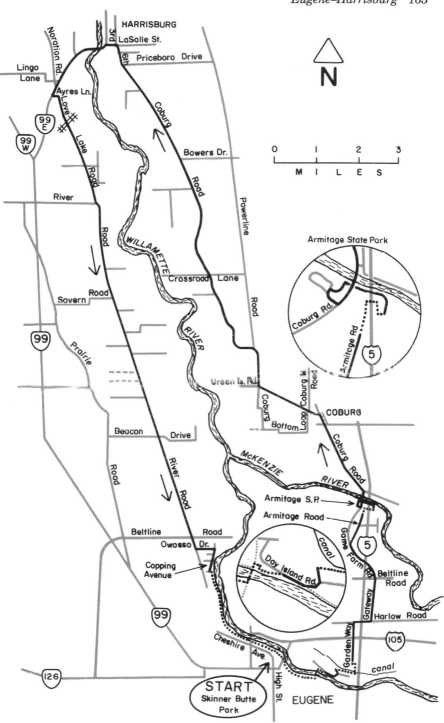

barriers in the road, and continue on Day Island Road at mile 1.9, even though the bike path exits on the right.

2.0   Bear left at an unmarked Y-intersection.

2.1   When the road ends, turn right on a bike path to follow a canal.

2.8   Turn left, cross the canal on a footbridge, and proceed north on a bike path along I-5. The path turns left (west) at mile 3.4.

3.5   Turn right (north) and follow a bike path along **Garden Way**. The bike path soon becomes a bike lane.

4.4   Turn right on **Harlow Road**.

4.9   Turn left on **Gateway Street**. This is a busy intersection. Use the crosswalks. Follow Gateway Street through a major intersection with Beltline Road, where Gateway Street becomes **Game Farm Road North**. A bike lane is available to this point.

6.9   Turn right on **Armitage Road**, which grows smaller and smaller, until it becomes a bike path. The bike path turns right at mile 8.1, passes under I-5, and then heads south along I-5.

8.2   Watch for a break in the fence on your left (under a very large tree), and then turn left into Armitage State Park (camping permitted; water available). Turn left again, and then follow the road back under I-5 to the main part of the park. Keep turning left to exit from the park to Coburg Road.

8.8   Turn left on **Coburg Road**. Be careful. Coburg Road is busy in the vicinity of the park. At mile 9.1, bear right to use the 1887 railroad bridge, now designated for bicycle/pedestrian crossings of the McKenzie River. After crossing the bridge, return to Coburg Road and turn right.

11.0   Coburg (founded 1847). Follow the arterial through the town, as Coburg Road becomes **Willamette Street**, turns west on **Van Duyn Street**, and then regains the name **Coburg Road**. The Van Duyn-Van Massey House (circa 1848–1850), at 238 W. Van Duyn Street, may be the oldest building in the county.

11.5   Continue west on Coburg Road. Do not turn right on Coburg North Road.

12.8   Follow Coburg Road as it turns right at an intersection with Green Island Road and Coburg Bottom Loop.

13.8   Stay on Coburg Road when it turns left at an intersection with Powerline Road. At mile 21.7, Coburg Road enters Harrisburg and becomes **Sixth Street**.

22.2   Turn left on **LaSalle Street**.

22.5   Turn left on **Third Street** (Highway 99E). (To visit the center of old Harrisburg, turn right here). At mile 22.6, the highway crosses the Willamette River. Use the sidewalk on the bridge. It continues for about 0.5 mile past the bridge. After leaving the sidewalk, Highway 99E is fairly busy, and the shoulder bumpy. Exercise care.

24.5   Turn left on **Ayres Lane**, just after passing through Lancaster. (Junction City, where Highway 99 east and west split, is visible through the trees.) At mile 24.7, Ayres Lane turns south and becomes **Love Lake Road**. At mile 25.4, the road passes under two very low railroad trestles. If the Willamette is flooding, beware of high water here.

27.3 Turn left on **River Road** at a T-intersection, and follow it into Eugene. (During harvest season, many opportunities to purchase produce are available along this route.) At mile 33.2, a bike lane starts on the right side of the road, and a bike path appears from time to time. Since traffic picks up in this area, the bike path is the better choice when available. After passing under Beltline Road at mile 35.8, watch for Owosso Drive on the left.

36.2 Turn left on **Owosso Drive**.

36.5 Turn right on **Copping Avenue** and follow it south.

36.9 Copping Avenue ends and a bike path begins. Follow the bike path as it turns left toward the river and then proceeds south downstream. Follow the river, ignoring various bike paths that turn right, away from the river. At mile 38.5, continue past a footbridge on the left over the river. After passing Skinner Butte at about mile 39, watch for the parking lot on the right.

39.9 Turn right to the parking lot. End of trip.

39 Lower Long Tom

Starting point: Kirk Park on Clear Lake Road at the western end of Fern Ridge Dam
Distance: 48.1 miles
Terrain: Generally flat with some moderate hills
Total cumulative elevation gain: 800 feet
Recommended time of year: Any season except during periods of flooding
Recommended starting time: 10:00 A.M.
Allow: 5 hours

Points of interest:
Fern Ridge Lake
Kirk Park
Richardson Park
Monroe City Park
Orchard Point Park

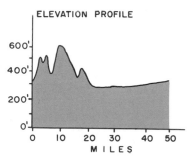

Draining the foothills of the Coast Range northwest of Eugene, the Long Tom River joins the Willamette near the town of Monroe. In the late 1930s the Long Tom was dammed near Alvadore, creating a huge 9000-

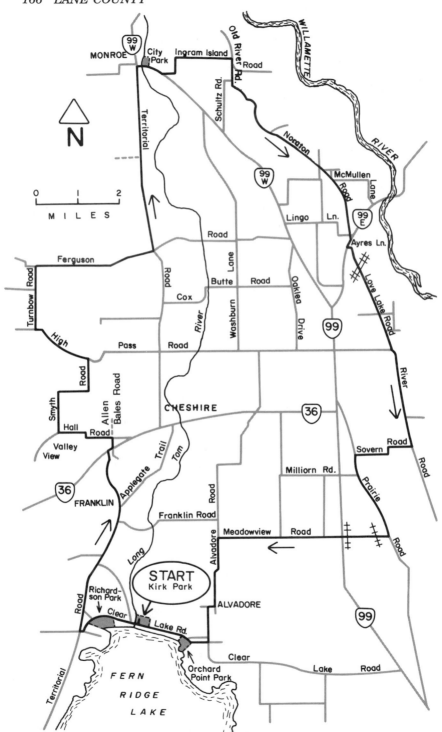

acre reservoir, Fern Ridge Lake. This ride starts near the dam spillway and circles the lower valley of the Long Tom.

The western half of the route climbs up and down foothills of the Coast Range, while the eastern half cruises flat farm roads along the Willamette. Most roads are quite narrow, but have little traffic to distract from pastoral surroundings.

Although the route is nearly 50 miles long, the general grid pattern of farm roads permits several shorter rides within the 50-mile loop. For example, High Pass Road roughly splits the loop in half horizontally at Junction City. By turning east, rather than west, at mile 10.7 and following High Pass Road to River Road at mile 33.7 of the regular route, the total length of the ride can be reduced to 32 miles.

For those wishing to avoid hills on the western part of the ride, a right turn on Applegate Trail Road at mile 4.7 accesses Territorial Highway near Cheshire, allowing the regular route to be rejoined at mile 16.9.

The Fern Ridge and Long Tom area offer superb birdwatching. Depending on the season, the area around the small lake near Kirk Park may contain a variety of hawks and owls, as well as gulls, ducks, and other shorebirds. In winter, the area near Amazon Creek north of mile 42.0 is home to hundreds of whistling swans.

If the winter has been particularly wet, and the Willamette is near flood stage, one section of the ride at mile 31.2 will be impassable, due to several feet of water on the road. Either wait for drier weather or work out a shorter loop to avoid the section.

Winter is also the least scenic time to view the reservoir, since the water level is lowered in late autumn to make room for rain. The water level is usually back to normal by late spring, when the lake becomes a sailing and water-skiing mecca for Eugene residents.

MILEAGE LOG

0.0 Kirk Park. Leave the parking lot, turn right on **Clear Lake Road**, and cross the bridge over the reservoir outlet (the Long Tom River). The entrance to Richardson Park is on the left at mile 1.3.

1.5 Bear right, following Clear Lake Road, at an intersection marked by a sign pointing left to the Eugene Yacht Club.

1.6 Intersection with **Territorial Road**. Turn right (north). At mile 4.7, follow Territorial Road (unmarked) as it bears left at the communities of Smithfield and then Franklin.

6.3 Turn right at a T-intersection with **Highway 36**.

6.4 Turn left on **Allen-Bales Road**. The sign points to Valley View.

6.7 Turn left on **Hall Road**.

8.1 Turn right on **Smyth Road**.

10.7 At a T-intersection with **High Pass Road**, turn left.

12.4 Turn right on **Turnbow Lane** and enjoy a short but beautiful section of roadway.

14.0 At a T-intersection with **Ferguson Road**, turn right.

16.9 Turn left on **Territorial Road** (unmarked) and follow it north to the town of Monroe.

21.4   Monroe. Turn right on **Highway 99W** and cross the Long Tom River. After the turn, Monroe City Park is on the left at mile 21.6. (To visit the city center, do not cross the river; continue straight.)

21.9   Turn left on **Ingram Island Road**.

24.1   Turn right (south) at a T-intersection with **Old River Road**.

24.3   Bear right at a Y-intersection, following Old River Road. The left fork is Ingram Island Road. At mile 28.4, Old River Road becomes **Noraton Road**.

30.0   Noraton Road joins Highway 99E at the community of Lancaster. Turn right (south) on **Highway 99E**.

30.2   Turn left on **Ayres Lane**. At mile 30.4, Ayres Lane turns south and becomes **Love Lake Road**. At mile 31.2 the road dips under two very low railroad trestles. If the Willamette is near flood stage, this will be under several feet of water.

33.0   Turn left (south) on **River Road**.

35.4   Turn right on **Sovern Road**.

37.0   At a T-intersection with **Prairie Road**, turn left (south).

39.3   Turn right on **Meadowview Road**. At mile 40.5, cross Highway 99.

43.5   Turn left (south) at a T-intersection with **Alvadore Road**. At mile 45.3, stay on Alvadore Road as it turns right, then left, and passes in front of the store in the small town of Alvadore.

46.2   Store. Turn right on **Clear Lake Road** (unmarked; sign points to Orchard Point). At mile 46.7, Orchard Point Park is on the left, and Orchard Point Marina is on the left at mile 47.0.

48.1   Turn right into Kirk Park. End of ride.

40 Fern Ridge

Starting point: Echo Hollow
Pool at 1655 Echo Hollow Road
in Eugene
Distance: 32.8 miles
Terrain: Rolling farmland with
one moderate hill
**Total cumulative elevation
gain:** 700 feet
Recommended time of year:
Any season
Recommended starting time:
Before 11:00 A.M.
Allow: 4 hours

Points of interest:
Orchard Point Park
Fern Ridge Lake
Kirk Park
Richardson Park

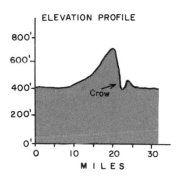

West of Eugene, where the Long Tom River once flowed through a
broad valley, now lies one of the largest lakes in western Oregon. Created
when Fern Ridge Dam was completed by the Army Corps of Engineers
in 1941, Fern Ridge Lake is nearly 5 miles long and 5 miles wide.

The lake is surrounded by farms, oak and evergreen forests, and small
towns like Elmira, Veneta, and Crow. This 33-mile ride starts on Eugene's
west side and follows backroads around the reservoir and into foothills
south of it. The ride is a gentle one, with the only significant hill a
moderate one over a pass between Veneta and Crow.

During the summer, when the water level in Fern Ridge Lake is at its
highest, the lake is very popular for swimming and boating, especially
sailing and water skiing. As a result, the ride from Eugene out to the
parks at the north end of the lake may be well trafficked. Once the west
side of the lake is reached, however, the roads should be free of most
traffic.

The ride starts and ends in suburban west Eugene. The first and last
few miles are on busy arterials, but, as is typical for Eugene, bike lanes
are provided.

Throughout the year Fern Ridge Lake is prime habitat for birds. Even
if you're not normally interested in birdwatching, some larger species are
hard to miss. Great blue herons, whistling swans, and turkey vultures
are common, and less-abundant species include osprey and several types
of hawks and owls. The two most frequently seen hawks are the marsh
hawk (a dark bird with a white rump) and the red-tailed hawk. Take your

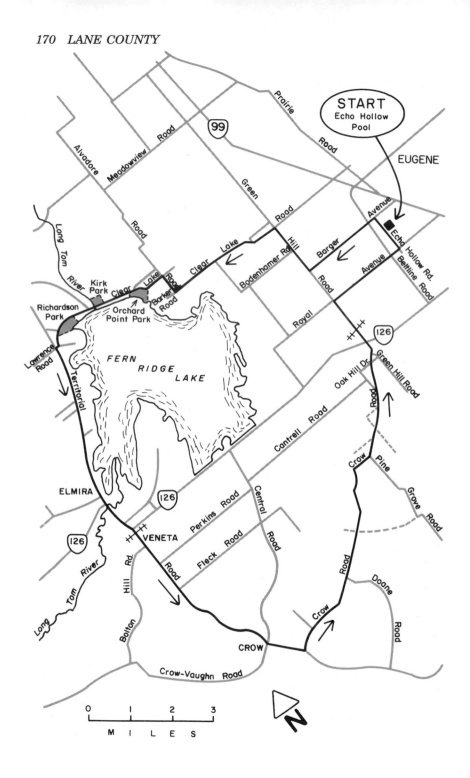

binoculars along, particularly in winter when many of the birds keep their distance across the expansive mudflats.

For those who would like to spend more time birdwatching or enjoying a swim in the lake after the ride, start the trip at Richardson Park, which is mile 10.0 in the log. History buffs may also be interested in reading about the Applegate Trail, which is crossed at mile 19.7 (in Crow) on this ride.

MILEAGE LOG

0.0 Echo Hollow Pool in Eugene. Leave the parking lot, turning right to ride north on **Echo Hollow Road**, using the bike lane.

0.3 Turn left on **Barger Avenue** and follow it west out into the country.

2.4 Turn right at a T-intersection with **Green Hill Road**.

3.6 Turn left at an intersection with **Clear Lake Road**.

6.4 Follow Clear Lake Road as it turns right (north) at an intersection with Barker Road.

6.9 Follow Clear Lake Road (Snyder Road) when it turns left (west) at an intersection with Alvadore South Road (store). At mile 7.4, Orchard Point Park is on the left, and then at mile 7.7 Fern Ridge Lake becomes visible to the left. The road traverses the dam's length. At mile 8.8 the entrance to Kirk Park is on the right, just before the road passes in front of the spillway. The entrance to Richardson Park is on the left at mile 10.0 (rest rooms; water available).

10.3 At an intersection of Clear Lake Road, Lawrence Road, and Territorial Road, turn left on **Territorial Road** and follow it south for several miles. Pass through the town of Elmira (store) at mile 14.0 and cross the Long Tom River at mile 14.3. At mile 15.3 pass through the town of Veneta (stores, restaurants). Between Elmira and Veneta, Territorial Road is Highway 126. At mile 18.0, the road begins to climb into hills south of the reservoir, reaching a crest at mile 19.0.

19.7 Crow (store). (Notice the sign in front of the store designating the 1846 route of the Applegate Trail.) Continue south on Territorial Road.

20.6 Turn left on **Crow Road** and follow it northeast for several miles. At mile 28.6 continue north through an intersection with **Green Hill Road**. At this point, Crow Road becomes Green Hill Road. Cross Highway 126 at mile 28.8.

30.1 Turn right on **Royal Avenue**. At mile 31.3 (Eugene City Limits), bike lanes begin on both sides of Royal.

32.1 Turn left on **Echo Hollow Road**.

32.8 Turn right into the parking lot at Echo Hollow Pool. End of ride.

41 Lorane Loops

Starting point: Acorn Park, at the intersection of W. 15th Avenue and Buck Street in Eugene. Park along Buck Street on the west side of the park.
Distance: Long loop, 64.4 miles; short loop, 34.6 miles
Terrain: Hilly
Total cumulative elevation gain: Long loop, 2780 feet; short loop, 1385 feet
Recommended time of year: Any season
Recommended starting time: Long loop, before 9:00 A.M.; short loop, 11:00 A.M.
Allow: Long loop, 7 hours; short loop, 4 hours
Points of interest:
Siuslaw River
Siuslaw Falls Park

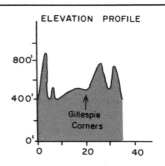

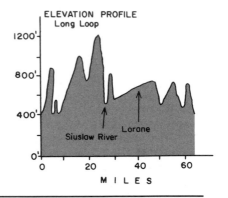

The flat Willamette Valley ends at Eugene, where the main stem of the Willamette is formed by the meeting of the Coast Fork, the Middle Fork, and the McKenzie. These three tributaries join the Willamette from the south and east, and provide relatively easy access into the Cascades.

For travelers headed into the Coast Range southwest from Eugene, however, no such broad valleys are available. Instead, a series of high ridges and small, but deep, stream valleys separate the Eugene area from the Siuslaw and Umpqua valleys to the southwest.

This bike ride climbs up and down those ridges on its way to visit the Siuslaw River. The route starts in West Eugene, near Amazon Creek, climbs over Murray Hill, and then follows Coyote Creek to the Crow area. From near Crow, the route climbs to a 1000-foot pass before dropping to Wolf Creek. This is followed by a climb to a 1200-foot pass and a steep descent to the Siuslaw River. After a gentle ride to the tiny town of Lorane, the route returns to Coyote Creek, and then climbs over one more pass on its return to suburban Eugene.

The southern section of the route, especially the descent to and the ride along the Siuslaw River, is one of the nicest rides in the state. The roads, while narrow, are shady, secluded, smooth, and free of traffic. Particularly when dropping down to the river, the endless curves through the woods are a joy. An autumn ride, after the foliage has turned colors, would be superb. Spring and early summer are highlighted by wildflowers, especially the lavender to deep purple, tough-leafed iris, which grows in abundance here.

Although the full loop to the Siuslaw and back to Eugene is nearly 65 miles, scenery makes it well worthwhile. If 65 miles is outside your range, a shorter loop of 35 miles is described, but it returns to Eugene well before reaching the Siuslaw. The remainder of the long loop could be ridden in a manageable 43.6 miles by starting, for example, in Lorane. Use the map and mileage log to ride north to Gillespie Corners, northwest toward Crow, and then southwest to the Siuslaw River, which could then be followed back to Lorane.

To ride a scenic, but hilly, route to the coast on backroads, turn west on the Siuslaw River Road at mile 26.0 and follow it along the river.

MILEAGE LOG

Long Loop

0.0 Acorn Park in Eugene. Ride south on **Buck Street**.

0.2 Turn right on **18th Avenue** and follow its bike lane west. At mile 1.4, the bike lane ends at an intersection with Bertelson Road. Continue west on 18th Avenue.

2.2 Turn left on **Willow Creek Road** (Williams Street). At mile 2.5, the road turns west and becomes **25th Avenue**, but later regains the name **Willow Creek Road**. The road climbs steadily up the side of Murray Hill. At mile 4.3, the road reaches its high point of 880 feet, and then turns north and becomes **Green Hill Road**.

5.7 Turn left at a T-intersection with **Crow Road**. The road climbs over a gentle pass and then enters a valley of flat farmland as it follows Coyote Creek toward the town of Crow.

13.9 Turn left at a T-intersection with **Territorial Road** (unmarked).

14.2 Turn right on **Wolf Creek Road**. (The short loop, which is described below, goes straight here.) Wolf Creek Road climbs to 1010 feet at mile 16.7, and then drops into the Wolf Creek Valley. Another climb brings the rider to a 1200-foot pass, after which the road becomes quite narrow as it drops to the Siuslaw River.

26.0 Turn left at a T-intersection with **Siuslaw River Road** and follow it east up the river. Although the gradient of the river is not steep, the road climbs up and down several small ridges.

34.9 Turn left at a sign pointing to Siuslaw Falls Park.

35.3 Siuslaw Falls Park (picnic facilities 0.5 mile down the park road). Return to Siuslaw River Road.

35.7 Turn left on **Siuslaw River Road**. Beyond this point the road is fairly gentle.

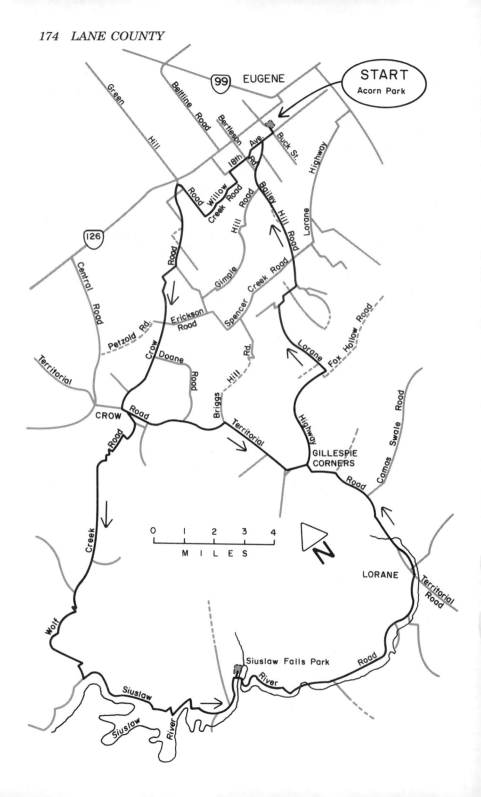

44.8   Lorane (store, cafe). Go straight on **Territorial Road**, which soon curves north.

50.9   Gillespie Corners. Turn right (east) on **Lorane Highway**. (The short loop rejoins the long loop at this intersection.) Lorane Highway proceeds east and north along a stream known simply as Fox Hollow. Stay left at mile 54.6, as Lorane Highway turns due north. Stay with it as it climbs over a small pass into the Spencer Creek Valley.

59.5   Intersection with Spencer Creek Road. Although Lorane Highway turns right here, continue straight (north) on **Bailey Hill Road**, which climbs to a 740-foot pass at mile 61.1.

62.6   Bear right at a Y-intersection with **Bertelson Road**. A bike lane is available on the right as you enter Eugene.

63.7   Turn right on **18th Avenue**.

64.2   Turn left on **Buck Street**.

64.4   Acorn Park. End of ride.

Short Loop

0.0   Acorn Park. Follow the mileage log for the long loop up to mile 14.2.

14.2   Do not turn on Wolf Creek Road, but continue straight (southeast) on **Territorial Road** and follow it as it continues up the Coyote Creek Valley.

21.1   Gillespie Corners. Although Territorial Road turns right (south), turn east on **Lorane Highway**. This intersection is mile 50.9 of the long loop. To return to Eugene, follow the mileage log for the long loop.

34.6   Acorn Park. End of ride.

42 Middle Fork

Starting point: Jasper County Park near Jasper. From the McKenzie Highway (126) in Springfield, take the Jasper Road/ Creswell Highway 222 toward Dexter Reservoir for about 7 miles. After crossing the Middle Fork at Jasper, watch for signs into the park.
Distance: 25.6 miles
Terrain: Relatively flat with some hills
Total cumulative elevation gain: 775 feet
Recommended time of year: Any season
Recommended starting time: 10:00 A.M.
Allow: 4 to 5 hours

Points of interest:
Four covered bridges
Dexter Reservoir
Dexter Park
Jasper Park

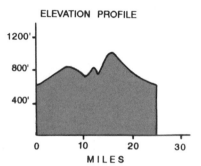

The Middle Fork of the Willamette River flows from the crest of the Cascades south of Willamette Pass to the Eugene/Springfield area, where it joins the Coast Fork. It drains an area of dense forests, small logging towns, and a few small farms. The valley is also home to a number of covered bridges.

Only two major roads enter the valley from the west. Highway 58 is the main thoroughfare, leading out of Eugene over Willamette Pass. The other highway is Jasper Road, which starts in Springfield as the Creswell Highway and winds its way along the river, joining Highway 58 at Dexter Reservoir. To avoid traffic on these busy highways, this ride concentrates on the backroads. It is short, but visits all four remaining covered bridges of the lower valley, in between passing through some picturesque back country.

The four bridges are located at Pengra, Unity, Lowell, and Dexter. The Pengra bridge, built in 1938, contains 126-foot timbers in its floor, and 98-foot timbers in its roof. The Unity Bridge, the only one of the four still open to automobile traffic, includes a full-length window on the upstream side.

The Lowell Bridge was built in 1945 to replace an older covered bridge damaged by an errant truck. Although one of the youngest covered bridges in the state, it must surely have nine lives. In 1953, when Dexter Dam and Reservoir were built and the area flooded, a causeway was built across the reservoir and the bridge raised several feet to accommodate the higher waters. Then, when heavy logging truck traffic necessitated a

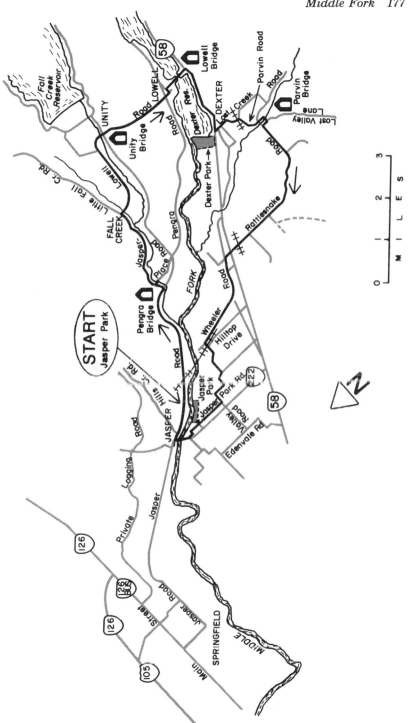

modern structure, the bridge was moved to one side and given a well-deserved retirement, although it is still open to pedestrians and bicyclists.

The last bridge, at Parvin, was similarly preserved for pedestrian and bicycle use when Rattlesnake Road was realigned and a new bridge built 0.25 mile downstream. In the last thirty years, apparently only one covered bridge in this area has been destroyed—the bridge at Fall Creek, replaced by a concrete structure. Perhaps the remaining four can be preserved indefinitely.

The ride begins in Jasper County Park, passes through Jasper, and follows Fall Creek past two covered bridges. It then climbs over a small ridge to Dexter Reservoir and the town of Lowell.

After crossing the reservoir, the ride follows Highway 58 for 2 miles. Although Highway 58 is quite busy, the shoulder is adequate here. Even so, ride with care, and minimize the time you spend on this section.

The last covered bridge is visited south of the reservoir, in the Lost Creek Valley. After a climb over an intervening ridge, the route passes through flat farmland and then returns to Jasper Park. Since the ride is short, plan to take a picnic to enjoy along the shores of the reservoir. Facilities are available to make it most enjoyable.

MILEAGE LOG

0.0   Exit Jasper Park. Turn right onto **Jasper Park Road** at mile 0.2. This road turns left and then right to join **Highway 222** (Jasper Road/Creswell Highway).

0.5   Turn right on **Highway 222** and cross the Middle Fork.

0.7   Turn right onto **Jasper-Lowell Road**.

5.0   Turn right on **Place Road**, to Pengra Bridge, and then return to Jasper-Lowell Road and turn right.

7.3   Fall Creek. Turn right, following Jasper-Lowell Road across Little Fall Creek.

9.8   Unity (store). Pass through the covered bridge and then continue straight on Jasper-Lowell Road.

11.6   Lowell. Ride straight through the major intersection with Pengra Road and then turn left on the next street (unmarked). A miniature covered bridge is on the left in the park.

12.0   Turn right on the next available street (unmarked; Lowell High School is on the southwest corner of this intersection). The road proceeds south, out of Lowell, and across Dexter Reservoir on a causeway. At the far end of the causeway, Lowell Bridge (no longer in use) stands on the right side of the road.

12.7   Turn right at a T-intersection with **Highway 58**, being careful of the moderate to heavy traffic on this main highway.

14.5   Turn left, onto **Lost Creek Road**, at the signs pointing to Dexter.

15.2   Immediately after passing under a railroad bridge, turn right on **Parvin Road**.

15.8   At an intersection with Rattlesnake Road, go straight, despite a sign for a dead end.

16.0 Parvin Bridge. Cross the bridge and then turn right on **Lost Valley Lane**.

16.2 Turn left at a T-intersection with **Rattlesnake Road**.

20.2 Cross Highway 58.

20.4 Turn left at a T-intersection with **Wheeler Road**.

22.8 Follow Wheeler Road when it turns left and passes under a railroad bridge. Stay on Wheeler Road as it works its way west and north.

24.6 Turn right on **Jasper Park Road**, one block before a stop sign.

25.4 Jasper Park is on the right.

25.6 End of ride.

MULTI-COUNTY RIDES
43 Scaponia

Starting point: West Union School, 12 miles west of Portland. From Highway 26, turn north on Helvetia Road and drive 1 mile, and then turn west on West Union Road.

Distance: 94.6 miles

Terrain: Extremely hilly with some flat sections

Total cumulative elevation gain: 3800 feet

Recommended time of year: Any season, except during periods of snowfall at elevations of 1000 feet or less

Recommended starting time: 6:00 A.M. if ridden in one day

Allow: 1 or 2 days

Points of interest:
Verboort
Nehalem Valley
Scaponia Recreation Area
Bonnie Falls

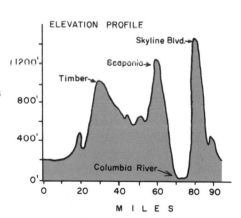

ELEVATION PROFILE

The Nehalem River carves a 100-mile arc across the north end of Oregon's Coast Range. From its source near the small town of Timber in Washington County, the river flows north through Columbia County before turning west and south to the Pacific.

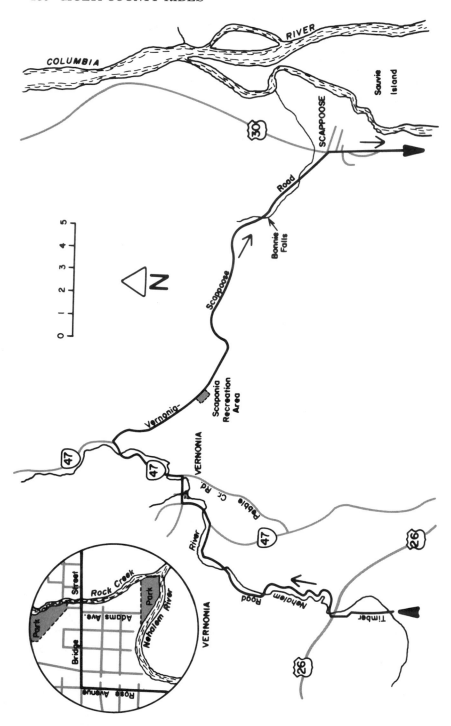

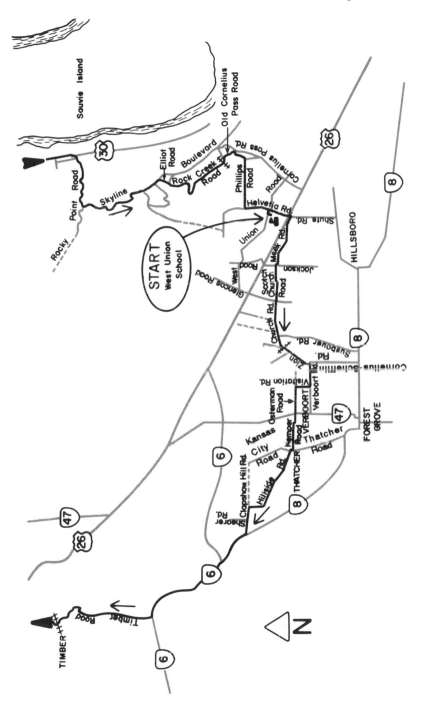

This ride, also nearly 100 miles in length, starts in the Tualatin Valley, climbs over a 1000-foot pass to join the Nehalem at Timber, and then follows the river through the town of Vernonia. A few miles north of Vernonia, the route turns east, away from the Nehalem, and climbs to 1200 feet before dropping to the town of Scappoose on the Columbia River. After an all-too-brief level section along the Columbia, the route returns to the hills by ascending Rocky Point Road. In 3.3 excruciating miles, the road climbs from the Columbia to Skyline Boulevard on the 1475-crest of the Tualatin Mountains. The effort does not go unrewarded, however, for the last leg of the journey is a long descent into the Tualatin Valley.

The 95-mile distance and the 3800-foot cumulative elevation gain combine to make this an extremely rigorous ride for even the best of cyclists. Some riders will be able to complete the route in a single day, but most will want to spread the work over two. Public campgrounds are available at two points along the route. At mile 44.5, Anderson Park, a city park in Vernonia, offers pleasant camping along the Nehalem River. At mile 57.6, Scaponia Recreation Area, a Bureau of Land Management campground, straddles the East Fork of the Nehalem. Obviously named for the two towns between which it lies, Scaponia is one of the prettiest campgrounds around. Hiking trails, a secluded location, and rustic bridges over a gurgling stream all add up to make Scaponia a fine place to camp.

If you are tempted instead to seek a motel, make reservations before you go. Overnight accommodations are extremely scarce in the Vernonia region.

A ride of this length and terrain requires a fit cyclist and a degree of careful planning. A 1-day ride gives the luxury of not carrying heavy overnight gear, but a 100-mile jaunt over steep hills should not be attempted by riders unsure of their stamina. Try several shorter rides first, and then get an early start and a favorable weather forecast on the chosen day.

A 2-day ride, even if requiring the burden of luggage, affords a much more leisurely pace, adding time for sightseeing and exploring along the way. Stop in Verboort, a little town of Dutch ancestry, famous for its annual sausage festival. Centered around the Visitation Catholic Church (1875), Verboort is a strongly religious community. Don't expect any stores to be open on Sunday.

Even smaller is Timber, in the Coast Range at the head of the Nehalem. The road literally switchbacks its way through this tiny logging town, which seems to be glued to the steep hillside.

You may also want to spend some time in Vernonia and Scappoose. While not large, they each have stores and restaurants. Vernonia has the distinction of being one terminus of Oregon's first "rail to trail" conversion. This as yet unpaved trail extends 20 miles southeast to Banks near Highway 26.

Leaving Scappoose, you will also be reminded of the most important reason to do this route in 2 days: It permits frequent stops to catch one's breath while climbing long hills.

MILEAGE LOG

0.0 West Union School. Leave the parking lot and turn right (east) on **West Union Road**.

0.1 Bear right at an intersection with **Helvetia Road** and follow it south.

1.0 Carefully cross Highway 26, after which Helvetia Road becomes **Shute Road**.

1.1 Turn right on **Meek Road** and follow it as it bears right and then parallels Highway 26.

3.6 Turn right at a T-intersection with **Jackson School Road**.

3.7 Turn left (west) on **Scotch Church Road**. After passing through an intersection with Glencoe Road at mile 5.4, Scotch Church Road becomes **Zion Church Road**, and then veers left and becomes Cornelius-Schefflin Road.

9.2 At a T-intersection, turn right (west) on **Verboort Road**.

10.2 Verboort. Turn right on **Visitation Road**.

11.1 Turn left (west) at a T-intersection with **Osterman Road**.

12.0 Cross Highway 47 and continue west on **Kemper Road**.

13.8 Thatcher. Turn right (north) on **Thatcher Road**.

13.9 Turn left on **Hillside Road** (unmarked).

17.4 Turn left (west) at a T-intersection with **Clapshaw Hill Road**. At mile 17.9, continue west on Clapshaw Hill Road through an intersection with Shearer Road, after which Clapshaw Hill Road drops rapidly into Gales Creek Valley.

18.8 Turn right on **Highway 8** (Gales Creek Road), which is unmarked at this point.

20.7 Turn left on **Highway 6**, which can be busy. Ride carefully.

24.1 Turn right (north) at a sign pointing to Timber and Vernonia. Follow this unmarked road (**Timber Road**) for the next 20 miles as it climbs up and down foothills to the town of Timber at mile 30.9, crosses Highway 26 at mile 34.1, and then follows the Nehalem River toward Vernonia.

44.5 Turn left at a T-intersection with **Highway 47** and then follow Highway 47 through Vernonia, where it becomes **Bridge Street**. Across Highway 47 at this intersection, the Banks-Vernonia Trail is visible through the trees. It can be ridden into Vernonia, but is not paved. Anderson Park (camping permitted; water available) is located three blocks south of the route as it passes through "downtown" Vernonia. To reach the park, turn right on Adams Avenue at mile 46.6. A day use park on Rock Creek is northeast of that same intersection.

47.7 Follow Highway 47 when it turns left immediately after crossing a bridge over the Nehalem River.

52.0 Turn right, leaving Highway 47, at a sign pointing to Scappoose and St. Helens (**Vernonia-Scappoose Road**).

57.6 Scaponia Recreation Area (camping, picnicking; water available). A 0.5-mile-long gravel road leads into the camping area. From Scaponia, the road continues to climb, reaching its highest point (1232 feet) at mile 60.0, after which the route begins a 12-mile descent to the Columbia River. At mile 68.5, Bonnie Falls is on the south side of the road.

72.8 Turn right on **Highway 30** and follow it through Scappoose. Although the shoulder of Highway 30 is quite adequate, the road is a busy one, so ride carefully. At two points (unmarked roads at miles 73.7 and 76.0), sections of the old highway parallel Highway 30, and can be used instead of the shoulder of the newer road.

76.8 Turn right on **Rocky Point Road** and prepare for several miles of very steep road.

80.1 Turn left on **Skyline Boulevard**. The elevation at this intersection is 1475 feet, the highest of the ride.

84.8 Turn right on **Elliot Road**. A few feet after this intersection, the road begins to drop into the Tualatin Valley.

85.5 Turn right at a T-intersection with **Rock Creek Road**.

89.8 Make a hard right turn onto **Old Cornelius Pass Road**.

91.2 Turn right on **Phillips Road**.

93.5 Turn left at a T-intersection with **Helvetia Road**.

94.5 Bear right (west) onto **West Union Road**.

94.6 West Union School. End of ride.

44 Three-Ferry Figure Eight

Starting point: Wheatland
Ferry, south of Dayton near
Maude Williamson State Park, or
drive west from I-5 exit no. 263
or 271. Park on either side of the
river.

Distance: Total, 147.5 miles
(first day, 59.3 miles; second day,
88.2 miles)

Terrain: Moderate—generally
level with some hills

**Total cumulative elevation
gain:** 3150 feet (first day, 1700
feet; second day, 1450 feet)

Recommended time of year:
Any season except winter and
early spring

Recommended starting time:
9:00 A.M.

Allow: 2 days

Points of interest:
Wheatland Ferry
Canby Ferry
Buena Vista Ferry
Four state parks
Willamette River Greenway
Parks
Numerous city and county parks
Ankeny National Wildlife Refuge

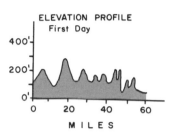

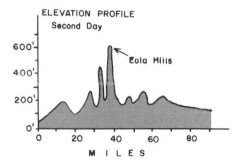

Back when the Willamette River had few bridges over it, the only way
across the river was by ferry. Small, primitive craft, the ferries were
privately owned by farmers attempting to supplement their income, or by
real estate speculators eager to lure commerce to their riverside communities.

Of the nearly two dozen ferries once operating across the Willamette,
only three remain. These flatbed craft resemble a sophisticated barge, but
are secured with underwater cables to provide stability in the river's swift
current.

The Buena Vista Ferry, located midway between Albany and Independence, has been operating since the early 1850s. Now primarily operated
for the benefit of area farmers, it is closed November through March, and
on Mondays and Tuesdays. The Wheatland Ferry, north of Salem, made

its first crossing in 1844. It is now a primary arterial for commuters between Yamhill and Marion counties. The youngest of the surviving boats, the Canby Ferry, was started in 1915. All are now operated by county governments. Each charges a nominal toll to motorists, but allows bicyclists and pedestrians to ride free.

This figure-eight loop includes all three ferries, with the Buena Vista Ferry at its southern end, the Canby Ferry at its northern end, and the Wheatland Ferry at the center crossroads. When the Buena Vista Ferry is not running, riders can cross a bridge a few miles downstream at Independence, shortening the second day of the ride by 18.4 miles.

The trip can be started at any point, and ridden in several different directions. However, several elements make careful planning necessary. The length of the ride, numerous ferry crossings, and lack of more than one campground along the route must be considered. The method described below is designed to roughly divide the riding into 2 days, with Champoeg State Park as the overnight stop. Accordingly, the route starts at the center of the figure eight, the Wheatland Ferry, and then proceeds north on the west side of the river.

In order to avoid Highway 99W in the Newberg/Dayton area, the route makes a detour through the Chehalem Valley. After crossing the Canby Ferry, the route turns south on the east side of the river to Champoeg State Park, for a first-day total of 59.3 miles. On the second day the route continues south to Wheatland, crosses to the west side and heads south to the Buena Vista Ferry (or the Independence Bridge), and then returns on the east bank to Wheatland, for a second-day total of 88.1 miles (69.7 miles, if the Independence Bridge is used).

The itinerary is also designed to deliver the rider to each ferry during its operating hours. At the time of publication, the operating hours were:

Canby Ferry: 7:00 A.M. to 10:00 P.M., every day except New Year's, Presidents', and Veterans days, Thanksgiving, and Christmas. (Open Memorial and Labor Day weekends and Independence Day.)

Wheatland Ferry: 6:00 A.M. to 9:45 P.M., every day except Christmas and Thanksgiving.

Buena Vista Ferry: 7:00 A.M. to 5:00 P.M., Monday through Friday; 9:00 A.M. to 7:00 P.M., Saturday and Sunday. (Closed last Sunday in October until first Wednesday in April.)

When planning the ride, verify operating hours for the ferries, especially during periods of high water. For the Wheatland and Buena Vista ferries, call Marion County Department of Public Works, (503) 588-7979 or 5304. The Canby Ferry information is available from (503) 655-8521. In addition to periods of high water, the Buena Vista Ferry may also be closed in late summer if the river's level is unusually low.

Despite these logistical challenges, this figure eight is well worth the effort. In the heart of the valley, it travels both sides of the river, passes through four counties, makes four ferry crossings, visits more than a

The ferry's decks certainly are slippery when wet.

dozen parks, and, with the exception of the Salem-center section, which has bike lanes, is relatively free of traffic.

On your second crossing at Wheatland, you can leave overnight gear in your car, which will be parked nearby. However, the gear might be safer on your bike.

Riders preferring shorter 1-day rides could use the mileage log below to ride the 79.4-mile loop between Wheatland and Canby, the 68-mile loop between Wheatland and Buena Vista, the 49.6-mile loop between Wheatland and Independence, or even the 19.4-mile loop between Independence and Buena Vista. Just make sure the ferries are running.

MILEAGE LOG

First Day

0.0 Wheatland Ferry. Park on either side of the ferry crossing, but start riding on the west side by heading west on **Wheatland Road**.

1.1 Turn right on **Highway 221**. The entrance to Maude Williamson State Park is across this intersection (day use only; water available).

1.4 Turn left on an unmarked road (**Hopewell Highway**). The sign points to Hopewell and McMinnville.

2.7 Hopewell. Follow the arterial through this very small community. The schoolhouse on the left dates from circa 1900. The church on the right is an 1880 remodeling of an older structure. At mile 2.8, follow the arterial (Hopewell Highway) as it curves right (north) at an intersection with Webfoot Road.

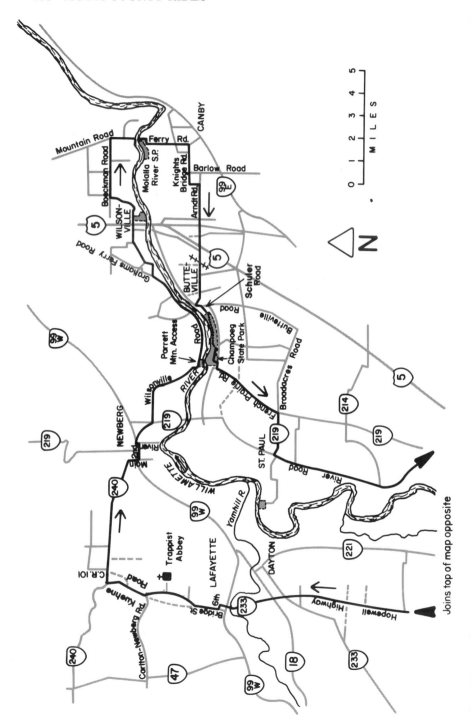

Joins top of map opposite

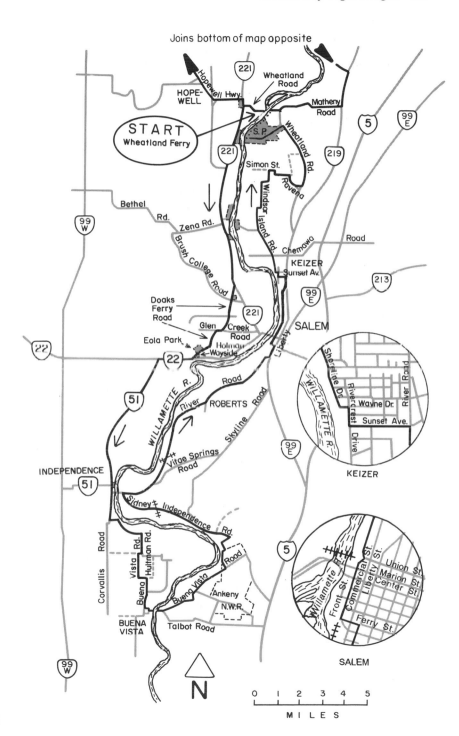

Joins bottom of map opposite

10.8   Ride straight (north) through this intersection. Hopewell Highway becomes **Highway 233** at this point. At mile 11.3, continue straight through an intersection with Highway 18. At mile, 13.3, the road crosses the Yamhill River on a bridge, followed by Terry Park on the left (day use only; water not available).

13.6   Lafayette. Highway 233 ends here. Continue north on **Madison Street** through an intersection with Highway 99W.

13.8   Turn left on **Sixth Street**. The Yamhill County Historical Society Museum is on the right.

14.0   Turn right (north) on **Bridge Street** and follow it as it becomes **Kuehne Road** and proceeds through the foothills and farmland north of Lafayette. Our Lady of Guadalupe Trappist Abbey is on the right at mile 16.9. At mile 18.0, bear right, staying on Kuehne Road.

19.9   At a T-intersection with **Highway 240**, turn right. At mile 20.5, continue east on Highway 240 at an intersection with **Ribbon Ridge Road** (County Road 101).

25.7   Highway 240 turns south and enters Newberg as **Main Street**. At mile 26.0, Main Street crosses two one-way streets that pass through Newberg as Highway 99W.

26.1   Turn left on **Second Street**.

26.6   At a T-intersection with **River Street**, turn left. On the left is the Hoover-Minthorn House, boyhood home of Herbert Hoover. Opposite is Hoover Memorial Park (day use only; water available).

26.7   Turn right on **Highway 99W**. A sidewalk is available on the south side of this busy road, or a path through Hoover Park may be used.

26.8   Turn right on **Highway 219**.

28.2   Turn left on **Wilsonville Road** and follow it east for several miles along the Willamette River. At mile 32.6, Willamette Greenway (Parrett Mountain Access) allows public access to the river. At mile 37.7, follow Wilsonville Road as it bears right at an intersection with Grahams Ferry Road. At mile 39.4, a bike lane becomes available on the right as the road enters Wilsonville.

40.4   Wilsonville (store). Continue east on Wilsonville Road. Wilsonville Memorial Park is on the right at mile 40.9 (day use only; water available).

42.6   Turn right (east) at a T-intersection with **Boeckman Road**.

42.7   Although the arterial turns left here, continue straight (east) on Boeckman Road. At mile 43.3, beware of a short, but very steep, hill that may have rough pavement.

45.4   Turn right (south) at a T-intersection with **Mountain Road**.

46.5   Follow the arterial by turning left, down a hill.

46.7   Canby Ferry Landing. After the ferry crossing, continue south on **Ferry Road** (Holly Road). Molalla River State Park is to the right, down a short road, at mile 47.2 (day use only; water available).

49.2   Turn right on **Knights Bridge Road** near a small city park. The road crosses the Molalla River at mile 49.9.

51.4 Road bends left and becomes **Arndt Road**. Cross the Pudding River on a bridge at mile 51.8 and follow Arndt Road west for several miles.

57.0 Butteville (store). Turn left on **Butteville Road**. A bike lane begins on the right one block later.

57.2 Turn right on **Schuler Road**, following the bike lane.

57.6 Follow the bike path when it bears left, leaving Schuler Road. The bike path proceeds west through the woods, along the Willamette to Champoeg State Park.

59.3 T-intersection with a paved road in Champoeg State Park. On the right is a bridge over Champoeg Creek. Turn left to the overnight campground. The park has several interesting features, including an excellent visitors center and several miles of bike paths.

Second Day

0.0 Leave Champoeg State Park overnight campground, following signs to the park entrance.

1.0 Park entrance. Turn right on **Champoeg Road**. At mile 0.9, the Robert Newell House museum is on the right.

1.2 At a T-intersection with **French Prairie Road** (Champoeg Road), turn left (south).

4.7 Turn right on **Highway 219**, following the signs to St. Paul.

6.6 St. Paul (store). Turn left (south) on **Main Street**, which soon becomes **River Road**

14.7 Turn right at a T-intersection with **Highway 219**.

16.4 Turn right on **Matheny Road**.

19.6 Turn right, following Matheny Road.

20.1 Wheatland Ferry. After crossing the river, continue west on **Wheatland Road**.

21.2 Turn left at an intersection with **Highway 221**. Maude Williamson State Park (day use only; water available) is directly west of this intersection. At mile 23.5, Spring Valley Access, a Willamette Greenway park, allows access to the river. Another access area can be reached by turning left on Lincoln Road at mile 26.7 (store), and a third is located at mile 27.7.

29.9 Turn right on **Doaks Ferry Road**. At mile 30.4, Brush College Park is on the left (day use only; water available).

31.9 Bear right, staying on Doaks Ferry, at an intersection with **Glen Creek Road**.

32.1 Turn left (south), following **Doaks Ferry Road**. Eola Park (day use only; water available) is on the right at mile 33.7.

34.3 At a T-intersection with **Highway 22**, turn right and proceed west using the bike path on the north side of this busy highway. Holman Wayside (day use only; water available) is northeast of this intersection.

35.7 Turn left on **Highway 51** and follow it to Independence, where it becomes **Main Street**. (If a break is in order, an authentic soda shop is here.)

42.2   Independence (store). Polk Marine Park (day use only; water available) is on the left at the foot of B Street.

42.7   The Independence bridge is on the left. If the Buena Vista Ferry is not running (the ferry is closed Mondays and Tuesdays and from November to April), or to shorten the ride by 18.4 miles, turn left here. At the east end of the bridge (it is 0.5 mile long), rejoin the route at mile 61.6 below. Otherwise, continue south on Main Street, which soon becomes **Corvallis Road**.

43.7   Turn left on **Buena Vista Road** (Hartman Road).

46.3   Turn right on Buena Vista Road (Davidson Road).

46.5   Turn left (south) on Buena Vista Road.

47.9   Follow Buena Vista Road when it turns right (south) at an intersection with Hultman Road.

49.5   Buena Vista. Turn left on **Sequoia Street** and follow it as it turns right and becomes **Riverview Street** at mile 49.6.

49.7   Turn left (east) following the signs to the ferry landing. Buena Vista Park (day use only; water not available) is one block south of an intersection at mile 49.8.

49.9   Buena Vista Ferry. After crossing the river, ride east on **Buena Vista Road**. Bear left, staying on Buena Vista Road, at an intersection with Talbot Road at mile 50.2.

53.9   Turn left on **Sidney-Independence Road** (County Road 852) immediately after crossing a small bridge over an irrigation ditch. This intersection is located within the Ankeny National Wildlife

Refuge. During the winter, watch for huge flocks of dusky Canada Geese. Follow this road through several ninety-degree turns as it works its way north.

61.5 Just before passing under the east approach to the Independence bridge, turn right (east).

61.6 Turn right on **River Road** and follow it east and north to Salem. Halls Ferry Access, a Willamette Greenway day use area, is on the left at mile 65.6.

68.1 Roberts (store). Follow River Road as it bears left. At mile 70.6, the entrance to Minto-Brown Island Park (day use only; water available) is on the left. A bike path begins on the east side of River Road at this point. At mile 71.6, River Road curves right (west) and becomes **Owens Street**.

71.9 Turn left at a T-intersection with **Liberty Street** and follow it north. Ride carefully on this busy street.

72.5 Turn left on **Ferry Street**.

72.7 Turn right on **Front Street**. A two-way bike lane leads through Salem.

74.8 Continue straight ahead on **Front Street** as Commercial Street comes in on the right.

75.2 Bear left as Front Street becomes **River Road** (Highway 219).

76.0 Keizer. Turn left on **Sunset Avenue**.

76.4 Turn right (north) on **Rivercrest Drive**. River Edge Park (day use only; water not available) is just west of this intersection.

76.6 Turn left on **Wayne Drive**, which curves north and becomes **Shoreline Drive**. At mile 77.4, Shoreline Drive crosses Chemawa Road and becomes **Windsor Island Road**. At mile 78.8, a 1-mile detour west on Naples Street leads to Spongs Landing Park (day use only; water available).

82.0 Turn right at a T-intersection with **Simon Street** and follow it as it becomes **Ninth Avenue** and then **Salmon Street**.

83.0 Turn right on **Ravena Drive**.

83.9 Bear left when the road forks.

84.1 Turn left on **Wheatland Road**. Willamette Mission State Park is on the left at mile 86.9 (day use only; water available).

87.8 Turn left (west) on **Matheny Road**.

88.2 Wheatland Ferry landing. End of ride.

45 Mount Hood Loop

Starting point: Mount Hood Community College, 17th and Kane streets, Gresham. From I-84 take Wood Village exit no. 16A. Obtain advance permission for overnight parking at the college (details below).

Distance: Total, 160.4 miles (first day, 54.7 miles; second day, 54.2 miles; third day, 51.5 miles)

Terrain: Flat to hilly and mountainous; not recommended for novice cyclists

Total cumulative elevation gain: 8400 feet (first day, 1050 feet; second day, 6850 feet; third day, 500 feet)

Recommended time of year: Late June through early September

Recommended starting time: 8:00 A.M.

Allow: 3 days

Points of interest:
Chanticleer Point (Portland Women's Forum State Park)
Historic Columbia River Highway
Multnomah Lodge and Falls
Bonneville Dam and Visitors Center
Bridge of the Gods
Cascade Locks and Marine Park
Authentic sternwheeler
Starvation Creek and Hole-in-the-Wall Falls
Columbia River windsurfers
Hood River Museum
Timberline Lodge
Sandy River Gorge

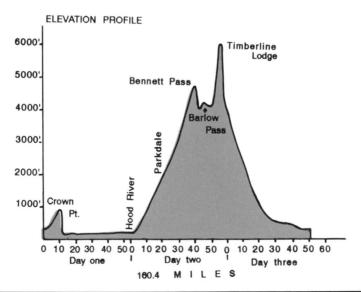

A bicycling tour offering opportunities to see natural and historic wonders over miles and miles of varied terrain can bring smiles and memories. This is such a tour.

A 3-day adventure that begins to unfold immediately, the route follows the historic Columbia River Highway nearly half of the first day. Completed in 1915, this highway was declared a national scenic area in 1986 and chosen by Rand McNally in 1991 as one of eight top scenic routes in the country. Passing eleven waterfalls in 12 miles, it offers plenty of choices for scenic lunch or rest stops along the way. A special favorite is Multnomah Lodge at mile 18.7, which has a snack bar, a restaurant, and outdoor picnic areas beside Oregon's tallest falls. Actually, at 620 feet, it is the second-highest falls in the country.

Shortly after leaving the lodge, the scenic highway gives way to Interstate 84, a freeway that replaced much of it in 1948. But enjoyment continues. Using the highway's wide shoulders, the ride visits Bonneville Dam, the oldest of four massive projects on the Columbia where giant turbines, fish viewing areas, and displays await. It then moves on to Cascade Locks, passing the Bridge of the Gods, said to be on the site of an ancient natural bridge, to enter Marine Park. At this location are historic photos, tickets for tours aboard a replica of an authentic sternwheeler, the 1896 locks that provided passage through what was once a 40-foot drop in the river, and a small museum. The route also visits Starvation Creek, a highway rest area commemorating an 1884 train incident that left passengers stranded in the snow, and delightful Hole-in-the Wall Falls on the same site. Day One will be complete only after rolling into Hood River with one eye on the confetti of windsurfers dancing on the waves of the Columbia. First settled in 1854, Hood River offers a variety of accommodations, a museum, train rides, historic Columbia Gorge Hotel, and many restaurants.

Adventure begins anew the second morning. The route leaves Hood River to rise abruptly toward Mount Hood. A 1700-foot plateau is reached by lunchtime, giving the rider fine views of the mountain and pleasant pedaling to prepare for what is to come. Grocery stores in Parkdale provide opportunities to replenish supplies before ascending Bennett Pass at 4220 feet, and Barlow Pass, a few miles later at 4151 feet. Important to Oregon pioneers seeking to avoid the Columbia's fierce rapids, these roads held perils of their own. The steep, rugged country made controlling covered wagons difficult and dangerous.

At Government Camp the rider has the option of an overnight stay or climbing more than 2100 feet in 6 miles through the pine-scented forest to historic Timberline Lodge. The choice isn't easy, given the splendor of the lodge and its surroundings at approximately 6000 feet. Timberline Lodge, a national historic landmark, was a Works Progress Administration (WPA) project from 1935 to 1937. A marvel of architecture set in awe-inspiring surroundings, the lodge serves America's only year-round ski terrain and burgeoning tourism on 11,235-foot Mount Hood. Free tours of the lodge, along with a self-operated video that tells the story of its construction and dedication by President Franklin Roosevelt, are available to guests. A swimming pool, a hot tub, and elegant dining can soothe and refresh cyclists for the final day of the tour.

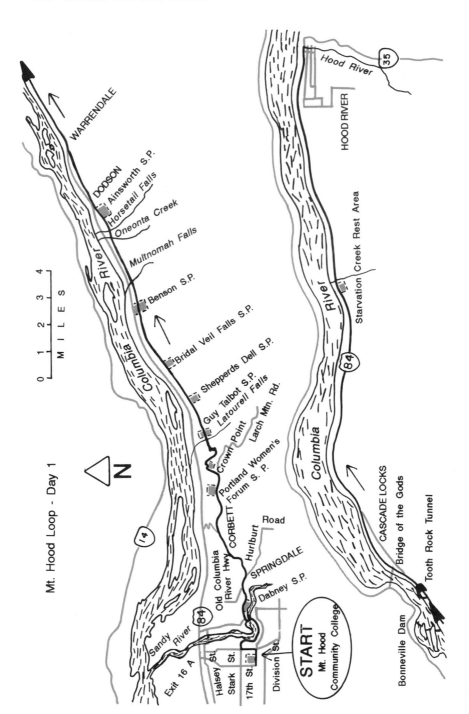

Mt. Hood Loop - Day 1

A thrilling plunge to Government Camp for huckleberry pancakes sets the pace for the third day. Mostly downhill, the route whisks along the shoulder of Highway 26, diverting to backroads at Zigzag for a ride on the route of the Old Oregon Trail. Cyclists may opt, instead, to stay with Highway 26 into Sandy. Leaving Highway 26 at Sandy, look into scenic Sandy Gorge at Jonsrud's Viewpoint, and then follow a winding course through acreage dedicated to nursery stock and farm products.

There will be ample excuses to savor the last miles of the 3-day tour. For example, choose July to enjoy the sweet smell of ripe raspberries while marveling at Mount Hood disappearing in the distance. Only smiles and wonderful memories will linger when you finally reach Mount Hood Community College, but a yearning for "next time" is virtually guaranteed. Before the car journey home, check the college's pool for a refreshing dip or shower.

Since the Gorge and Mount Hood are subject to sudden weather changes, choose your tour dates carefully. If the winter has been cold or late, check with the Hood River Ranger Station in Parkdale (503-352-6002) before heading out. September is often a beautiful time for this trip, but advance planning is necessary. It also is advisable to carry maps of the area, food, and extra supplies for the bicycle.

Recommended as a motel trip, Mount Hood Loop easily attracts non-riders who may wish to drive. They can provide a "sag" car to carry overnight gear. This would make camping a more viable option for those wishing to avoid the added weight on the mountain passes. The ride also can be done in 4 days by adding an overnight stay in the Parkdale/Cooper Spur area. Whichever option is chosen, advance reservations for people and bikes definitely are advised. This is a popular area.

Riders planning to leave a car or cars at Mount Hood Community College should write for permission to the Coordinator of Public Safety/ Plant Services, Mount Hood Community College, 26000 SE Stark St., Gresham, OR 97030. While not accepting responsibility for autos parked there (or their contents), the college seeks to accommodate requests for use of the fenced parking area.

MILEAGE LOG

First Day

0.0 Mount Hood Community College, Gresham. Park and secure your car in the assigned parking area (advance permission required). Begin by riding east on **NE 17th Street**, which becomes **Cochran Road**.

0.6 At a T-intersection, turn left on **Troutdale Road**.

1.2 Turn right on **Stark Street**, heading downhill.

3.3 Cross the Sandy River on a bridge and turn right onto the old **Columbia River Highway** (Highway 30). The entrance to Dabney State Park (day use only; water available) is on the right at mile 3.6.

3.9 Bear left on **Nielson Road**, climb a short hill, and ride past the

Columbia Gorge Ranger Station.

4.2   Turn right at **Woodard Road**.

4.6   Springdale. Bear right, following the signs to Crown Point.

4.8   Bear left at the intersection with Hurlburt Road.

7.8   Corbett (store).

9.0   Portland Women's Forum State Park (day use only; water available). Probably the most famous view of the Gorge is from this park at Chanticleer Point.

9.4   Bear left at an intersection with Larch Mountain Road. Watch for oncoming traffic as the road narrows.

10.2   Crown Point State Park (rest rooms; water available). Consisting of the Vista House, it was used until recently as a souvenir shop. The Vista House is now serving as an interpretative center. On summer and holiday weekends, displays of gorge fauna and flora and photos of the area in earlier days can be seen. Also, a "mountain man" often is in residence with stories of Old Oregon. The highway curves around the front of Vista House and then drops under an archway of trees through a series of 100-foot curves. Proceed with caution on the narrow curves.

12.6   Latourell Falls (day use only; water available). This is part of Guy Talbot State Park. For a full view of the falls, walk your bike up a short path. Also note craftsmanship of the highway bridge over Latourell Creek. It is probably the only braced-spandrel, concrete, arched bridge in the state, and one of the first built in the United States.

13.9   Shepperds Dell State Park (day use only; water not available). A short path at the east end of the bridge gives excellent views of the bridge and Shepperds Dell Falls as well as closeups of small plants.

14.9   Bridal Veil Bridge. This small bridge is supported by its solid railings, rather than from below, to allow clearance for the three log flumes and the small dam that once lay beneath it.

15.5   Bridal Veil. Continue east on the Columbia River Highway, rather than turning left to the freeway.

18.1   Wahkeena Falls, part of Benson State Park.

18.7   Multnomah Falls; at a combined height of 620 feet, this is Oregon's highest (store, restaurants, informational brochures; water available). On both sides of the falls, the highway traverses steep ground on concrete viaducts. The lodge was constructed in 1925.

21.0   Oneonta Creek. The present highway bridge was built in 1948 to replace the original 1914 structure, which is now used as a wayside. Note evidence of the tunnel to the east, which was closed when the new bridge was built. In this area there is said to be a submerged fossil forest caught between lava flows.

21.3   Horsetail Falls.

21.8   Ainsworth State Park. An overnight camping area is located at mile 22.3 (water available).

22.6   Intersection with **I-84**. Turn right, following signs for eastbound traffic. A short section of the old highway was destroyed by construction of this interchange.

22.9 Bear right on **Frontage Road**. At mile 22.8, Frontage Road rejoins the old alignment of the Columbia River Highway.

23.3 Dodson. The large barn on the south side of the road is circa 1870. Above it sits a basalt formation known as Saint Peters Dome.

24.2 Warrendale. In 1882 Frank Warren used a device called a fishwheel to scoop salmon from the river for processing here in his cannery.

25.2 Frontage Road ends. Enter I-84. Beacon Rock, a monolith mentioned in Lewis and Clark journals, is across the river.

27.7 Turn right at exit 40 to visit Bonneville Dam, the oldest and largest electrical power generators on the Columbia. Turn left at the stop sign. Carefully cross the tracks by the powerhouse and continue toward the Bradford Island visitors center at mile 29.2. After viewing the exhibits, stop by the shore to the west of the dam. Early-morning fishermen seek to lure sturgeon or salmon here. Also watch for boats and barges headed to the lock.

31.0 Exit Bonneville by passing under I-84 and onto the ramp to I-84 eastbound (toward Hood River). Travel with care through a lighted tunnel at mile 31.9, watching for grates on the extreme right. The sidewalk is dangerous and should be avoided in the tunnel.

35.1 Turn right at exit 44 (U.S. 30 East) to Cascade Locks (food, stores, rest rooms, lodging). Pass under the Bridge of the Gods. This structure, built in the 1930s, stands near a rock slide created by volcanic eruptions. Indian legends named it. Oregon Trail pioneers made a 6-mile portage here and, in later years, a crude mule-powered train helped.

36.1 Cascade Marine Park on the left offers an interesting museum, photos of the old town, and passage on the sternwheel boat that plies the river (rest rooms; water available).

36.8 Turn left on **Forest Lane Road** (unmarked) toward the airport and industrial park. Pass a KOA Campground at mile 38.0.

38.8 Cross I-84, bearing left toward Herman Creek Road. At mile 39.8, continue on the shoulder of I-84 toward Hood River.

47.5 Starvation Creek Rest Area. Walk or ride the path near the rest rooms to visit the beautiful waterfall and picnic area.

54.7 Turn right at exit 62 (Westcliff Drive) and enter Hood River. Lodging is available on the opposite side of the highway and along the route into town. To reach downtown Hood River, proceed straight ahead about 3 miles on **W. Cascade Drive**, which becomes **Oak Street** (restaurants, stores, motels). The downtown marina offers a museum and interesting views of all stages of windsurfing. The downtown train station has been refurbished. Roundtrip train rides to Parkdale are available daily.

Second Day

0.0 In downtown Hood River (Second and Oak) begin riding south on **Second Street**. This is uphill and away from the river. Proceed one block on **Second Street** and then turn right (west) on **State Street**.

1.0 Turn left at a T-intersection on **13th Street** and immediately right onto **Sherman Avenue**, continuing west. (A nice view of Mount Adams may be visible on the right).

1.7 Turn left on **Rand Road** and then right on **May Street** at mile 1.9.

2.7 Turn left (south) on **Frankton Road.**

3.5 Turn right onto **Belmont Drive.** (A nice view of Mount Hood may be visible to left of this intersection.)

3.8 Turn left at a T-intersection on **Methodist Road.**

4.9 Turn left on **Barrett Drive**.

5.7 Turn right toward Parkdale on **Tucker Road** (unmarked) (store). Descend the hill and cross the Hood River.

7.7 Bear right on **Dee Highway 281** at a Y-intersection, continuing toward Tucker Park. The park entrance is passed at mile 7.9 (rest rooms; water available). This is a popular camping area for sailboard enthusiasts who frequent the area.

10.6 Cross railroad tracks and continue straight ahead.

13.9 Lumber Mill and the junction to Lost Lake is on the right. (This fully paved road leads about 18 miles to the lake on Mount Hood's southwest side.) Continue straight ahead toward Parkdale.

15.4 Cross the east fork of Hood River.

15.5 Cross the rail tracks again, watching for a view of Mount Hood at mile 16.7 (store).

19.4 Parkdale (stores, restaurant). This is a good place to buy supplies. There are no services for the next 28 miles.

19.9 Continue straight ahead (east) on **Baseline Road** as **Cooper Spur Road** heads off to the right (south).

22.2 Turn right at a T-intersection on **Highway 35**, riding the shoulder. At mile 26.4 the entrance to Rouston County Park is on the left.

28.6 Cooper Spur Road joins the highway from the right. Continue straight ahead on **Highway 35**.

30.7 Sherwood Campground appears on the right (rest rooms; water available).

32.0 Junction with **Highway 44**. Continue straight ahead on **Highway 35**.

34.7 The entrance to Robinhood Campground is on the right (rest rooms; water available).

35.6 Cross Newton Creek.

37.9 The entrance to Mount Hood Meadows Ski Area is on the right. Continue straight ahead.

39.1 On the left is Bennett Pass Road and Mount Hood Meadows Road is to the right. Continue straight down the highway, crossing Bennett Pass Summit (elevation 4647 feet) at mile 39.6.

41.2 Cross the White River. This is a good location to view Mount Hood. A month after this highway opened in 1925, a freak storm brought

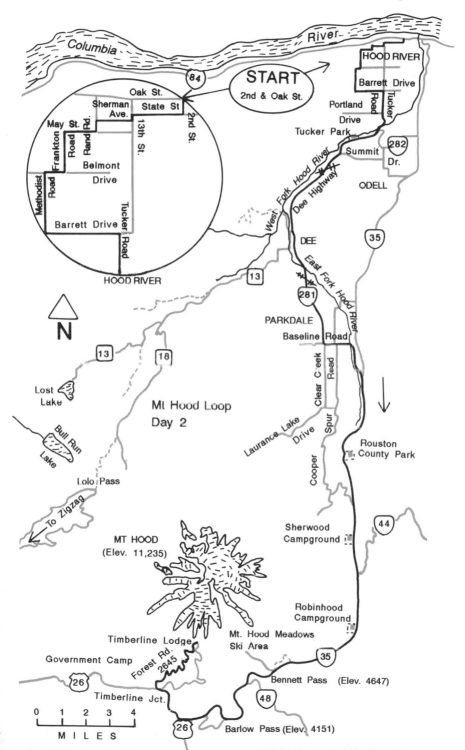

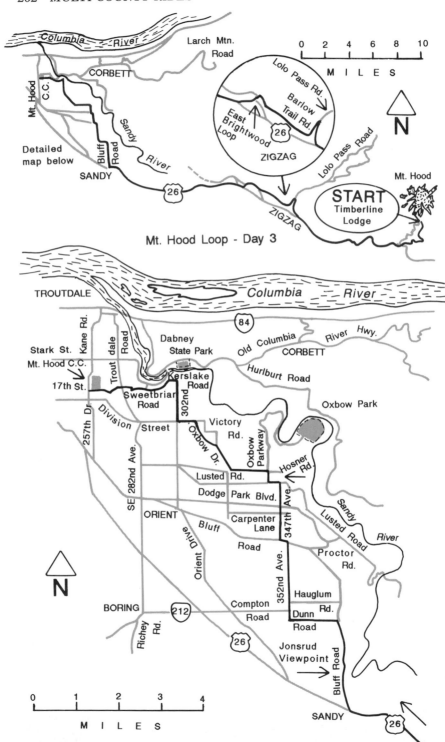

Mt. Hood Loop - Day 3

mud and boulders off the glacier and took out the new bridge here. It was estimated that a mass of 100 tons a second swept down the White River Gorge.

43.4 Cross the summit of Barlow Pass. Once a toll road for wagons headed to the fertile Willamette Valley, much of the Barlow Road today is part of Highway 26.

45.6 Madras Junction. Stay right on **Highway 26** (toward Portland).

46.4 Pass the Trillium Lake exit on the left, continuing straight on Highway 26.

48.2 Timberline Junction. Turn right on **Timberline Road**, but *immediately* cross over it to turn left onto **Forest Road 2645**. This intersection may be unmarked and the road may appear to be a gravel driveway. However, within 0.25 mile, it is paved. Follow it as it switchbacks up toward Timberline.

48.7 Mazama Club Lodge is on the right. This outdoor club is based in Portland.

53.8 Turn left at a T-intersection with **Timberline Road** and wind around to Timberline Lodge. (Reservations should be made for lodging and for bicycle storage. Bikes are not allowed in rooms.)

54.2 End of day.

Third Day

0.0 Exit Timberline by crossing the parking lot and turning right. Sail down **Timberline Road**, taking care on the curves.

6.0 Turn right on **Highway 26**.

6.6 Enter Government Camp (stores, restaurants).

7.0 Turn right onto **Highway 26** and begin the downhill ride.

15.2 Tollgate Campground is on the left. This was the site of the tollgate for the Barlow Road, which became free in 1915.

15.6 Pass through Rhododendron (restaurants).

16.1 Cross the Zigzag River.

16.9 Turn right on Lolo Pass Road (Zigzag Store). You also have the option of continuing to Sandy on Highway 26.

17.1 Cross the Zigzig River.

17.9 Cross the Sandy River.

18.1 Turn left on **Barlow Trail Road**, following the route of the Old Oregon Trail toward Brightwood.

23.1 Turn left toward Highway 26 on **Brightwood Bridge Road**.

23.2 Cross the Sandy River.

23.4 Turn right on **East Brightwood Loop**.

24.2 Cross the Salmon River.

25.5 Turn right onto **Highway 26**.

35.9 Sandy (restaurants, stores).

37.0 Turn right on **Bluff Road**. Sandy High School is to the right. At mile 37.9 is Jonsrud's Viewpoint, offering a spectacular view of Sandy River Gorge.

39.2 Turn left on **Dunn Road**, which bends right and becomes **352nd Avenue** at mile 40.5.

42.1 Turn left on **Bluff Road**.

42.4 Turn right on **347th Avenue**, which becomes **Cottrell Road**.

43.4 Cross Carpenter Lane and continue on **Cottrell Road**. Also stay with **Cottrell Road** at mile 43.5 after crossing Dodge Park Road.

44.0 Turn left on **Lusted Road**.

44.3 Turn right on **Hosner Road** (342nd Avenue). (The sign may be hidden by a tree.)

44.7 Turn left onto **Oxbow Drive**. (To make a side trip into Oxbow Park, go about 1.5 miles straight ahead here down a long hill.) The route follows Oxbow Drive as it eventually becomes **Division Street**.

47.2 Turn right on **302nd Avenue** and bear left at mile 48.2 as it becomes **Kerslake Road**.

50.0 Bear left up a short, steep hill on **Sweetbriar Road**.

50.9 Cross Troutdale Road and follow **Cochran Road** to **17th Street**.

51.5 Turn right into the Mount Hood Community College parking area. End of ride.

APPENDICES

Trip Junctions

To help connect two or more of the described routes, use this list of towns, parks, or other sites where the routes cross paths. In a few cases, the routes do not actually cross, but pass within a mile or two.

Junction	Trip Number	Junction	Trip Number
Airlie	30, 36	Lebanon	32, 34
Amity	21, 22	Lewis and Clark	
Brownsville	33, 34, 35	State Park	1, 3
Buena Vista Ferry	28, 30, 44	Maude Williamson	
Butteville	24, 44	State Park	21, 22, 44
Canby Ferry	14, 18, 44	Meadowbrook	17, 18
Carlton	19, 20	Molalla River State Park	18, 44
Champoeg State Park	24, 44	Mount Angel	25, 26
Corvallis	36, 37	Needy	18, 26
Crabtree	31, 32	Newberg	19, 44
Crow	40, 41	Perrydale	22, 23, 29
Dabney State Park	1, 3	Portland Women's Forum	
Estacada	15, 16	State Park	1, 2, 6
Eugene	38, 40, 4	St. Louis	24, 25
Fern Ridge Lake	39, 40	St. Paul	24, 25
Feyrer Park	17, 18	Scholls	7, 13, 19
Forest Grove	8, 10, 43	Sherwood	7, 13
Gervais	24, 25	Skyline Boulevard	5, 43
Harrisburg	35, 37, 38, 39	Springdale	1, 3
Hillsboro	8, 43	Springwater	15, 17
Hillside	10, 43	Suver	30, 36
Holman Wayside	29, 44	Troutdale	1, 3
Hopewell	21, 22, 44	Verboort	8, 43
Independence	29, 30, 44	West Union	5, 9, 43
Jefferson	28, 31	Wheatland Ferry	21, 22, 25, 44
Lafayette	20, 40	Whiskey Hill	18, 26
Lancaster	37, 38, 39	Wilsonville	13, 44
Larwood	31, 32	Yamhill	19, 20

Mileage Index

Miles	Trip Name	Number	Miles	Trip Name	Number
11.6	Hagg Lake	11	22.0	Sherwood–Scholls	7
12.4	Sauvie Island	4	22.3	Mountaindale	9
19.4	Petes Mountain	14	24.2	Lolo Pass	12

Mileage Index

About the Authors

Philip N. Jones is the author of *Canoe Routes: Northwest Oregon*, and the editor of *Columbia River Gorge: A Complete Guide*, both published by The Mountaineers. He is an avid cyclist, paddler, and photographer, and is an active member of several outdoor organizations in the Northwest. He practices law in Portland.

Jean Henderson discovered the joys of Northwest bicycling through longtime memberships in The Mountaineers and the Cascade Bicycle Club. An organizer and leader of many cycling trips, she has traveled by bike through Europe, and recently completed two years as chair of the Mountaineers Bicycle Committee. A public relations consultant, Jean resides in Seattle.

THE MOUNTAINEERS, founded in 1906, is a non-profit outdoor activity and conservation club whose mission is "to explore, study, preserve, and enjoy the natural beauty of the outdoors . . . ." Based in Seattle, Washington, the club is now the third largest such organization in the United States, with 12,000 members and four branches throughout Washington State.

The Mountaineers sponsors both classes and year-round outdoor activities in the Pacific Northwest, which include hiking, mountain climbing, ski-touring, snowshoeing, bicycling, camping, kayaking and canoeing, nature study, sailing, and adventure travel. The club's conservation division supports environmental causes through education activities, sponsoring legislation, and presenting information programs. All club activities are led by skilled, experienced volunteers who are dedicated to promoting safe and responsible enjoyment and preservation of the outdoors. The Mountaineers Books, an active, non-profit publishing program of the club, produces guidebooks, instructional texts, historical works, natural history guides, and works on environmental conservation. All books produced by The Mountaineers Books are aimed at fulfilling the club's mission.

If you would like to participate in these organized outdoor activities or the club's programs, consider a membership in The Mountaineers. For information and an application, write or call The Mountaineers, Club Headquarters, 300 Third Avenue West, Seattle, Washington 98119; (206) 284-6310.

Send or call for our catalog of over 200 outdoor books:
The Mountaineers Books
1011 SW Klickitat Way, Suite 107
Seattle, WA 98134
1-800-553-4453